Marriage, Sex, and the Family in England 1660-1800

A Forty-four Volume Facsimile Series

edited by
Randolph Trumbach
Baruch College

A Garland Series

Prostitution Reform

Four Documents

Garland Publishing, Inc.
New York & London
1985

For a complete list of the titles in this series see the final pages of this volume.

The facsimile of *An Account of the Rise, Progress, and Present State of the Magdalen Hospital* was made from a copy in the Francis A. Countway Library of Medicine, Boston. The other facsimiles are from copies in the British Library.

Library of Congress Cataloging in Publication Data

Main entry under title:

Prostitution reform.

(Marriage, sex, and the family in England, 1660-1800)
Reprint (1st work). Originally published: Proposals for establishing a public place of reception for penitent prostitutes, etc. / Robert Dingley. London : Printed by W. Faden, 1758.
Reprint (2nd work). Originally published: A proposal to render effectual a plan to remove the nuisance of common prostitutes from the streets of this metropolis / by Saunders Welch. London : Printed for C. Henderson at the Royal Exchange, 1758.
Reprint (3rd work). Originally published: An account of the origin and effects of a police set on foot by his Grace the Duke of Newcastle in the year 1753, upon a plan presented to his Grace by the late Henry Fielding, Esq.; to which is added a plan for preserving those deserted girls in this town, who become prostitutes from necessity / by John Fielding. London : Printed by A. Millar, 1758.
Reprint (4th work). Originally published: An account of the rise, progress, and present state of the Magdalen Hospital, for the reception of penitent prostitutes, together with Dr. Dodd's sermons, to which are added The advice to the Magdalens, with the psalms, hymns, prayers, rules, and list of subscribers. 5th ed. London : Printed by W. Faden, 1776.
1. Prostitution—England—London. 2. London (England)—Moral conditions. I. Series.
HQ186.L66P76 1985 306.7′42′0942 83-48597
ISBN 0-8240-5921-2 (alk. paper)

The volumes in this series are printed on acid-free, 250-year-life paper.
Printed in the United States of America

Prostitution Reform

1. Proposals for Establishing a public Place of Reception for Penitent Prostitutes (1758)
Robert Dingley

2. A Proposal to render effectual a Plan, to remove the Nuisance of Common Prostitutes from the Streets of this Metropolis (1758)
Saunders Welch

3. An Account of the Origin and Effects of a Police Set on Foot by His Grace the Duke of Newcastle in the Year 1753, upon a Plan presented to his Grace by the late *Henry Fielding*, Esq; to which is added a Plan for preserving those deserted Girls in this Town, who become Prostitutes from Necessity (1758)
John Fielding

4. An Account of the Rise, Progress, and Present State of the Magdalen Hospital, for the Reception of Penitent Prostitutes (1776)

PROPOSALS

FOR ESTABLISHING

A PUBLIC PLACE of Reception

FOR

PENITENT PROSTITUTES, &c.

LONDON:

Printed by W. FADEN, in Wine-Office-Court, Fleet-Street.

MDCCLVIII.

PROPOSALS, &c.

NOBLE and extenſive are the Charities already eſtabliſhed in this CITY: Unfortunate Females ſeem the only Objects that have not yet catched the attention of public Benevolence: but, I dare ſay, it will appear on reflection, a work of as great Compaſſion and Conſequence, Neceſſity and Advantage to provide a Place † of Reception for them, as for any under the protection of the Public.

Humanity in its utmoſt efforts pleads their cauſe more powerfully than any thing I can offer on the ſubject; and I appeal to every mind, from its own experience, if there can be greater Objects of Compaſſion, than poor, young, thoughtleſs Females, plunged into ruin by thoſe tempations, to which their very youth and perſonal advantages expoſes them, no leſs thanthoſe paſſions implanted by nature for wiſe, good

† There are many ſuch Eſtabliſhments in ſeveral Cities of Italy, France, *&c.*

and great ends? Surrounded by ſnares, the moſt artfully and induſtriouſly laid, ſnares laid by thoſe endowed with ſuperior faculties, and all the advantages of Education and fortune, what virtue can be proof againſt ſuch formidable Seducers, who offer too commonly, and too profuſely promiſe, to tranſport the thoughtleſs Girls from Want, Confinement, and Reſtraint of Paſſions, to Luxury, Liberty, Gaiety, and Joy? And when once ſeduced, how ſoon their golden dreams vaniſh? abandoned by the Seducer, deſerted by their Friends, contemned by the World, they are left to ſtruggle with want, deſpair, and ſcorn, and even in their own defence to plunge ſtill deeper and deeper in ſin, till Diſeaſe and Diſtreſs conclude a miſerable Being. It is too well known that this is the caſe with moſt of the Proſtitutes in their ſeveral degrees, ſooner or later, from thoſe pampered in private Stews, to the common dregs infeſting our Streets: and that far the greater part of them, having taken to this dreadful way of life, thus ſeeking diſeaſe, death, and eternal deſtruction, not of choice, but through fatal neceſſity: the ſeeds of virtue would exert themſelves, but alas! the poſſibility is removed.—The ſame neceſſity, obliging them to prey on the unwary, diffuſes the contagion, even through both ſexes, propagating profligacy, and ſpreading ruin, diſeaſe

diſeaſe, and death, if I may ſo ſay, almoſt through the whole human ſpecies.

What act of Benevolence, then, can there be greater than to give theſe truly compaſſionate objects, an opportunity to reclaim and recover themſelves from their otherwiſe loſt State; an opportunity to become of peſts, uſeful members of ſociety, as I doubt not many of them may and will?

Numbers, I am perſuaded, amongſt my Countrymen, famed through every nation for their extreme Humanity, will readily and gladly bear a part in ſo benevolent a Deſign, and rejoice to promote an undertaking that will at once be a Bleſſing to the Commonwealth, and an Honour to human nature.

Theſe and ſuch like Conſiderations induced me ſome years ſince to wiſh and hope, that an Eſtabliſhment of this kind might take place, and be bleſt with the ready Patronage and Protection of the humane and compaſſionate of both Sexes. And, not reſting in hopes and wiſhes only, I have at various times intimated my thoughts and warm deſires on this ſubject to ſeveral of my friends: many of whom, though I found ready to contribute the good aid of their wealth; yet more objections and difficulties were ſtarted againſt the practicability

ticability of its firſt Eſtabliſhment, than offers were made of the Aſſiſtance of time and attention to carry it into Execution. —— The Tenderneſs of my own Conſtitution, and many other neceſſary Avocations, made it a Taſk far beyond my ſingle Abilities; yet my Hopes and Wiſhes ſtill continued moſt ardent. But as two worthy Magiſtrates, Mr. FIELDING and Mr. WELCH have given their thoughts on this ſubject to the Public †, and as the latter has lately mentioned my name in the moſt obliging manner, relating to my latent wiſhes, my hopes revive, and I judged it incumbent on me to communicate my Thoughts to the World.

The Neceſſity and Utility of ſuch an Eſtabliſhment I have juſt touched upon; other circumſtances occur: It will be a means of employing the idle, of inſtructing them in, as well as habituating them to work; of reforming their Morals; of reſcuing many bodies from Diſeaſe and Death, and many Souls from eternal Miſery.——It will do more good with much leſs expence than any other Charity; the objects being in

† My Friend Mr. HANWAY too has been pleaſed to addreſs a Letter on this ſubject to me; which, I hope, will have its due effect, in awakening the attention of the humane to conſider this uſeful Deſign.

their prime of life; capable of working; and ſuch, as I doubt not, may even wholly maintain the Houſe, after a little time, when well eſtabliſhed. For they will want but very few Officers, and their own Expences lie in a narrow compaſs; being only ſuch as will ariſe from Cloathing, plain Food, and MEDICINES, (at firſt to make ſuch of them clean as are diſeaſed:) Temperance and Sobriety, it is to be hoped, will afterwards render them of little uſe.

There is another Set of Objects, which may indeed be conſidered, as compriſed in this Deſign, though under a diſtinct Head, the Female Children, from Twelve to Fifteen Years, of the lower Claſs of people, who are often abandoned by their Parents, and even ſometimes ſold by them to PROCURESSES, names indeed too ſoft for ſuch unnatural excreſcences of the human Species.—Whenever the Eſtabliſhment is ſet on foot, the ſame Rules, in general, may ſerve for theſe, as for the former, remembering always that a particular care muſt be taken to keep them abſolutely ſeparate.—But I ſhall at preſent confine myſelf to the firſt, and conſider the propoſed Eſtabliſhment under three diſtinct Branches.—1. The Government.—2. The Eſtabliſhment.—3. The Method of Admiſſion, and

and Domeſtic Oeconomy; offering hints only, to be properly enlarged hereafter, for I do not preſume at all to dictate or obtrude my Sentiments on ſuch as will unite their endeavours in ſupport of the Undertaking.

I. The Government

SHould be, by a President, Vice-President, and Committee, ballotted for, as in other Eſtabliſhments of a ſimilar nature; always having a ſtrict regard to the Ability, Character, and Diſpoſition of the Gentlemen, to be ballotted for, to conduct the affairs of this Charity.

II. The Establishment.

THE firſt Establishment muſt be made at ſome convenient place, to be found and propoſed— (one offers, in Goodman's-Fields, lately the London-Infirmary.) For I ſhould think it by no means adviſeable, to begin with Building, which would be a vaſt Expence, before a fair eſſay is made. The proper Eſtabliſhing, and apparent Utility being the only means of recommending it to the Public; and experience will beſt point out, on what plan a future Building

Building ſhould be compoſed. Perhaps it may be found adviſeable to have more than one; and even the principal one at a diſtance, from the Metropolis. —The Houſe, to be called, 'The MAGDALEN CHARITY HOUSE,—or, as ſhall be thought moſt expreſſive. — The Officers neceſſary, will be,

1. A Chaplain.

2. A Matron.

3. A Phyſician.

4. A Surgeon and Apothecary.

5. A Steward, who may alſo be the Secretary.

6 A Porter.

Theſe are all the Officers requiſite. No Servants will be wanting. The MATRON may be Wife to the STEWARD. — All theſe muſt be of fit age, and diſcretion, and unblemiſhed Characters. — They muſt attend all Committees, to make their Reports, and receive all neceſſary Orders. This in general. In particular,

1ſt. The CHAPLAIN muſt attend all Admiſſions, to influence Decency; who, by a little practice and obſervation, will be qualified to judge of the real good Diſpoſition of the Object.—He muſt read Morning and Evening Prayers, Pray and Preach twice every Sunday, at certain fixed hours, as ſhall be judged moſt convenient; adminiſter the Sacrament, at certain appointed ſeaſons; and, as occaſion requires, attend the Sick and Uninformed, taking eſpecial care of their Inſtruction in the Eſtabliſh'd Religion, and to have no other Preferment or Employ.

2d. To enlarge on the Buſineſs of PHYSICIAN, SURGEON, and APOTHECARY, would be needleſs; application, tenderneſs, and ſkill, will ever be required.

3d. The MATRON, muſt govern and regulate the domeſtic affairs; take in, and deliver out work; ſet the Taſks, employ the Objects, and ſee that every one diſcharge their Duty.

4th. The STEWARD and SECRETARY muſt provide Proviſions, Cloaths, &c. for the Houſe, and keep all Accounts and Correſpondence.

5th. The PORTER, muſt attend the Gates; receive and carry Meſſages, do Errands, and all other matters in his province.

N. B.

N. B. Neither of theſe ſhould have any communication, or the leaſt CONNECTION with the WOMEN in the Houſe.

III. Of ADMISSION, and the DOMESTIC OECONOMY.

1ſt. PROPER OBJECTS FOR ADMISSION.

SUCH as apply by PETITION; which ſhould firſt be referred to the Committee; and their Enquiries be made in ſuch Manner as ſhall be thought beſt. The Petition being thus examined, if approved, to be wrote on, "Found proper," and ſo preſerved, as a Proof of the Petitioner's Sincerity; who accordingly muſt be bound Apprentice, or articled Servant to the MATRON, for ſeven Years; but with a reſerve to be diſmiſſed, if afterwards, an apparent impoſition ſhould be diſcovered; and when diſmiſſed, never more to be re-admitted.—— That the ſaid Articles be ſo drawn, as to have a power of cancelling them, at three or five Years, or any other intermediate time, as circumſtances require, or a fit viciſſitude may offer, to the ſatisfaction of the PRESIDENT, &c.—— ſuch as Reconciliation of Parents, and Relations, Change of Fortune, and the like. For to keep thoſe who can be provided for, would be burdening the Charity, to the prejudice of others that may want it; and to receive thoſe, who return to their Shame, would be making it only a Retreat for Iniquity.

That Perſons to be admitted produce, if poſſible, a Certificate of their place of Settlement, real Name, Age, &c.

Cure. 2. The Objects thus admitted, (within ſuch an age as ſhall be determined) to be rendered clean and healthy, either in a ſick Ward for that purpoſe, a Houſe at a diſtance, or at the public ſick Hoſpitals already eſtabliſhed, and this at the Expence of the Houſe.

Names. 3. The Patients thus taken into the care of the Houſe, and made clean, ſhall have their Names regiſtered, and take on them ſome other name, by which Name only they ſhall be called and known, when entered

tered into the House itself.—That they wear an uniform of light grey, black, or sky blue; and in all their Dress, be as plain and neat as possible: their own cloaths being laid by, to return them, when they leave the House.—That they be classed in TWELVES in each Ward; sleep in separate Beds, without Curtains, except in case of Sickness: —— That there be a ROOM for their Working, &c. at the End of, or adjoining to each Ward. —— That one in each Ward preside in turn weekly, and be answerable to the Matron for the Behaviour of the rest.—That the Wards be numbered and named.—That they watch in turns one every night, and traverse the Wards at least every hour, to see all is in good order, &c.—That they eat all in one room, though at different tables, each ward dining by themselves.—That there be a Superiority or preference of Wards.—That the Objects, in general, be cloathed and fed meanly, though with cleanly and healthful provision: Yet according as the Matron, &c. shall judge best, a Preference be given to some Wards before others, according to the Behaviour and Education of the Objects; and that they be clothed and fed accordingly.—That the inferior Wards consist of the inferior Objects, and those degraded for misbehaviour. —That

Dress. Classes. Beds. Working-Room. Wards. Watching. Eating. Distinction. Business of the House.

—That they do all the servile Offices of the House, and be subject to Dismission, on gross Misbehaviour; as there must be no compulsion, or censorial punishment inflicted; but the strictest order and humanity be observed in every respect.—That they rise according to their time of being in the House, and their good behaviour, especially from the INFERIOR to the SUPERIOR Wards. And that, if possible, a small Closet or apartment might be provided for each of the most serious and best-behaved, for their Retirement: and that these also be made the immediate reward of good conduct.

Devotion. —That they all be kept strict to the hours of Devotion, Eating, *&c.*—Work so many hours every day,

Reading. as may be judged fit, and that one read while the rest work, every hour alternately, during the time of their Work, and at Meals— But only such Books of PIETY and INSTRUCTION, as the CHAPLAIN or Committee shall allow; and that for this purpose a small and useful collection of Books be provided.—That every Ob-

Work. ject work, or do something, according to her Ability, and have half the Benefit accruing from her Labour or Ingenuity; part whereof to be deposited in the Committee's Hands for her Benefit, when dismissed, on proper Behaviour,—which Sum may also be increased, by by the bounty of the Houſe, as favourable opportunities offer of eſtabliſhing them in the World.—That the Breakfaſt and Supper of the ſix inferior Wards be Water-gruel, Milk, or Milk-pottage, Bread and Butter or Cheeſe—Their Dinner, Broth, Beef, and Herbage, except Sundays, then to have white meat and Mutton. The ſuperior Wards may have Tea, if they buy it themſelves, and white meat, Tueſdays, Thurſdays and Sundays: the beſt pieces of Beef on other Days, each better, according to the ſeniority of the Ward: That the Superintendant of each Ward dine at the upper end of each Table, and the inferior Wards wait on the reſt at Meals.—That thoſe of the ſenior Ward may be permitted to dine with the Matron, at the diſcretion of the Matron.—That no one whatever be admitted to ſee, or have any Converſation with them without a Leave firſt had and ſign'd, by the Preſident, or two of the Committee.—That no Letters be received into the Houſe, without being inſpected by the MATRON.

Breakfaſt. Supper.

Dinner.

Not to be ſpoke with without leave.

Letters.

4. For their EMPLOY—It may be either making or mending of Linen—Scowering Pewter——Making Bon-Lace—Black Lace—Artificial Flowers——Children's Toys—Spinning fine Thread, &c. and Woollen

Employ.

Yarn

Yarn for Clothiers, Callimanco's, and Cruels —— Winding Silk —— Embroidery, and all branches of Millinery, Lady's Shoes, Mantua's, &c. Coat-making, Stays —— Cauls for Wigs —— Knitting Hose and Mittins — Making of Gloves, leathern and silken — Weaving of Hair — Making Garters — Drawing Patterns, &c. or whatever EMPLOY their several Abilities and Geniuses shall lead to. —— Ever observing, as well in this, as in every other Circumstance, the utmost Care and Delicacy, Humanity and Tenderness; so that this Establishment may be coveted, and not thought an House of Correction, but an happy Asylum, and desireable Retreat from their wretched and distressful Circumstances.

Conclusion. Thus having thrown my Thoughts together, in a general manner, — for I would by no means be thought to dictate to such worthy and able persons as I am persuaded will readily assist so good a Work — I submit them entirely to their and the public Consideration: And such Hints as regard its better Regulation, and particularly how to employ them properly, and prevent all possible Imposition, will be most gratefully acknowledged. My utmost Efforts shall not be wanting to carry this Design into Execution; and for such

as

as will unite their Hearts and Hands in the Cauſe, their Reward, I truſt, will not fail them here; their works of Benevolence, we are aſſur'd, ſhall not miſs of their Reward hereafter. And I know not how I can more properly conclude my Addreſs, than by two apt Paſſages of ſacred Writ:——

THEY THAT ARE WHOLE, NEED NOT A PHYSICIAN BUT THEY THAT ARE SICK: I CAME NOT TO CALL THE RIGHTEOUS, BUT SINNERS TO REPENTANCE.

LET HIM KNOW, THAT HE THAT CONVERTETH A SINNER, FROM THE ERROR OF HIS WAY, SHALL SAVE A SOUL FROM DEATH, AND HIDE A MULTITUDE OF SINS.

St. Helens,
March 27, 1758.

ROBERT DINGLEY.

A

PROPOSAL

To render effectual a

PLAN,

To remove the Nuisance of

Common Prostitutes

FROM THE

STREETS of this METROPOLIS;

To prevent

The INNOCENT from being seduced;

To provide

A decent and comfortable Maintenance for those whom Necessity or Vice hath already forced into that infamous Course of LIFE;

And to maintain and educate

Those CHILDREN of the Poor, who are either ORPHANS, or are *deserted* by wicked Parents.

To which is annexed,

A LETTER upon the Subject of Robberies, wrote in the year 1753.

By *SAUNDERS WELCH*,

One of his Majesty's Justices of the Peace for the County of *Middlesex*, and for the City and Liberty of *Westminster*.

LONDON:

Printed for C. HENDERSON, at the *Royal Exchange*, and sold at the Booksellers and Pamphlet Shops of *London* and *Westminster*. 1758.

TO THE

RIGHT HONOURABLE

CHARLES Lord Visc. *Folkstone*,

PRESIDENT,

The Vice-Presidents and Members

OF THE

SOCIETY for encouraging ARTS and MANUFACTURES:

This humble Attempt in the Service of the PUBLIC is with all possible Humility dedicated

By their most respectful,

Most humble

And obedient Servant,

SAUNDERS WELCH.

INTRODUCTION.

THE publication of my thoughts upon the ſubject of providing for proſtitutes, &c. which at preſent ſeems to ingroſs the attention of ſo many worthy minds, ariſes not from either a deſire to diſtinguiſh myſelf, or the thirſt of applauſe; much leſs is it done to depreciate the labours of others, who have publiſhed their ſentiments upon the ſubject, particularly thoſe two worthy gentlemen, Mr. Dingley, and Mr. Hanway: I know I ſhall not offend them by offering my mite towards this great and benevolent deſign. So far are theſe gentlemen from being tenacious of their own opinions, or arbitrarily inforcing any particular plan as the ſtandard of perfection, that with a modeſty inſeparable from real merit, they deſire that the ſentiments of all who are inclined to write upon the ſubject, may be collected, as the beſt means of carrying their benevolent deſigns into execution; thereby preferring the public intereſt to the paltry conſideration of being eſteemed the projectors of a ſcheme.

My intention in the following eſſay, is to point out thoſe previous meaſures, which ſeem to me to be eſſentially neceſſary to a plan of this kind;

for, upon conſidering this matter with the utmoſt attention, it appears to me impracticable to render the deſign of public uſe without the aid of the legiſlature. The plan which has been ſome time publiſhed for a *public laundry*, and for which ſome ſubſcriptions have been raiſed, has not, I think, been ſo much attended to, either in its conſtruction, or in the method of executing it, as the ſubject deſerved. But this does not take away the merit of the attempt; neither ought the propoſing of a remedy for its defects to provoke envy or reſentment.

By this plan, bawdy-houſes are left untouched; they may ſtill ſeduce the Innocent, and continue their miſchief to ſociety with their uſual impunity; nor is any proviſion made to remove the nuſance of common proſtitutes from our ſtreets; except ſuch of them as ſhall voluntarily offer themſelves to the intended hoſpital: what thoſe will be, is eaſy to foreſee: no doubt, many will offer, when their bodies are corrupted by diſeaſes, and want and miſery has ſurrounded them, and rendered them dreadful objects to warn others from treading in the ſame wicked paths. But after they are received into the hoſpital, are cured of their diſeaſe, clothed, and their health and ſpirits retrieved by comfortable nouriſhment, is it not in their option to continue, or to demand their diſcharge? and without the interpoſition of the legiſlature, a ſubject cannot be impriſoned in this, any more than in any other hoſpital: they may therefore return to their

their former lewd practices, and render the charity little other, than a Lock hoſpital for curing venereal diſtempers.

The method of binding the orphan and deſerted children of the poor to the matron, as propoſed by the *Preſervatory and reformatory* plan, will appear impracticable, when it is conſidered that by our laws forty days continuance under an indenture of apprenticeſhip will give ſuch children an undoubted ſettlement in the pariſh where ſuch hoſpital is erected: but what pariſh will be able to ſupport the expence ſuch hoſpital muſt render it liable to? The proſtitutes are alſo, by the ſame plan, to be indentured apprentices to the matron, and *ſuch indentures to be dated back*; a propoſal which either ſlipped from the author, or he did not duly conſider the law, in as much as it implies fraud upon the face of it; as it is well known that ſuch indentures muſt be dated the day they are executed, and for the term of ſeven years at leaſt from the date, by the ſtatute of 5 Eliz. And ſurely the fathers of this intended charity will not ſuffer, or give their ſanction to a practice contrary to law.

But when this plan is further conſidered, with reſpect to the proſtitutes, it will appear productive of very evil conſequences to the Public, by increaſing their number, which is already too great in our ſtreets, and be the means of bawds ſupplying themſelves with girls more eaſily than at preſent.

It ſeems to me a miſtake to aſſert, that the

bawdy-houſes and ſtreets are furniſhed with proſtitutes from the children of the laborious Poor: this, I believe, is not the caſe of one in twenty of theſe unhappy creatures. The wrong turn of education of the children of thoſe in the next ſphere of life to labourers, is the plentiful ſource from whence the bagnios and bawdy-houſes are conſtantly ſupplied. And when diſeaſe and diſtemper render them incapable to ſee company (as it is termed) the ſtreets receive them. The maxim of the parents of theſe children is, to give them what they call a good education; and if Miſs happens to be pretty, her vanity is indulged by dreſs, &c. in hopes that ſhe may mend her fortune by captivating ſome rich gudgeon, or be qualified to wait upon a lady, or at leaſt to be a chamber-maid. The truth of this obſervation will ſufficiently appear, from the great difficulty of getting *ſervants for all work*; and the vaſt number of candidates for higher ſtations. Thus a uſeful education is ſacrificed, and the fond deluded parent lays the foundation of the child's deſtruction in pride and idleneſs: Unuſed to do the meaner offices of life, and unable to get a ſtation ſuitable to her education, pride united to neceſſity throws her as a miſtreſs into the arms of the firſt man who is willing to ſupport her in idleneſs and extravagance; or elſe ſhe falls an eaſy prey to the artifices of bawds.

Others, who have the good luck to be placed in ſtations ſuitable to their education, are ruined by by the falſe good-nature of their ſuperiors; how often is the lady's woman ſeen flaunting in her miſtreſs's left-off cloaths, and ridiculouſly affecting the airs of a woman of quality? Thus the mind is puffed up by vanity; that diſtinction and reſpectful diſtance which ſhould always ſubſiſt, is weakened if not deſtroyed; and the giddy girl becomes much fitter to be the miſtreſs of a man of quality, than a wife in her own ſtation. This might be eaſily remedied, if perſons of faſhion, at the ſame time that they give their cloaths to their ſervants, would interdict their wearing them. As the caſe ſtands at preſent, the ſervant who applies for a place, reſembles rather a viſiter to the perſon ſhe applies to, than one ſolliciting employment. Their finery induces them to inſiſt upon high wages, to the great injury of all ranks of people who ſtand in need of their ſervice; and inſtead of being of advantage to them, it involves them in difficulties from which they are unable to extricate themſelves; for the whole of their wages being generally ſpent in cloaths, if by accident they are thrown out of place, what recourſe have they for ſupport, but firſt to pawn or ſell their cloaths, and then to proſtitute their perſons?

The dread of the conſequences to which the diſſolute lives of proſtitutes unavoidably ſubject them, namely, univerſal contempt, diſeaſe and want, may, indeed, have its influence over the minds of many, whoſe inclinations lead them to give a looſe to their paſſions, or whoſe proneneſs to idle-

idleneſs tempts them to prefer a life of eaſe and debauchery, to that of induſtry and virtue. But, remove the dread of periſhing in the ſtreets by diſeaſe and want, and point out to them a certain *aſylum* at all events, not attended with the certain puniſhment of confinement, labour or correction; and will not the looſely-inclined be induced to liſt themſelves in the troops of proſtitutes, under this reflection, that let what will happen, there is a certain retreat for them: and thus the hoſpital, inſtead of redreſſing the evil, will actually increaſe it.

The author's motive for publiſhing this imperfect eſſay, is a ſincere deſire to ſerve the Public, by removing theſe and other objections to this charity, in a manner agreeable to the genius of our laws. The truth of this declaration he believes none will queſtion, who know either him or his views. To raiſe an honeſt fame by a faithful, active, and uncorrupt diſcharge of his truſt, is the utmoſt of his ambition; and he modeſtly hopes, that in near thirteen years execution of his public offices, at the riſque of his health, and hazard of his life, none can juſtly charge him with an arbitrary or corrupt action.

Mr. WELCH's

PROPOSALS

To render effectual a PLAN *to remove the nuſance of* COMMON PROSTITUTES *from the ſtreets of this metropolis; to prevent the Innocent from being ſeduced, and to provide a decent and comfortable maintenance for thoſe whom neceſſity or vice have already forced into that infamous courſe of life; and to maintain and educate thoſe children of the Poor, who are either orphans, or are deſerted by wicked parents.*

PROSTITUTES ſwarm in the ſtreets of this metropolis to ſuch a degree, and bawdy-houſes are kept in ſuch an open and public manner, to the great ſcandal of our civil polity, that a ſtranger would think that ſuch practices, inſtead of being prohibited, had the ſanction of the legiſlature, and that the whole town was one general ſtew.

The complaint is as univerſal as the diſorder; the conſequences ariſing from it being ſenſibly felt by a general depravity of morals, a conſtant ſupply of ſharpers and robbers to infeſt our ſtreets, and a train of other evils, which naturally flow from minds depraved by lust and enervated by debauchery.

Acts of lewdness were always punishable at the common law by indictment, and the general sentence upon bawds is, fine, imprisonment, and pillory; and in this case the law punishes the wife equally with the husband, as this offence relates to the government of the house, in which the wife has a principal share.

But tho' the law always punished this offence, the difficulty of conviction was very great, from the various arts and stratagems of the keepers of such houses, who sometimes occupied the house in the name of an unknown person, entered appearances in the crown office, gave bail, bought off the evidence, and threatened the parties with mischief to their persons. These and various other arts, joined to the delay of the law, and difficulty of proving the fact, so effectually disheartened prosecutors, that bawds carried on their houses as openly as if they had a licence for it; and thus with a kind of impunity went on, until their practices occasioned a most dangerous riot, which threatened the peace of the whole town; for a sailor going to one of these dens of lust in the Strand, was there beat in a cruel manner and robbed: instead of applying to a magistrate, he carried his grievance, and applied for redress to his brother tars at Wapping, and they came in numbers and gutted the houses of three of the bawds in the Strand, and made a bonfire of the goods before their doors. This

occa-

occaſioned a juſt, though unpopular execution: and the riot was with great difficulty and danger quelled by the then high-conſtable of Holborn diviſion.

This outrage induced the legiſlature to take the nuſance of bawdy-houſes into conſideration; and by the ſtatute of the 25th of his preſent Majeſty, it is enacted, " That, to encourage " proſecutions againſt perſons keeping bawdy-" houſes, gaming-houſes, or other diſorderly " houſes, the conſtable, on notice given him " in writing by any two inhabitants of the pa-" riſh paying ſcot and lot, of any perſon keep-" ing ſuch bawdy-houſes, &c. ſhall forthwith " go with them to a juſtice of the peace, and (on " their making oath that they do believe the " contents of ſuch notice to be true, and enter-" ing into a recognizance of twenty pounds each " to produce evidence of the offence) the con-" ſtable ſhall enter into a recognizance of thirty " pounds to proſecute the law with effect againſt " ſuch bawdy-houſe keeper, &c. at the next " ſeſſions or aſſizes; and the juſtice is required " to iſſue his warrant for bringing the accuſed " perſons before him, and ſhall bind them o-" ver to appear at the ſaid ſeſſion :or aſſizes; " and ſhall alſo, if he think fit, demand and " take ſurety for their good behaviour in the " mean time.

" And if the conſtable ſhall neglect or re-" fuſe, upon ſuch notice, to go before a juſtice, " or to enter into recognizance, or ſhall be

" wilfully negligent in carrying on the prose-
" cution, he ſhall forfeit twenty pounds to each
" of the ſaid inhabitants.

" And on trial, any perſon may give evi-
" dence againſt the defendant, notwithſtanding
" his being a pariſhioner, or having entered in-
" to ſuch recognizance.

" And the conſtable ſhall be allowed all the
" reaſonable expences of the proſecution, to be
" aſcertained by two juſtices, and ſhall be paid
" the ſame by the overſeers of the poor: and
" if ſuch perſon be convicted, the overſeer ſhall
" alſo forthwith pay ten pounds to each of ſuch
" inhabitants, on pain of forfeiting double that
" ſum to the ſaid perſons.

" And no indictment of ſuch offence ſhall be
" removed by *certiorari.*"

It was generally hoped that this act would effectually ſuppreſs, at leaſt, the open and bare faced bawdy-houſes; as the proceſs againſt them upon this ſtatute not only ſhortens the proceedings, but prevents that kind of chicanery, by which they had formerly eluded puniſhment; and alſo aſſigns a pecuniary reward to enforce its execution. The conſequence of this act was ſo much apprehended by the bawds of Covent Garden, that upon its commencement, and ſome little time after, they ſtopped their infamous practices. But unhappily the execution of this excellent law requires the information of two houſe-keepers who pay ſcot and lot in the pariſh where the offence is committed:

ted: and ſuch is the dread every man is under of incurring the odious name of informer, that few proſecutions have been commenced upon this act. This the bawds ſaw, and availed themſelves of it, by returning openly and publickly to their trade of proſtitution; and one of them, with an impudence agreeable to her calling, advertized in the news papers, that ſhe was removed from the piazzas, Covent-Garden, *to Bow-Street*, which ſhe alſo inſcribed under her ſign; and that ſtreet is now almoſt filled *with infamous houſes.*

To enumerate all the practices of bawds, the artful means by which innocence is decoyed into dens of luſt, and the meaſures practiſed to impriſon deluded girls; and render their return to induſtry and virtue impoſſible, ſo long as health and beauty render them proper objects of gainful proſtitution; would fill volumes.

It is well known that agents are conſtantly employed by bawds to attend the coming into town of waggons and other carriages; and when a young creature arrives, whoſe age, ſhape, and features are likely to raiſe deſire, ſhe is accoſted by ſome agent of corruption, with queſtions concerning her country, and cautions to be very careful of herſelf in this wicked town. After much inſinuating diſcourſe, the ſeducer takes a note where the deſtined victim lodges, and promiſes to inquire for a place for her. If the poor wench knows not of a lodging, the procureſs very luckily recollects a gentlewoman, who boards young ladies, and as her maid went away yesterday, ſhe may go into her place without loſs of time or any expence. This ſpecious addreſs, gilded by a hypocritical pretence to goodneſs, has intrapped many hundred innocents. At her arrival at the bawd's, after ſtrict enquiry concerning character (which the procureſs ſatisfies by averring her knowledge of the girl and her friends) ſhe is hired; and from that moment the unhappy wretch is a priſoner, and either by perſuaſion, or force, ſoon becomes one of the family. When this is effected, her cloaths are taken from her as not elegant enough to ſee gentlemen in; and the bawd procures a flimſey ſuit of either ſecond-hand ſilk, or fine linen, for which a ſufficient price is ſet down; and if the wretch, tired of her wicked courſe of life, even but attempts to depart, a Marſhalſea-Court writ for the cloaths and board is directly executed upon her, and a priſon is her portion, where ſhe is kept until the bawd releaſes her, which is never done but upon a promiſe of implicit obedience; and the debt is immediately augmented by the coſts to ten pounds and upwards, and a note for that ſum is obtained from the unhappy girl, who is threatened with a county writ and Newgate in caſe of a ſecond elopement. Thus ſhe continues until diſeaſes occaſioned by a continued courſe of debauchery, diſqualifies her for houſes of coſtly leudneſs, and then ſhe is diſcharged as a miſerable outcaſt to infeſt the publick ſtreets.

To

To give ſome idea of the horrid ſcenes carried on in theſe brothels, where robberies, drunkenneſs, curſing, ſwearing, and luſtful practices, of which modeſty permits not the bare mention, reign thro' all the waking hours, and recollection is totally buried in one continued riot, till diſeaſe awakens, and deſpair ſeizes upon the guilty mind, take one inſtance. An account being brought me, a few months ſince, that a murder had been committed at an infamous bawdy-houſe in Exeter-Street, I went to apprehend the bawd and her girls for examination; in one of the rooms lay a fine young creature exceſſive ill, who, inſtead of the language of repentance, vented horrid imprecations, and in a little time in deſpair threw herſelf out of the window, and ended her wretched being.

But to conſider the conſequences of this debauchery to the other ſex, what evils is it not productive of? Youth are debilitated, their conſtitutions are deſtroyed, and their morals corrupted: What kind of huſband is ſuch a man like to make a virtuous modeſt woman, if her unhappy fate throws her into his arms? * Add to this,

* If the number of women in the bills of mortality, whoſe ſole dependance is upon proſtitution, be computed at only 3000, a number which, I am convinced, falls far ſhort of the truth; and when it is duly conſidered that more than 2500 of theſe are rendered barren by their infamous courſe of life; thoſe who underſtand political arithmetic, muſt allow this to be no leſs a national than a moral evil; eſpecially if the thought be further purſued, and it be conſidered that

this, that the expence incurred by frequenting bawdy-houſes, is too great for moſt people who connect themſelves with whores and bawds; and yet when their fortunes are ruined by it, habit renders it extremely difficult to break this connexion: money muſt be had to ſupport the extravagance; the highway, or the ſtreets preſent themſelves; whoring is ſucceeded by robbery; and theſe houſes, as they are a certain nurſery of robbers, are alſo the concealers of them, and in them is riotouſly ſpent at night, what the violence of the day has procured. To ſuppreſs theſe houſes by puniſhing the keepers, the law ſeemed to be framed with wiſdom; but experience evinces that many things which appear demonſtrable in theory, often fail in practice. Thus it has happened to the ſtatute of the 25th of the king for the reaſon abovementioned.

My ſentiments of the evil ariſing from common proſtitutes, both to the public and themſelves;

that ſuch criminal converſe alienates the mind from matrimony; for it is hard to conceive that thoſe men who have contracted habits of converſing with every woman they like, will be brought to confine themſelves to one modeſt woman; and too many of them who do are ſo debilitated and weakened by diſeaſe and debauchery, that if any children are procreated by ſuch marriage, they are too generally weakly and infected with the *Evil* and other diſeaſes, from the corrupted ſtate of the father's conſtitution. And ſurely the maxim that a reformed rake makes the beſt huſband muſt be falſe, unleſs it can be proved, that it is a benefit to the fair ſex to have, inſtead of a vigorous conſtitution, the dregs of a broken one.

ſelves ; I ſet forth in the year 1753, by command of a noble duke in a very high ſtation, in a letter to his grace, in which was the following paſſage : Thoſe who have had the ſame opportunities, which the office I then held gave me, of ſeeing the miſery of theſe unhappy wretches, and have attended to the conſequences of their actions, well know that much more might have been ſaid with the ſtricteſt regard to truth.

" Common proſtitutes are another cauſe of
" robberies. Little needs be ſaid to prove that
" theſe wretches, who are lurking at every
" corner of our ſtreets, are an intolerable nu-
" ſance : Here I would be underſtood to mean,
" thoſe unhappy creatures, who, having neither
" a houſe to ſhelter them, nor protector to ſup-
" port them, are under a neceſſity of wander-
" ing up and down the ſtreets to make a prey
" of the unwary apprentice, and intoxicated
" huſband. The bodies of theſe women are
" generally a complication of diſorders, their
" language made up of dreadful execrations, and
" their behaviour infamous beyond compariſon.
" Theſe wretches by their open proſtitution
" make ſin cheap. By theſe the apprentice is
" ſeduced to criminal converſe, which generally
" ends in pilfering from the maſter : Detection
" follows, and if his maſter has the humanity
" to diſcharge him without proſecution, repu-
" tation being deſtroyed, it is odds but he aſſo-
" ciates

" ciates himſelf with the wretch who ſeduced " him, who rarely fails to put him upon rob- " bery for her ſupport. Theſe wretches can- " not be ſaid only to corrupt youth, but like a " virulent contagion precipitate the body into " immediate deſtruction. Great numbers of " theſe have been apprehended upon private " ſearches, and have been ſent, ſome to Bride- " well to hard labour, others, too diſeaſed for " puniſhment, to hoſpitals : Little good, if any, " has aroſe from theſe ; for upon being diſ- " charged from one, and cured at the other, " having no means of recommendation, or ho- " neſt method of ſupporting themſelves, ne- " ceſſity, united to a mind abandoned to de- " bauchery, drives them to their former prac- " tices for ſupport. Hard indeed is that duty " whoſe tendency is uſeleſs ſeverity ; and where " puniſhment only prevents for the time it ope- " rates, but hardly ever produced one reforma- " tion. I have often wiſhed with an aching heart, " that there was among the noble charities, " which diſtinguiſh this age in hoſpitals for al- " moſt every human calamity, one inſtituted " by the legiſlature to receive and provide la- " bour for theſe true objects of compaſſion, as " well as deteſtation. Poſſibly the making " the army cloaths and linen might be intro- " duced, whereby theſe unhappy fellow-crea- " tures might be reſcued from diſeaſe and mi- " ſery, and inſtead of being a nuſance to the

" publick,

" publick, become uſeful to it, and prevent the " ruin of thouſands*."

As acts of bawdry are by the common law deemed breaches of the peace, and bring the actors of them under the denomination of perſons of evil fame; ſo thoſe who offer themſelves for proſtitution, juſtly fall under the deſcription of looſe, idle, and diſorderly perſons, and come within the cognizance of the civil magiſtrate; and upon proof upon oath of the fact, are liable to be committed to priſon as perſons of evil fame, for want of ſureties for their future good behaviour; or, what is more generally practiſed in this caſe, to Bridewell *in execution* for a time not exceeding one kalendar month to hard labour. When ſearch warrants have been granted, founded upon the ſtatute of the 17th of his preſent majeſty, great numbers of theſe unhappy creatures have been apprehended, and committed *in execution to Bridewell for a month to hard labour*; but the puniſhment of the far greater number is generally but of ſhort duration: thoſe who are proper furniture for a bawdy-houſe ſeldom remain twen-

* Since the writing of the above letter, the evil has increaſed: proſtitutes of a higher rank, and gayer turn, ſome from bawdy-houſes, others who have private lodgings of their own, publickly ply in the Strand and Fleet-Street at noon day; and except ſome parliamentary remedy be applied to ſtop the evil, it will not only be impoſſible for modeſt women to walk the ſtreets, as theſe harlots take every opportunity to affront and inſult them; but an univerſal debauchery will alſo ſpread among our youth.

ty-four hours in prifon; for by *bail* and other means the bawds get them releafed, and they return directly and commit the fame offence for which they were imprifoned: But thofe whom difeafe and poverty have rendered friendlefs, are left to pine and languifh out their month's imprifonment under the feverity of the law. This is a fact well known by the gentlemen in the commiffion of the peace who attend goal-deliveries, and the truth of it will be demonftrated by the annals of Bridewell. At the laft general goal-delivery, upon a commitment of this kind, wherein many names were inferted, only two poor wretches, almoft naked, remained; and upon being afk'd by a gentleman who does honour to the commiffion, how they came not to be difcharged as well as the reft? one of them in a feeble languifhing tone of voice anfwered, *Becaufe we had no friends*; upon which the court difcharged them.

It will readily be feen that the law has not provided a remedy adequate to the mifchief thefe unhappy women bring upon themfelves and fociety; and that an amendment of the law is neceffary before this flagrant evil can be redreffed*.

The

* The effect which open proftitution has upon unwary youth is but too well known. Thoufands have been tempted and feduced, to their utter ruin, in their paffage thro' the ftreets where thefe infamous houfes abound; into whofe minds lewdnefs would not have found its way, had not the temptation been placed in this barefaced manner before their eyes.

The reformation of abuſes long practiſed with a kind of impunity, requires good ſenſe and judgment matured by experience. Zeal too often miſleads the underſtanding of the reformer. Great care ought to be taken, that while we haſtily remove one evil, we do not render the remedy worſe than the diſeaſe by introducing a greater. The preſent depravity requires delicacy in it's management. The imagination of the writer is not ſo filled with the idea of reforming that he ſhould ſuppoſe it practicable totally to ſuppreſs whoreing; the conſequence of which, were it poſſible to effect it, might be the encreaſe of a horrid vice too rife already, though the bare thought of it ſtrikes the mind with horror; poſſibly the having waſte ground, may prevent the *razing the ſanctuary and pitching our evils there*, as our excellent poet expreſſes it. But certainly there is a wide difference between vice hiding its head and ſkulking in corners, and vice expoſing its face at noon-day. What idea muſt foreigners have of our policy, when in almoſt every ſtreet they ſee women publickly expoſing themſelves at the windows and doors of bawdy-houſes, like beaſts in a market for publick ſale, with language, dreſs, and geſture too offenſive to mention; and find themſelves tempted (it may be ſaid aſſaulted) in the ſtreets by a hundred women between Temple-Bar and Charing-Croſs, in terms ſhocking to the ear of modeſty. To remove this publick proſtitution, reſtore decency to our ſtreets, provide comfortably by uſeful labour for unhappy wretches now ſunk in luſt and diſeaſe, and by preventive meaſures, to ſecure others from falling a prey to bawds and panders, the author modeſtly offers his ſentiments, to be improved by others, whoſe leiſure hours may be well employed in this benevolent undertaking.

In order to render the law leſs difficult in the execution, and more effectual for the ſuppreſſion of common bawdy-houſes, and thereby to prevent the innocent from being ſeduced, to remove the nuſance of common proſtitutes from the ſtreets, to provide a comfortable maintenance for thoſe who ſhall be deſirous to quit that infamous courſe of life, and to reclaim thoſe who ſhall be apprehended in common bawdy-houſes, or in the public ſtreets, the following outline of an act of Parliament is moſt humbly offered to thoſe of greater abilities and in ſuperior ſtation, to be by them altered and amended, as they ſhall think proper.

Let it be enacted, THAT the keepers of common bawdy-houſes, their agents, and ſervants acting in ſuch bawdy-houſes, being convicted thereof, ſhall be tranſported for the term of ſeven years, according to the laws made for tranſporting felons; excepting thoſe ſervants or agents who ſhall voluntarily offer themſelves to give evidence in his Majeſty's behalf, and be accepted by the juſtice before whom the charge

2 ſhall

ſhall be made; ſuch evidences to be impriſoned until the parties ſo charged ſhall be tried *.

THAT every juſtice of the peace, in his reſpective juriſdiction, be impowered to convene before him the conſtables or any other peace or pariſh officers of the pariſh or place where he ſhall ſuſpect any bawdy-houſes to be kept, and upon their oaths † enquire of the truth of ſuch ſuſpicion; and if ſuch ſuſpicion be confirmed by the oath of any peace or other pariſh officer, ſuch juſtice of the peace ſhall be impowered to enter into ſuch ſuſpected bawdy-houſe, and upon his own view apprehend the occupier of ſuch houſe, together with the ſervants or agents there acting, and commit them to priſon for a time not exceeding three days; when the parties ſo committed ſhall be brought up before the ſaid juſtice for further examination; and the ſaid juſtice ſhall be impowered to ſummon before him ſuch perſon or perſons whom he ſhall deem to be material evidence in his Majeſty's behalf, to prove the truth of the fact againſt ſuch bawds,

* When it is duly conſidered, that our law tranſports for very ſmall ſums feloniouſly taken, tho' perhaps real neceſſity was the motive of the crime; it is hoped that the ſubjecting of theſe wretches, who are the inſtigators to highway robberies and theft, to the ſame puniſhment, will not be deemed too harſh and ſevere, as there ſeems hardly any proportion in the offences with reſpect to the Public.

† As it might be thought too great a power to enable the juſtice to enter any houſe ſolely upon his own ſuſpicion, to obviate this objection the circumſtance of an oath is here ſet down. The power given to convene proper perſons to be examined, is agreeable to our laws.

bawds, their agents, and ſervants; and if ſuch pariſh or peace officers, or ſuch perſons whom the juſtice ſhall deem material evidence, ſhall neglect or refuſe to appear before the juſtice according to the ſummons; then ſuch juſtice ſhall iſſue his warrant to bring ſuch perſons before him: and if the parties ſo convened and ſummoned, or brought before him by warrant as aforeſaid, ſhall refuſe to be examined upon oath touching the premiſes (except the people called Quakers) the juſtice ſhall be impowered to commit ſuch perſons ſo refuſing to anſwer, to priſon, there to reman until ſeſſions, or until they ſhall ſignify to the juſtice that they are willing to be examined as the law directs.

AND if upon ſuch further examination the juſtice ſhall deem the evidence before him ſufficient to put the parties ſo charged to their trials, then the juſtice ſhall take the informations of the evidences, and bind over the conſtable in a recognizance of thirty pounds to proſecute the law with effect at the next or general quarter ſeſſions of the peace; and the other parties in a recognizance of twenty pounds each, to appear and give evidence*. And if the conſtable ſhall be wilfully negligent in carrying on the proſecution, he ſhall forfeit forty pounds to the poor of the pariſh where the offence is committed, to be accounted for as other monies raiſed for the uſe

* This clauſe being founded upon the ſtatute of the 25th of his preſent Majeſty, needs neither comment to explain it, nor reaſons to inforce it.

ufe of the poor are accounted for. And all charges accruing to the conftable in carrying on fuch profecution, and a reafonable allowance for his time and trouble, being fettled by two juftices of the peace in or near the parifh where the offence is committed, fhall be paid him by the overfeers of the poor of the parifh where the offence is committed, out of the monies collected, or to be collected, for the poor, within forty days after the fervice of the faid order of the juftices (which faid allowance fhall be allowed fuch overfeers in paffing their accounts) upon penalty of forfeiting double the fum mentioned in the faid order, to be levied by warrant of diftrefs under the hands and feals of the two juftices who figned the faid order. And fuch juftice fhall commit the parties fo charged to the county goal, there to remain and take their trials at the next general or quarter feffions of the peace to be held for the county in which the offence fhall be committed.

THAT upon the apprehending any proftitute in the ftreet, or in any bawdy-houfe, and the fact being proved, the juftice before whom fhe is brought fhall take the examination of fuch proftitute, upon her oath, touching the place of her legal fettlement, and tranfmit the fame to the next general or quarter feffions, and commit fuch proftitute to † Bridewell, there to remain until the

† A particular ward might be appropriated in the hofpital, for the reception of the committed proftitutes, until the next feffions, and the goals have nothing to do with them.

the next feffions, when the prifoner fhall be brought into court, together with her commitment; and, if the fact charged upon her be proved to the fatisfaction of the court, the feffions fhall have power to commit her to the hofpital hereafter named for any time not exceeding years, nor lefs than one year; and with the commitment annex the examination touching her fettlement taken before the committing juftice; which commitment and examination fhall be forthwith filed, and kept in fuch hofpital for the purpofes hereafter mentioned. And for the future fuch proftitutes as fhall be found plying in the public ftreets, or other public places, fhall and may be apprehended by any perfon who fhall be witnefs of the fact, without any procefs, and be delivered over directly into the cuftody of any conftable, or other peace officer; and fuch conftable or peace officer fhall be required to receive the charge, and immediately convey fuch proftitutes before fome juftice of the peace, to be dealt with as before mentioned†.

The

† This claufe is founded upon the ftatute of the 17th of his prefent Majefty, commonly called the vagrant act, and it will be readily admitted, that common proftitutes are greater offenders againft the public peace, than thofe who through real want feek alms in the ftreets; for which offence they are liable to be committed until feffions, and after that for a time not exceeding fix months to hard labour, and fubject to be whipped at fuch times and places as the court fhall order.

THE means here pointed out for ſuppreſſing lewdneſs, it is hoped, will produce the effect deſired, namely, the putting a ſtop to the open and public traffick of bawds in houſes ſolely appropriated to that purpoſe, by expoſing women at their windows and doors, as tradeſmen do their goods for ſale.

But as a regulation of this ſort muſt of courſe reduce a great number of unhappy young women, who now live only by proſtitution, to abſolute diſtreſs,

It's humbly propoſed for their relief,

That a voluntary ſubſcription be opened for erecting an hoſpital for the reception of Proſtitutes, and the orphan and deſerted children of the Poor, by the name of

That every perſon ſubſcribing fifty pounds at once, be a governor for life; and every perſon contributing five pounds *per ann.* be an annual governor ſo long as ſuch ſubſcription is continued.

That when a fund is raiſed ſufficient for that purpoſe, application be made to parliament to procure an act for the purpoſes beforementioned, and for incorporating the ſaid governors, by the name of *the governors and ſupporters of the hoſpital for the reception and reformation of common proſtitutes, and for the reception of the orphans and deſerted children of the poor*; and that ſuch governors be inveſted with power to receive, confine, put to labour, and provide neceſſaries for, ſuch proſtitutes as ſhall be committed to the ſaid hoſpital by the general or quarter ſeſſions of the peace; and to receive and provide for ſuch penitent proſtitutes as ſhall voluntarily offer themſelves to the ſaid hoſpital; under ſuch terms and reſtrictions as ſhall be from time to time ſettled and agreed to between the governors of the ſaid hoſpital and ſuch penitent proſtitutes: And to receive, maintain, educate, and apprentice out, or place out in ſervices, the orphan and deſerted children of the Poor, according to ſuch rules and orders as ſhall from time to time be made by the governors of the ſaid hoſpital.

And that the ſaid governors, or the majority of them, ſhall have power to make ſuch rules and orders for the better governing and regulating ſuch hoſpital, as from time to time to them ſhall ſeem proper.

That in caſe the ſaid committed proſtitutes ſhould at any time ſo encreaſe in number, that convenient room could not be found for them in the ſaid hoſpital, or the income of the hoſpital be inſufficient to ſupport them: That then and in ſuch caſes the ſaid governors, or any three of them, certifying the ſame to the next court of general or quarter ſeſſions, and producing the commitment of ſeſſions of ſuch proſtitutes, and the examinations thereto annexed, touching the ſettlements of thoſe proſtitutes, whoſe ſettlements ſhall be at the greateſt diſtance from this metropolis, the ſaid court of ſeſſions ſhall paſs ſuch proſtitutes to their legal ſettlements in the ſame form and manner as rogues and

and vagabonds are directed to be paſſed by the ſtatute of the 17th of his preſent Majeſty†.

And if ſuch proſtitutes ſhall, after being ſo paſſed, return back, and be convicted at the general or quarter ſeſſions of committing the like offence, ſuch proſtitutes ſhall be tranſported for ſeven years*.

That if any proſtitute, who ſhall have been ſo committed as aforeſaid, manifeſt an abandoned diſpoſition, by frequent ſwearing, curſing, indecent behaviour, or by being guilty of frequent miſdemeanors, by refuſing to work the hours appointed by the governors, or being idle and negligent in their reſpective labour, quarrelling, or making waſte in her work or proviſions: That then it ſhall and may be lawful to and for ſuch governors, or any three of them, to cauſe ſuch woman to be brought before them at their next meeting; and, the facts being proved, the

E 2 gover-

† The paſſing of proſtitutes to their ſettlement, with the penalty of tranſportation upon their return, will not only thin the ſtreets of theſe wretches, but prevent the hoſpital from being over-charged, either in reſpect of the income, or room in the houſe: and the terror of the puniſhment, it is hoped, will alſo deter others from the purſuit of ſuch practices.

* When every ſtep taken for the reformation of theſe wretches proves ineffectual, no exception can ſurely be taken to their being removed, from being a nuſance to the Public, and bringing deſtruction upon themſelves, to a place where their iniquities cannot be practiſed, and where they will be compelled to be uſeful; ſuch proſtitutes being cured, if they have the venereal diſtemper upon them, before they are ſent abroad.

governors ſhall have power to order her reaſonable corporal puniſhment immediately, or to mulct her in her meals until the next meeting, and alſo place ſome badge or mark of ignominy on her for a week, to be removed, or continued, as her behaviour ſhall deſerve.

That if any woman, after receiving ſuch reaſonable correction or puniſhment as aforeſaid, ſhall continue her abandoned behaviour, ſo as to appear to the governors to be irreclaimable by the reaſonable correction ordered by them at the weekly board; ſuch woman ſhall, upon the fact being certified to the next general or quarter ſeſſions, under the hands of three of the governors, be paſſed in ſuch manner and form as rogues and vagabonds are paſſed, to her ſettlement, as aforeſaid; and if after ſhe ſhall be ſo paſſed, ſhe ſhall return, and commence common proſtitute, upon a proof thereof at the next general or quarter ſeſſions, ſuch woman ſhall be tranſported for ſeven years.

That if any woman ſo committed and confined in the ſaid hoſpital as aforeſaid, ſhall endeavour or attempt to break the ſaid hoſpital, with an intent to eſcape therefrom; or if any other perſon or perſons ſhall break into the ſaid hoſpital, with intent to reſcue any perſon who ſhall be there under confinement, or ſhall attempt to reſcue any perſon who ſhall be in cuſtody by virtue of this act, and conveying either before a magiſtrate, or to this hoſpital, or ſhall

aſſault

assault any officer in the discharge of his duty relative to this hospital, or who shall be conveying such offenders as aforesaid; she, he or they, shall be deemed offenders against law and the public peace; and the court before whom such offenders shall be tried, shall, in case she, he or they be convicted of any of the said offences, order such offender or offenders to be fined and imprisoned, or to be put in the pillory, or publicly whipped, or to be transported (as aforesaid) for the term of seven years, as the court in which any such offender or offenders shall be convicted, shall think fit and order*.

That if any person or persons shall wilfully and maliciously set fire to, or attempt to set fire to, or otherwise destroy the said hospital, or any part thereof, he, she, or they, being convicted thereof, shall be adjudged guilty of felony, and shall suffer death as felons, without benefit of clergy†.

By the method here pointed out of striking at the root of the evil, and uniting this noble in-

* This hospital will have few servants to conduct it, as the prostitutes will be employed alternately to do the whole houshold work, this clause is therefore but a necessary security to protect the matron, and the rest of the servants from any attempt of violence, either from those confined in the hospital, or any person without, with whom they may have been connected.

† As the lives of numbers of people may be involved in such diabolical act, no punishment can be too severe upon the perpetrators of it.

ſtitution with an amendment of the police of this metropolis, the governors will be enabled to purſue their plan with effect; and poſſibly time may remove the nuſance of common proſtitutes from the ſtreets; and by decreaſing the objects intended to be relieved, leave the governors more at liberty to extend their benevolence to the orphan and deſerted children of the poor, whoſe caſe is thus briefly repreſented in the before mentioned letter wrote in 1753.

" Another cauſe of robberies I apprehend to " be the want of a proviſion for maintaining and " educating in good principles aud habits of " induſtry, the children of the poor.

" The children of the poor may be reduced " to three claſſes.

" *1ſt*, The families of the Induſtrious, too " numerous for their parents to maintain with " decency, much leſs provide for their educa" tion in good principles, or labour ſuitable to " their tender age.

" *2dly*, The children of the extravagant diſ" ſolute Poor. Theſe are indeed miſerable; " for ſo far are theſe wretches from taking " proper care of their offspring, that they them" ſelves encourage and inſtruct their children in " the pilfering trade, and are ready to receive " whatever they ſteal.

" *3dly*, Orphans of the Poor, left deſtitute " and friendleſs from the age of ſeven years

to

" to that of fourteen: Unnoticed, and unre-
" lieved by pariſh officers, they are left to
" wander under the cruel alternative of beg-
" ging, ſtealing, or ſtarving.

" What other conſequence can ariſe to the
" Public, from children turned adrift in a
" town wicked as this, with minds untutored,
" and pinched by neceſſity, but a conſtant ſup-
" ply of pick-pockets, pilferers from ſhops,
" and inſtruments in the hands of greater vil-
" lains, to lie concealed in houſes till the dead
" of night, and then let them in to plunder,
" perhaps murder an innocent family? Chil-
" dren thus bred up in ſloth and naſtineſs un-
" til ſeven years of age, at the time when edu-
" cation and habits of induſtry ſhould com-
" mence, become thieves by neceſſity; and if
" they are bold and daring, if they eſcape
" tranſportation, or being cut off by diſeaſe and
" rottenneſs, turn ſtreet robbers, and perhaps
" murderers. The ſacred name of God is no
" otherwiſe known to them, but by dreadful
" execrations; and Religion is firſt taught them
" by the ordinary of Newgate.

" If I am rightly informed, in our manu-
" factory towns children ceaſe to be a burthen
" to their parents at leſs than ſeven years of
" age: And ſure little need be ſaid of the ne-
" ceſſity and utility of ſome hoſpital to receive
" theſe innocents, educate and employ them;

when,

" when, inſtead of their being a dreadful nu-
" ſance to ſociety, as they now are, ſuch a
" foundation would prove a ſeminary of excel-
" lent ſervants to the publick."

By this ſtate of the children of the Poor, it will readily be ſeen that the writer regarded the male part only, as the then proper object of his diſquiſition; and indeed, boys left orphans, or totally deſerted by their parents and friends, are much likelier to become thieves at that age, than the girls are to become whores; and the evils brought upon ſociety by them, more to be dreaded: To extend this charity to the girls only, will therefore be a partial proviſion; humanity and good policy claim the like protection for theſe unhappy innocent boys, who may ſoon be taught to labour in ſome ſimple manufacture, and apprenticed out afterwards to ordinary tradeſmen, artificers, *&c.* or placed out to huſbandmen in the country, where hands are greatly wanting; as the girls may be to middling tradeſmen, artificers, *&c.* as ſoon as they are qualified by their age, ſtature, and abilities.

Thoſe who are well acquainted with the laborious poor in this town, and their mannner of behaviour, know that the generality of them do ſeldom extend their labour beyond what is abſolutely neceſſary to the bare ſupport of their family; and this is the true reaſon why we encounter

counter the children of the Poor at a diſtance from the metropolis, clean, and their cloaths however ordinary, whole and decent; while thoſe in town are too generally ragged, and hurt the eye by their filthy appearance; altho' the parents of the firſt can earn but ſix ſhillings a week, and thoſe of the latter are able, were they willing, to earn fifteen. To take in the children of the Poor indiſcriminately, might not only tend to weaken parental affection, a circumſtance well worthy ſerious conſideration; but it might alſo tend to increaſe that general idleneſs univerſally complained of by maſters in moſt manufactures. Moderate dearneſs of proviſions, however it may affect individuals, is poſſibly far from being a publick detriment; for as it increaſes the national ſtock by additional labour and induſtry, ſo it alſo ſtops the current of exceſs and debauchery; and a frugal uſe of the neceſſaries of life as naturally tends to their increaſe, as wanton profuſeneſs leads to ſcarcity.

But the innocent orphans and deſerted children of both ſexes extend their arms, and particularly call upon the Public to be their common parent, and reſcue them from miſery and deſtruction; Heaven pleads their cauſe; and humanity and good policy unite to demand protection for them. By making this hoſpital a place of general reception of chil-

 dren,

dren, we might, by graſping at too much, defeat the noble deſign; whereas by prudently beginning with theſe deſtitute orphans, the charity may ſoon be carried into execution; and if room be found, and the fund prove ſufficient, the governors may extend their patronage to the children of the diſſolute.

There is an inſtitution of this kind at Paris, the utility of which has been thoroughly experienced.

This hoſpital was founded about the year 1202 by two friars, for the reception of poor paſſengers, and continued under their, and other direction, until the year 1545; but abuſes having crept in, "the "parliament obliged the paſſengers to re- "move, and put in their ſtead the children "of the poor of both ſexes, born in Paris "in lawful wedlock; to give them educa- "tion, and teach them a trade. This hoſ- "pital conſiſts of 100 beds for boys, and "thirty-ſix for girls, who have different a- "partments; their cloathing a blue uniform. "The youngeſt are taught to read and write; "and as ſoon as they are ſix or ſeven years "of age, they are taught ſome trade in the "hoſpital, all ſorts of trades having been ſet "up in this hoſpital. And, in order to en- "courage tradeſmen to come and exerciſe "their trades here, and to teach the chil-

"dren,

" dren, the parliament declared, that ſuch " journeymen as ſhould have taught theſe " poor children ſix years in this hoſpital, " ſhould have the freedom without any coſt " or trial *. And thoſe children who " ſhould be arrived to the age of 25, and " have taught others during ſix years ſince " they were out of their apprenticeſhip, " ſhould have the ſame privilege. This " wiſe eſtabliſhment has procured the city " of Paris a vaſt number of very able artifi- " cers of all ſorts, who might otherwiſe have " paſſed their lifetime in a ſhameful and " burthenſome poverty [the author might " have added, perhaps turn'd robbers and " murderers.] This hoſpital is governed by " five eminent perſons choſen by the parlia- " ment out of ten, whom the attorney- " general preſents †."

But if a plan of this nature ſhould not be approved, a correſpondence might be ſettled with the manufacturing towns of Birmingham, Sheffield, Mancheſter, &c. for transferring the children, at a proper age or ſtature, from this hoſpital, to the artificers and mechanics of thoſe towns, who ſhould apply for apprentices.

 The

* The author has omitted to mention whether the freedom is of Paris only, or extends to the whole kingdom.

† General Syſtem of Geography, Vol. I. p. 48.

The *Prefervatory* Plan, it is apprehended, is too confined in limiting the objects for this hofpital to children of feven years of age and upwards. It is a melancholy fact that many boys are now thieves and pilferers under that age: And Covent-Garden, St. Giles's, and other places, afford too many inftances of girls, not yet feven years old, curfing, fwearing, and making ufe of obfcene expreffions. If therefore the girls even fo young are to be uncorrupt in their morals to intitle them to be candidates for this charity, it is much to be feared that thofe who need it moft will be excluded, and the hofpital be but thinly inhabited. The younger the children are admitted, the greater the profpect of their future happinefs will be; nor poffibly would it be attended with any material inconvenience, if fuch children as fhould be rejected by the Foundling-houfe, on account of age, were here admitted, upon proof before the governors, that fuch children were orphans, or deferted by their parents or friends*.

It is not my intention, nor indeed, although I have been long converfant in the management of hofpitals, is it within the compafs of my

* It will readily be feen that great care ought to be taken, that this hofpital be not made ufe of to eafe the work-

my abilities, to preſcribe a ſyſtem for the interiour government of this charity. Rules and orders muſt be made as incidents ariſe. But a few miſcellaneous hints will, I hope, be rather interpreted a deſire to promote this excellent charity, than an impertinent dictating to a ſet of gentlemen who intend to dedicate a part of their time to the management of it; more eſpecially as a plan has already been ſketched out by Mr. Dingley, of whoſe abilities I have a far better opinion, than of my own.

To the labour * propoſed by Mr. Dingley's plan, I beg leave to add, that of making the ſoldiers

workhouſes of the ſeveral pariſhes of the children whom, their legal ſettlements are known, and whom the law has ſufficiently provided for. But as numbers of vagabonds, as well as induſtrious Iriſh poor, ſwarm in this town, and moſt of the Iriſh are papiſts, the providing for the orphan and deſerted children of theſe, and bringing them up in the proteſtant religion, will render them uſeful and loyal ſubjects, and ſtrengthen the proteſtant cauſe.

* It deſerves ſerious conſideration what kind of labour is moſt proper to be introduced into this hoſpital: The governors will, no doubt, be careful that while they relieve one ſet of objects, they do not bring diſtreſs and miſery upon others by depriving them of the means of ſupport. The laundry plan is obviouſly productive of this ill conſequence, by ruining a great number of people whoſe ſole ſupport is waſhing linen. But as the execution of Mr. Dingley's plan is in the hands of a body of merchants, the moſt reſpectable in the kingdom,

ſoldiers cloaths and linen; as this work will not only be certain, but ſo eaſy, that the moment a woman comes into the hoſpital, ſhe will be capable of earning more than the expence of her apparel and maintenance: and the contractors for cloathing the army, would gladly embrace the opportunity of having their work done here, as they would be not only certain of having the cloaths finiſh'd in due time to perform their contracts, but alſo the injury they ſuſtain by their cloaths being made away with, by giving them out to numbers of bad people, would be prevented. Upon a ſurvey of the expence of the poor in St. Giles's workhouſe, in a year when the price of proviſions was at a medium with a number of years before, I found that, all expences included, the charge was under two ſhillings a week a head: And of my own knowledge, a woman who is but tolerably quick at her needle, may earn upwards of three ſhillings and ſixpence per week at ſoldiers work.

It ſeems neceſſary that the hoſpital for the proſtitutes ſhould conſiſt of two parts; one for the reception of penitent proſtitutes, which

dom, it is not to be doubted, that their extenſive knowledge in trade will enable them to introduce ſome new manufacture into the hoſpital, whereby the nation may be benefited, and no individual hurt.

which in good policy ſhould be made rather the object of deſire, as an agreeable retreat from temptation, than of dread, as a place of puniſhment. It ſhould be appropriated to thoſe only upon whoſe minds Grace ſhould work a change, and induce to forſake their evil courſes; or others who might be deſirous to quit their miſerable ſituation on account of temporal miſchiefs attending it. The other part of the hoſpital may be for thoſe apprehended in their crimes, who, though they excite commiſeration as diſtreſſed fellow-creatures, ought to be dealt with in a different manner, ſo as to render their confinement in the eyes of the vulgar a kind of puniſhment. This would prevent ſome from deviating from virtue, and induce the penitent who might be ſincerely deſirous to be kept from temptation, voluntarily to preſent herſelf to be received into this hoſpital as a place of retreat from contempt and miſery, and thereby avoid the ſhame of being apprehended and expoſed in a court of juſtice, and abiding it's ſentence. Any communication between this part and that allotted for the reception of the orphan and deſerted children, ought to be rendered abſolutely impracticable.

The governors being ſatisfied of the ſincerity of the penitent proſtitutes, may appoint thoſe whoſe abilities may qualify them for the

the office, to be ſub-matrons of the committed proſtitutes wards, for the more orderly and regular government thereof, under ſuch regulations as from time to time ſhall be made by the governors; or the governors may transfer them as ſervants into the Orphan-Hoſpital. The repentant proſtitutes might alſo be permitted to do any kind of work they might be qualified for; and after one year's continuance in the hoſpital might be ſuffered to depart upon preſenting a petition to the board; or ſooner than a year, if they could be provided for to the ſatisfaction of the governors; the governors giving them ſuch certificate as their conduct and behaviour ſhould deſerve.

Upon the commitment or admiſſion of ſuch proſtitutes to the hoſpital, an uniform cloathing for thoſe committed might be ſettled by the governors, and another of better materials for the penitents; and the cloaths they come to the hoſpital in, if they be worth preſerving, be got up in a decent manner, and label'd with the perſon's name, and ranged in a warehouſe in the order of their admiſſion, except ſuch cloaths as the governors ſhould deem too fine for their ſtation, which might be ſold for the beſt price, and an account of the produce of ſuch cloaths be entered into a book, together with the neat produce of the labour

of

of every proſtitute during the time of her continuance in the hoſpital.

Twice every year a general account of the expence of the hoſpital might be made up, in order to aſcertain the expence of every individual; and the expence of ſuch individual be entered on the debtor ſide of her account.

After the continuance of any woman in the hoſpital for one year, upon the modeſt and virtuous demeanour and induſtrious conduct of ſuch woman, and upon application of her parents or friends; or of any houſe-keeper, who upon enquiry ſhould be found to be of ſufficient credit, and in want of a ſervant; if ſuch friends declare, that they will forgive the paſt offences of ſuch woman, and will provide for her; or if ſuch houſe-keeper will receive ſuch woman as a ſervant; in either of thoſe caſes the governors might diſcharge ſuch woman.

Upon the diſcharge of ſuch woman, her cloaths, or, if ſold, the neat produce of them ſhould be returned to her, together with whatever balance might be due upon her account; and a certificate given her, under the hands of three or more of the governors, of her conduct and behaviour during the time of her being in the hoſpital.

Every proſtitute, whether repentant or committed, who ſhould be placed in a ſervice from this hoſpital, and ſhould continue one whole year in ſuch ſervice to the ſatisfaction of the maſter or miſtreſs; upon the fact being made out to the ſatisfaction of a board of the governors at their next meeting; the governors might give ſuch woman, by way of encouragement, the ſum of two guineas.

At the firſt general meeting of the governors, a preſident, vice preſidents, and a treaſurer might be choſen by ballot. And alſo a committee of twenty-four governors † to manage and conduct the affairs of the hoſpital; who, with the preſident or vice preſidents, might meet weekly or oftener at the ſaid hoſpital. Nevertheleſs every governor ought to be at liberty to attend, and act, at ſuch weekly or other meeting, five to be a quorum.

A

† The appointment of a committee of fathers for life, to the total excluſion of every other governor, as propoſed by the *plan for a laundry*, appears to me falſe policy; for it is hard to conceive that any 24 gentlemen will accept of the fatigue of a government for life, where no profit can ariſe, and where it muſt neceſſarily break into their own domeſtic affairs, except ſuch as are fond of power indeed; a quality which certainly ought to exclude them; for in this caſe the management of the hoſpital might fall under a junto of very improper people. And the moſt reſpectable ſocieties have kept open the direction by frequent elections, witneſs the Bank, Eaſt India company, and all other ſocieties of rank and eſtimation; ſuch frequent elections, as it prevents the ill uſe men are too apt to make of power, ſo it is a check upon their conduct, and is preventive of inſolent behaviour.

A preſident, vice preſidents, treaſurer, and committee, as aforeſaid, as alſo the ſeveral officers of the hoſpital who ſhould rank above the degree of common ſervants, might be annually choſen by ballot, at the annual general meeting, by the majority of the governors preſent.

Any five or more of the committee or governors at their weekly or other meeting, might be empowered to call a general meeting of the governors as often as they ſhould judge it requiſite for the benefit of the hoſpital; but not leſs than four times a year; of which the annual general meeting ſhould be one; notice of which meetings ſhould be advertiſed in the public papers three days at leaſt before.

At every annual general meeting, there ſhould be laid before the governors the general ſtate of the hoſpital reſpecting the year's receipts, and diſburſements, caſh in hand, &c. the number of repentant proſtitutes in the hoſpital; the names of thoſe admitted ſince the laſt annual meeting; the names of thoſe provided for, and the manner how, in the compaſs of the laſt year, and the time they continued in the hoſpital. And the ſame account of the committed proſtitutes; and the orphan and deſerted children of the Poor, and all other matters and things relating to the hoſpital. And an abſtract of the ſaid account might be published in ſuch manner as the governors ſhould deem moſt ſatisfactory to the Public.

Three or more of the committee might, at their weekly or other meeting, go through the ſeveral wards of the proſtitutes and the children, to enquire into the conduct of the officers and ſervants towards the proſtitutes and children, and the behaviour of the proſtitutes and children themſelves, and inſpect into the goodneſs of the ſeveral proviſions and goods ſent, and ſuch other matters as ſhould occur to them reſpecting the good government and order of the charity, and report their obſervations to the board. And no perſon, excepting a governor, ought to be permitted to go into any proſtitute ward, in the intervals of the ſitting of the committee, except the chaplain, phyſician, ſurgeon, or apothecary, nor any governor but in the company of the chaplain or matron.

Thus have I endeavoured to model an inſtitution, which by a due mixture of mildneſs and ſeverity may redreſs an enormity which has long infeſted our ſtreets, and diſgraced our government; which has brought to the *grave* multitudes of the young by diſeaſe, and of the old by ſorrow. I have laid down rules of an hoſpital, in which penitence may be ſheltered, and corruption be reclaimed; where honeſt induſtry may be inculcated by inſtruction, or inforced by chaſtiſement: where thoſe who were once educated in the know-

ledge

ledge of religion, may gradually revive the principles which had been almoſt extinguiſhed by intercourſe with bad example, and by ſucceſſive viciſſitudes of riots and diſtreſs: and the light of inſtruction may be imparted to thoſe, whoſe minds have been hitherto clouded with ignorance, whom poverty has reſigned to guilt without a check, and whoſe intellectual powers have ſerved them to no other purpoſe than thoſe of fraud, and rapine, treachery and ſeduction.

From the reformation of guilt, if it can be happily effected, the proſpect goes on to its prevention in ſucceeding generations. The unpleaſing employment of puniſhing thoſe who have already tranſgreſſed the laws of virtue, will be changed to that of preſerving thoſe who muſt hereafter tranſgreſs, if charity does not ſnatch them out of the ſnares of poverty. If there are any who hate vice more than they love virtue, and in their zeal for vindictive juſtice, conſider all thoſe as unworthy of their favour whoſe miſery may be imputed to their crimes; yet not even theſe can refuſe compaſſion to them who are about to ſuffer by the crimes of others; whom the poverty or negligence of their parents expoſes to the temptation of hunger and nakedneſs; whom diſtreſs unavoidably mingles with robbers and profligates; and whoſe minds, untaught and unſettled, are open to the influ-

ence

ence of every tongue which perſwades them to relieve their wants at the expence of their innocence.

This charity is therefore recommended by every conſideration, civil and religious: whoever contributes to it, may ſolace his mind by reflecting, that his charity frees the ſtreets from annoyance, reſcues his ſervants and children from temptation, ſecures his goods from robbery, and his life from violence; and, what ought to prevail beyond all other motives, preſerves ſouls from everlaſting miſery.

The following letter, written in the year 1753, and from whence two quotations are made in the foregoing propofals, by fome accident made its appearance in the *London Chronicle*, in *January* laft, and was republifhed in *Lloyd's Evening Poft*, foon after, but very incorrectly in the latter: feveral gentlemen of worth and candour, defirous to have a copy, and not able to get one, have, fince the printing of this pamphlet, follicited Mr. Welch to reprint, and annex it thereto entire. As the writer had not any copy, he has reprinted it from the *London Chronicle*; to the author of which paper he is, at leaft, obliged, for his care in fending it abroad correct.

This letter is annexed. with fomewhat the more propriety, as the author had unaccountably forgotten to mention bawdy-houfes among the nurferies of robbers; and therefore none of the remarks contained in the letter are anticipated in the foregoing Effay, except in the quotations, which would not have been made, had there been then any defign of publifhing the letter itfelf. Thefe two pieces contain what the author's obfervation has fuggefted to him, concerning the caufes and remedies of corruption among the lower orders of the people.

MY LORD,

" IN obedience to your Grace's commands, fignified to me by Mr. Sharpe, I moft humbly prefent to you what has occurred to me, me, in my confined ſphere of life, relating to the frequent murders and robberies ſo juſtly and univerſally complained of.

"The grand ſpring of the whole may perhaps be with ſome degree of juſtice aſcribed to the irreligion, idleneſs, almoſt total want of morals, and diſſoluteneſs of manners of the common people, together with the too remiſs execution of the laws in being, and the bad examples of too many in higher ſtations.

"*The unlimited wandering of the Poor of our own kingdom, and the uncontrouled importation of Iriſh vagabonds, are two great cauſes of the ſupply of rogues to this town.*

"The great diſproportion of the births and burials in this metropolis, ſufficiently demonſtrates the neceſſity of frequent ſupplies of ſervants and labourers from the country; and it is of the laſt importance that thoſe ſupplies be the honeſt and induſtrious: and ſome method to induce theſe to come, and reſtrain the idle and diſſolute, would be of great conſequence, not only to private families who muſt be ſupplied from this ſource, but to the police of the town. Indiſcriminate migrations are in their conſequences bad; for as the good ſervant may be here greatly improved and rendered more uſeful, ſo the mind enervated by bad principles and an idle diſpoſition, will ſoon improve in the arts of villainy, to the public nuiſance, and its own deſtruction. The motives of theſe two for coming

to

to London, are these: the first, desirous to improve himself and his circumstances, comes with an honest and laudable intention: the other, finding his continuance in the country unsafe, flies to town to conceal himself, and practise his knavery. It is therefore humbly apprehended, that a law ought to be made to prevent the servant and labourer from removing from their legal settlement, or other place of residence, without a certificate, describing the name, age, stature, and person of the party, and that he or she have behaved with honesty and industry, and that their purpose is to go to London, or whatever place it be, to become servants or labourers: such certificate to be signed either by a magistrate, minister, or churchwardens; and, to prevent such certificates being counterfeited, to have the cheapest stamp possible; the counterfeiting of which should receive the punishment of death, as for counterfeiting other stamps; and the counterfeiting of the names of those by law impowered to sign such certificates, should subject the parties to the punishment of rogues and vagabonds. And all servants or labourers, upon their passing through any city, town, or village, being thereunto required by any mayor, justice of the peace, or other officer, should produce his or her certificate, and upon refusal to produce it, or if upon examination it shall be found that they have wandered without one, it ſhould be lawful for any juſtice of the peace, mayor, &c. to paſs ſuch parties back to their ſettlement, as rogues and vagabonds are paſſed.

" It is humbly conceived, that ſome method of this kind will be of the greateſt uſe to the honeſt and induſtrious ſervant and labourer, who will come with much greater confidence to aſk for employment ſo certified, than otherwiſe: and this may in time produce a valuable reformation in the behaviour of the ſervants and labourers in the country, eſpecially in the riſing generation; for when they ſee that good conduct will enable them to go where their intereſt or inclinations may lead, and a bad one will ſubject them to a kind of impriſonment in their own particular pariſh, it may ſo ſtrongly operate upon their minds, that the idleneſs and pilfering, ſo much complained of in the country, may totally ceaſe, and this town be no farther annoyed and peſtered by looſe and diſordered fellows from thence.

" The Iriſh imported into this kingdom of the lower claſs are thoſe who annually come to harveſt work; and, when that is over, return with the ſavings of their labour to their own country. Theſe are uſeful, faithful, good ſervants to the farmer; and as they are of real uſe to the kingdom, deſerve protection and encouragement. The others are a ſet of fellows

lows made desperate by their crimes, and whose stay in Ireland being no longer safe, come to London to perpetrate their outrages: and it may be justly asserted, that most of the robberies, and the murders consequent upon them, have been committed by these outcasts of Ireland. To prevent these desperado's coming here, will be to prevent many robberies. There is indeed a law which from the long non-execution of it, almost requires a republication: this enacts, That any master of a ship who shall import any vagabond, either from Ireland, or any of his Majesty's islands or plantations, into this kingdom, shall be liable to a penalty of five pounds, and all costs and charges arising from the apprehending and reconveying such vagabonds. Might not certificates of the honest and industrious behaviour of Irish servants and labourers be made the necessary passport to be produced to the master of the ship before he presume to admit the party on board, and the master of the ship produce it to the custom-house officer at the port where he lands? Such certificate to be signed by the magistrates, &c. as before described; and the same power of demanding the sight of it in every city, town, or village, through which such labourer or person may pass, upon pain of being sent back as a rogue and vagabond.

"That London is the asylum of those rogues

and vagabonds, as well Iriſh as Engliſh, who are driven by their rogueries to ſeek ſhelter and concealment, is a truth beyond diſpute; and when the houſes to which they reſort are conſidered, it is matter of wonder that a night paſſes without numbers of robberies and burglaries. There have, within a few years, ariſen in the out-ſkirts of this town, a kind of traffic in old ruinous buildings, which the occupiers fill up with ſtraw and flock beds, which they nightly lett out at two-pence for a ſingle perſon, or three-pence a couple; nor is the leaſt regard paid to decency. Men and women are promiſcuouſly entertained; and in my ſearches after villains, I have found two or three couple in one room, who were perfect ſtrangers to each other before the preceding night, then in bed together. Indeed I have ſeen debauchery in theſe houſes carried farther than this; for ſometimes two women have been in bed with one man, and two men with one woman. Four or five beds are often in one room; and what with the naſtineſs of theſe wretches, and their numbers, ſuch an inconceivable ſtench has aroſe from them, that I have been hardly able to bear it the little time my duty required my ſtay. Spirituous liquors afford means of intoxication for the wretches here received; and the houſes are kept open all night to entertain rogues and receive their plunder. Great

numbers

numbers of desperate villains have been taken out of these houses and executed. One woman occupies, in the parish of St. Giles's, near twenty of these houses. Black-boy Alley abounds with them; and they were the shelter of that dreadful gang of villains, who, about nine years since, robbed and wounded people at noon day. The bringing them to justice cost the Government great sums: and several of the civil officers were dreadfully wounded. Shoreditch has also numbers of them. A few years ago I assisted Mr. Henry Fielding in taking from under one roof upwards of seventy lodgers of both sexes. Suppose the number of these houses to be only two hundred, and compute only twenty persons to a house, the number is 4000; and, much I fear, not one fourth could obtain a just character of honesty and industry: the rest consisting of rotten whores, pick-pockets, pilferers, and others of more desperate denominations. What evils are the Public not liable to from such a villainous mixture as this?

" *Another cause of robberies I apprehend to be, the want of provision for maintaining and educating in good principles, and habits of industry, the children of the Poor.*

" The children of the Poor may be reduced to three classes:

1. The

" 1. The families of the Induſtrious, too numerous for their parents to maintain with decency, much leſs to provide for their education in good principles, or labour ſuitable to their tender age.

2. The children of the extravagant diſſolute Poor. Theſe are indeed miſerable; for ſo far are theſe wretches from taking proper care of their offspring, that they themſelves encourage and inſtruct their children in the pilfering trade, and are ready to receive whatever they ſteal.

" 3. Orphans of the Poor, left deſtitute and friendleſs from the age of ſeven years to that of fourteen: unnoticed, and unrelieved by pariſh officers, they are left to wander under the cruel alternative of begging, ſtealing, or ſtarving.

" What other conſequences can ariſe to the Public, from children turned adrift in a town wicked as this, with minds untutored, and pinched by neceſſity, but a conſtant ſupply of pick-pockets, pilferers from ſhops, and inſtruments in the hands of greater villains to lie concealed in houſes till the dead of the night, and then let them in to plunder, perhaps murder an innocent family? Children thus bred up in ſloth and naſtineſs until ſeven years of age, at the time when education and habits of induſtry ſhould commence, become thieves by neceſſity; and, if they are bold nd daring, if they escape transportation, or being cut off by disease and rottenness, turn street robbers, and perhaps murderers. The sacred name of God is no otherwise known to them, but by dreadful execrations; and religion is first taught them by the Ordinary of Newgate.

" If I am rightly informed, in our manufactory towns children cease to be a burthen to their parents at less than seven years of age: and sure little need be said of the necessity and utility of some hospital to receive these innocents, educate and employ them: when instead of their being a dreadful nusance to society, as they now are, such a foundation would prove a seminary of excellent servants to the Public.

" The offspring of beggars are thieves and whores from both precept and example: the children of these wretches might be provided for as above; and happy would it be for the Public, if their sturdy fathers and mothers were transported; and the objects of age and infirmity were confined to their proper settlements. The laws indeed are amply sufficient; but laws unexecuted, and no laws, are the same thing. Were the magistrates of London, Westminster, and Southwark, to unite in putting the laws into vigorous execution, and at one time to signify their resolution, requiring those beggars who were unable by

age

age or infirmities to apply for paſſes to the officers of the reſpective pariſhes where they reſide by a certain day; and a declaration that thoſe found wandering and begging after that day, ſhould receive the utmoſt chaſtiſement of the law; and to affix their reſolutions in printed papers to the corners of the ſtreets, and ſpirit up their under-officers by giving the rewards the law allows for apprehending vagabonds; I will be bold to ſay, that not a beggar would be ſeen in our ſtreets; and poſſibly this example might be followed by the reſt of the kingdom, to the total ridding of ſociety of theſe burthens to our minds, as well as purſes. By this means thoſe who were able would be compelled to labour; real objects would be decently provided for at a tenth part of the expence they now are; and the whole abridgment to the begging tribe, would be the two incentives to begging, idleneſs and ſpirituous liquors."

" *Common proſtitutes are another cauſe of robberies.*

" Little needs be ſaid to prove that theſe wretches, who are lurking at every corner of our ſtreets, are an intolerable nuiſance: here I would be underſtood to mean, thoſe unhappy creatures who having neither a houſe to ſhelter them, nor protector to ſupport them, are under a neceſſity of wandering up and down the ſtreets to make a prey of the unwary apprentice, and intoxicated huſband. The bodies of theſe women are generally a complication of diſorders; their language made up of dreadful execrations; and their behaviour infamous beyond comparison. Theſe wretches by their open proſtitution make ſin cheap. By theſe the apprentice is ſeduced to criminal converſe; which generally ends in pilfering from his maſter: detection follows, and if the maſter has the humanity to diſcharge him without proſecution, reputation being deſtroyed, it is odds but he aſſociates himſelf with the wretch who ſeduced him, who rarely fails to put him upon robbery for her ſupport. Theſe wretches cannot be ſaid only to corrupt youth, but like a virulent contagion precipitate the body into immediate deſtruction. Great numbers of theſe have been apprehended upon private ſearches, who have been ſent, ſome to Bridewell to hard labour, others, too diſeaſed for puniſhment, to hoſpitals: little good, if any, has aroſe from theſe; for upon being diſcharged from one, and cured at the other, having no means of recommendation, or honeſt method of ſupporting themſelves, neceſſity, united to a mind abandoned to debauchery, drives them to their former practices for ſupport. Hard indeed is that duty whoſe tendency is uſeleſs ſeverity; and where puniſhment only prevents for the time it operates, but hardly ever produced one reformation. I have often wiſhed with an aching heart, that there was among the noble charities, which diſtinguiſh this age in hoſpitals for almoſt every human calamity, one inſtituted by the legiſlature to receive and provide labour for theſe true objects of compaſſion, as well as deteſtation. Poſſibly the making the army cloaths and linnen might be introduced, whereby theſe unhappy fellow-creatures might be reſcued from diſeaſe and miſery, and inſtead of being a nuiſance to the Public, become uſeful to it, and prevent the ruin of thouſands.

" *Gaming-houſes are another cauſe of robberies.*

" This is a truth too glaring to need any illuſtration. A remedy for this evil has at times taken up the attention of the legiſlature for two centuries: but ſo long as great men ſubſtitute falſe honour to defeat the laws of their country, and prefer the graſping at another man's fortune, while they neglect the true enjoyment of their own, it is no wonder that every intention of the legiſlature is fruſtrated. Happy would it be if gaming were confined to people of quality and fortune; for however they may uſe little

tle arts againſt one another, there is no danger of their turning either highwaymen, or ſtreet robbers. But, alas! the example deſcends, and the minds of the common people are become infected; and here indeed gameſter and highwayman are almoſt ſynonimous. Poſſibly ſubjecting the keepers of gaming-houſes and their helpers, except ſuch as ſhould give information and evidence, to be tranſported as felons, and whipping at the cart's tail every perſon under the degree of a gentleman, proved to have gamed, might cure this accurſed practice.

" Under the article of gaming, a ſet of men denominated gamblers comes properly. Theſe are fellows who have ſubſiſted in this kingdom more than forty years; and uſing every trick and cheat to defraud the Unwary, have reigned, if I may ſo term it, almoſt with impunity. Theſe cheats attend at every avenue of the town, and at moſt of the fairs in the kingdom, where, by the arts of card-playing, pricking at the belt, falſe dice, ſelling pretended gold rings, and numberleſs other ſtratagems, they live upon the plunder of the Innocent, and that often to the total deſtruction of families. As theſe often aſſume the dreſs of gentlemen, by that diſguiſe they introduce themſelves to the gaming-tables of the Polite, and ſome thouſands of guineas have been brought from the gaming-tables at the masquerade by these gentry, by arts now well known. These men are very numerous: and they are said to be formed into a kind of body corporate, and to have their treasurer and sollicitor, whose business it is either to buy off prosecution, or procure false evidence to defeat a just one. Indeed, when the artful trade has failed, these nurseries produce genteel highwaymen, who being learned and practised in every disguise, are the hardest of all others to detect and bring to justice. The true reason of the long and successful reign of gamblers in this kingdom is, that there is not a punishment in the law adequate to the offence: for if any of them is detected in their frauds, it is a bailable offence, being a misdemeanor only: bail is easily got by the treasurer; and before the time of trial comes, the prosecutor is reimbursed his loss, and there ends the prosecution. But as they have various arts of disguising themselves, they are successful twenty times to one that they are detected. Shopkeepers suffer prodigiously by being defrauded of their goods by false messages and other arts. These fellows are so well known, that if the magistrates had a power to apprehend them, and, upon their being unable to prove that they subsist by lawful means, to commit them to hard labour as vagabonds till the ſeſſions, then to be dealt with according to their demerits; a ſtop would ſoon be put to theſe peſts to the harmleſs, unwary, honeſt country people and ſhopkeepers."

" *Accomplices in robberies who are admitted evidences, being left at liberty after the conviction of their comerades, is a great cauſe of a conſtant ſupply of robbers.*

" As robbing in the ſtreets of London is of all enterprizes the moſt bold and daring, gangs are frequently formed for this purpoſe; and I have known them fourteen or ſixteen in number. They divide themſelves into parties to rob, and are ready to unite to ſupport and procure the eſcape of their companions even with murder. Theſe gangs have been as conſtantly broke as they have got together: But to effect this benefit to the Public, it has unhappily been neceſſary to admit one or more of theſe villains as evidences, as well to get at the knowledge of the reſt, and their lurking-places, as by a diſcovery of the manner of the robberies to procure proſecutions, and legal evidences to bring them to juſtice. Theſe evidences, as ſoon as their accomplices are convicted, are diſcharged, and with this addition of infamy are turned into the ſtreets to remain the contempt and terror of ſociety. This ſort of of reception from the Public never fails to induce the unhappy criminal to endeavour to raiſe a freſh gang, which he can eaſily do by reſorting to the houſes I have before deſcribed. He ſoon finds proper aſſociates; and there hardly paſſes a ſeſſion when one or more are not convicted, who perhaps the preceding one were evidences. A glaring inſtance of the truth of this obſervation I knew in the caſe of one Lewis, concerned in robbing Lady Albemarle: being admitted an evidence, he committed a robbery in Southampton fields within two hours of his diſcharge from Newgate, in company with one Campbell. Indeed I have obſerved that generally the evidence is the moſt notorious villain. Would it not be charity to the criminal, as well as beneficial to the Public, to ſend them, under ſome reſtraint, abroad for ſeven years? Their haunts and habits of idleneſs and vice might be broke, and a reformation rendered probable; which is impoſſible whilſt they ſtay in England. Indeed, theſe fellows are rarely intitled to the benefit of the ſtatute in its utmoſt extent; for they are generally apprehended before they are admitted evidences: whereas the ſtatute requires a voluntary ſurrender.

" *A better regulation of the priſons, by preventing*

venting debaucheries and all exceſſes; ſeparating murderers, ſtreet-robbers, burglars, and highwaymen, from any communication with thoſe committed for aſſaults, breaches of the peace, or petty thefts: and that the keepers of gaols ſhould ſubſiſt upon ſalaries, and not perquiſites, would be a great means of preventing the increaſe of robberies.

" In the preſent ſtate of our priſons, they are far from being that object of dread and terror they ought always to be: for the greater conſumption of wine and beer (the legiſlature by a late act having baniſhed ſpirituous liquors) made by a priſoner or his friends, the greater profit ariſes to the gaoler: and a good priſoner in the gaoler's language, is he, who has the greateſt means of exceſs, or who being a prodigy in villainy, numbers croud to ſee him; and he is exhibited to view for the profit of his keeper. Sometimes this furniſhes the felon with inſtruments to effect his eſcape. If this fails, perhaps he is by wine, &c. kept in a ſtate of continued intoxication, glories in his villainies to the time of his trial, and then determines to dye a hero. Thus the intention of public juſtice is defeated; for inſtead of being a dreadful example to deter others, his bold and daring behaviour renders him, as he from experience knows, the darling of the mob, and delight of his brethren in villainy,

lainy, who are more encouraged in their practices, by the conduct of one of these, than they are deterr'd by that of twenty penitents.

I would here suggest a hint to prevent this daring behaviour of convicts going to and at the place of execution. The bodies of those criminals are at the King's disposal; if my Lords the Judges, upon passing sentence, would mention this enormity, and give direction to the sheriff in the hearing of the prisoners at the bar, that upon any improper conduct, either in the prison after sentence, or going to or at the place of execution, the body of such criminal should not be delivered to his friends for burial, but be conveyed to Surgeons Hall; this, I am satisfied, would produce outward penitence at least, and cure this absurd heroism. Our Bridewells, those schools of labour, wisely instituted as the proper punishment and cure of idleness, are, I fear, little better than nurseries of debauchery. Labour and correction, the sentence of the law, are never put into execution, except poverty be annexed to the crime; for, as I have before observed, the profit of the gaoler arising from the consumption of liquors, it is absurd to imagine that he will correct his friends. What necessity is there either for wine or strong beer in prisons? The being debarred from means of excess and intempetemperance, might have ſome effect to render a priſon an object of terror to many, and bring thoſe to thinking, and a ſenſe of their crimes, who are ſent thither. A cook's ſhop, and a ſmall-beer tap, would furniſh the means of ſupport; and no farther ought it to go: and the keepers ſhould be paid ſalaries adequate to the truſt and danger they run, inſtead of ſubſiſting by perquiſites. As there is certainly a wide difference in offences, ſo is there in offenders: it is for this reaſon that thoſe committed for aſſaults, and petty offences, ſhould either not be ſent to the ſame priſon with the greater villains; or there ſhould be ſome barrier there to effectually ſeparate them. Such dreadful examples to minds perhaps juſt ſtept into iniquity, cannot fail to complete their ruin.

" *The better enlightning and watching the public ſtreets would render robbery very unſafe.*

" Light and a watch are the greateſt enemies to villains. Excepting ſome local acts of parliament, the lightning of the ſtreets ſtands upon a ſtatute of William and Mary, which, as it makes no diſtinction between perſons of great propertyand thoſe of narrow circumſtances, requiring every houſekeeper to put out a light every night from dark to twelve o'clock from Michaelmas to

 Lady-

Lady-Day, unleſs they contribute to public lamps to be ſet out by two juſtices of the peace; but as there is no method preſcribed how the charge of public lamps is to be defrayed, and the intermediate time between Lady-Day and Michaelmas is totally unprovided for, and at the time that ſtatute was made ſtreet robberies were unknown, it ſeems neceſſary that a better proviſion ought to be made; and this is the ſenſe of the legiſlature, as many pariſhes have obtained acts of parliament for this purpoſe, and for providing an able and ſufficient watch. But ſtill the out-pariſhes, where the greateſt danger from robbers and burglars may juſtly be apprehended, have only the unexecuted ſtatute above-mentioned for lighting the ſtreets, and the ſtatute of Wincheſter for watching, and this only provides, "that watch and ward "ſhall be kept from Aſcenſion-Day to Mi- "chaelmas from ſun to ſun." Indeed, cuſtom, eſtabliſhed by neceſſity, has prevailed in this town for a nightly watch all the year, and this cuſtom has introduced a pecuniary compound for perſonal ſervice between the conſtable and the inhabitant; and this from time is grown into a kind of rate, and a ſum demanded by the conſtable quarterly to defray the expence of paying his beadle and the watchmen he hires. The total want of lights in the out-parts, and the inſuf-

insufficiency of the watch, is a grievance greatly and justly complained of; and it is hoped a general law will provide for an effectual light and able watch for the security of the night, as most of the street robberies have been perpetrated in the dark out-skirts of the town, through which the coaches of persons of quality and others must necessarily pass.

" Some methods of rendering low mechanics, servants, and labourers in this town, known, would be of the utmost consequence to the good government of it, as by this means it might be ascertained where to find them, and how, and in what manner, their time is employed. In a place so extensive, its inhabitants so numerous, various and fluctuating, it seems almost impossible to fix this with any tolerable certainty: but are not the inhabitants of small towns and large villages known, and may not this town be portioned out into districts not exceeding thirty houses, and officers annually chosen under the denomination of *conservators*, or other title, under whose care such districts might be placed; and proper books of entry made of the names and family of each inhabitant. Sure the charges would not be difficult to raise. Such inhabitants may be forbid under severe penalties, to receive any lodger, servant, or labourer, as a lodger, until such labourer

bourer or ſervant has been produced before ſuch conſervator, and entered into ſuch book, with ſome particulars, as, where he came from, whether he was in work, and where; if not, what means of ſubſiſtance he had; and if it ſhould appear that the perſon applying can give no ſatisfactory account of him or herſelf, ſuch conſervator might have power to deliver the party to a conſtable, who ſhould convey him to a juſtice of the peace to be dealt with as the law directs.

There are many other things neceſſary for better regulating a town vaſt as this is; poſſibly time may ſhew it neceſſary that a body of laws ſhould be enacted, different as the vices of this town are from thoſe in the country: but this is a ſubject too great for my humble ſtation: I ſhall eſteem myſelf happy if I have furniſhed any hint of uſe to the Public, in the ſervice of which your Grace is ſo eminently diſtinguiſhed. I am, with all poſſible humility, &c.

F I N I S.

AN

ACCOUNT

OF THE

ORIGIN AND EFFECTS

OF A

POLICE

Set on Foot by

His GRACE the DUKE of NEWCASTLE in the Year 1753, upon a Plan presented to his Grace by the late *Henry Fielding*, Esq;

To which is added

A PLAN for preserving those deserted Girls in this Town, who become Prostitutes from Necessity.

By JOHN FIELDING, Esq;

LONDON:
Printed for A. MILLAR, in the *Strand*.
MDCCLVIII.

[Price 1 s.

To His GRACE the

DUKE of NEWCASTLE,

Custos Rotulorum of the County of Middlesex.

My LORD,

AS the following Sheets contain an Account of some Advantages that have arose to the Public in general, and to this Metropolis in particular, from an Institution which owes its Birth to your Goodness, and its Continuance to your Care, I think that they have a special Claim to your Patronage; and the more so, as they reward you at the same time as they solicit your Countenance: For whenever Benevolence exerts itself for the Good of others, Succeſs is its moſt acceptable Reward.

Indeed, conquering Countries, fighting Battles, and ſuch like extraordinary Atchievements, are the Actions that make the greateſt *Eclat* among Mankind; and ſeem the only Ones that intitle a Man to the Appellation of *Great*: But he who preſerves the Lives, Property, and the Peace of thouſands, by encouraging the Execution of a Police adequate to theſe Purpoſes, as far exceeds the Conqueror, as the preſerving ſurpaſſes the deſtroying Mankind.

An Attention to domeſtic Quiet, eſpecially in a Metropolis, which is the Seat of Government, is, to the laſt Degree, praiſe-worthy, as it is productive of the happieſt Effects; and when ſuch a Police is brought to due Perfection, it will not only prevent common Acts of Violence between Man and Man, but such a Vigilance will ever defeat any Attempts that Malice, Extravagance, or disappointed Ambition, may contrive against the Government itself.

That this Police, now in its Infancy, so happily begun, and so warmly encouraged by your Grace, may answer the good Ends you proposed by it, is the sincere Wish of him whose highest Ambition is to deserve well of his Country, and whose singular Pleasure it will ever be to approve himself,

My Lord,

Your Grace's no less respectful,

Than grateful Humble Servant,

JOHN FIELDING.

INTRODUCTION.

IN large and populous Cities, eſpecially in the Metropolis of a flouriſhing Kingdom, Artificers, Servants and Labourers, compoſe the Bulk of the People, and keeping them in good Order is the Object of the Police, the Care of the Legiſlature, and the Duty of the Magiſtrates, and all other Peace-Officers. The Reſtraints on the Conduct of Mankind in general, eſpecially that Part of them who are happy enough to be Chriſtians, are the Laws of the Goſpel, and the Laws of their Country. Indeed ſuch a Compliance with the former, as lays a Foundation for a well-grounded Hope in the Life to come, makes their Reſtraints by human Inſtitutions unneceſſary; but Experience teaches us that thoſe Objects act the ſtrongeſt on our Fears and our Hopes that promiſe immediate Advantages, or threaten immediate Puniſhments: Hence it is, that the common People ſtand more in Awe of the Laws made by Men, than of thoſe which come from the Fountain of all Laws; and the Priſon, Whipping-Poſt, Pillory, and Gallows, make more Men honeſt than may at firſt be imagined.

Religion, Education, and Good-breeding, preſerve good Order and Decency among the ſuperior Rank of Mankind, and prevent thoſe Diſturbances, Irregularities and Injuries to our Fellow-Creatures, that happen among the illiterate and lower Order of the People: Good Laws, therefore, are neceſſary to ſupply the Place of Education among the Populace; and ſure no Nation in the World can boaſt of better for this Purpoſe than England.

The common People, when compared to thoſe of a higher Rank, are as the Neceſſaries of Life, when compared to the Conveniences or ornamental Part of it. The Riches and Strength of a Nation are the Number of its Inhabitants; the Happineſs of that Nation, their being uſefully and conſtantly employed. Time is the Labourer's Stock in Trade; and he that makes moſt of it by Induſtry and Application is a valuable Subject. A Journeyman can no more afford to give or throw away his Time than the Tradeſman can his Commodity; and the beſt Way of preventing this uſeful Body of Men from this Species of Extravagancy, is

to

to remove from their Sight all Temptation to Idleneſs: And however Diverſions may be neceſſary to fill up the diſmal Chaſms of burdenſome Time among People of Fortune, too frequent Relaxations of this Kind among the Populace enervate Induſtry.

In the Country, the Plowman, the Labourer, and the Artificer, are ſatisfied with their Holydays at Eaſter, Whitſuntide and Chriſtmas. At the two former they enjoy their innocent Sports, ſuch as a Cricket-Match, or a Game at Cudgels, or ſome other laudable Trial of Manhood to the Improvement of Engliſh Courage. At Chriſtmas, they partake of the good Cheer of that Seaſon, and return ſatisfied to their Labour: But in this Town, Diverſions calculated to ſlacken the Induſtry of the uſeful Hands are innumerable: To leſſen therefore the Number of theſe is the Buſineſs of the Magiſtrate. Bull-baitings, Bear-baitings, Cock-matches, and ſuch Races as are contrary to Law, are in the Number of out-door Diverſions that call for Redreſs. The firſt indeed are inhuman, and, for that Reaſon, it is to be hop'd, are leſs frequent; but the Amuſements of the greateſt Conſequence are thoſe that are carried on in the Public-Houſes in Town; ſuch as Cards, Dice, Draughts, Shuffleboards, Miſſiſippi Tables, Billiards, and cover'd Skittle-Grounds. Theſe are the Thieves that rob the Journeymen and Labourers of their precious Time, their little Property, and their leſs Morals. And it is very certain, that theſe Evils are in the Power of the Publican to prevent. At leaſt it is to be hoped, that the Act paſs'd laſt Seſſions for preventing gaming in Publick-Houſes, will induce them, for their own Sakes, to put an entire Stop to this Inlet of general Corruption of the common People. And tho' Habit makes many things appear neceſſary, that are not only in themſelves ſuperfluous, but injurious, I am perſuaded, that the putting down entirely of the above Species of Gaming would ſoon be found to be a conſiderable Advantage as well to the Publican as his Cuſtomers.

Among the various Truſts repoſed in the Magiſtrates of this City, there is none, in my Opinion, of greater Importance than that of granting Licenſes to Ale-Houſes; for it is on their Care, in this Reſpect, that the Peace and good Order of this Town abſolutely depends. At the Ale-Houſe the Idle meet to game and quarrel; here the Gamblers form their Stratagems; here the Pick-pockets hide themſelves till Duſk, and

Gangs of Thieves form their Plots and Routs; here Conſpirators contrive their helliſh Devices; and here the Combinations of Journeymen are made to execute their ſilly Schemes. Cannot the Publican then, who knows his Gueſts, prevent theſe Miſchiefs? Is it not therefore his Intereſt to preſerve the Credit of his Houſe; and is it not the Duty of the Juſtice to examine well to whom he grants a Licence? For when that is in good Hands, every Ale-Houſe-Keeper becomes an honeſt and watchful Centinel over the Peace, Safety and Regularity of the City.

For my own Part, I think no Man ſhould have a Licence who is not a Proteſtant, nor any one who has been bred to a Trade, unleſs he is diſabled; for the Moment the healthy Artificer gets a Public Houſe, he generally becomes a Sot himſelf; he is a Decoy-Duck to his old Shop-Mates of the ſame Trade, and one uſeful Hand at leaſt is lopt off from that Trade. There is a large Body of Men who, when they marry and have Families, have ſcarce any other Reſource for Livelihood but keeping an Ale-houſe; I mean Servants of all kinds, who have never been bred to any Trade; perhaps diſabled Soldiers and Mariners may be proper Objects of this Truſt; but it is certain that the good Order of this

Town,

Town, and Happineſs of the common People and their Families, muſt ariſe from the good Order obſerved in Public Houſes. And here I cannot omit taking Notice of an unobſerved, tho' conſiderable Advantage to the Populace, ariſing from the late Regulations to prevent the Uſe of Corn among the Diſtillers, which has anſwered two Ends, firſt, by lowering the Price of the Staff of Life; and, ſecondly, by raiſing the Price of Poiſon; for Gin is now ſo dear, or elſe ſo very bad, that good Porter gains the pre-eminence, and I doubt not, but at the Year's End, there will be found a conſiderable Increaſe in the Conſumption of that Commodity, a Liquor not only more wholeſome in itſelf, but when drank to Exceſs, does not inflame the Paſſions to that violently Degree as Spirituous Liquor do, which rather enrages than inebriates, and makes Men mad and miſchievous rather than merry. And I am firmly perſuaded, that moſt of the haſty and precipitate Murders that have been committed among the Common People, in Family Quarrels, have aroſe from the direful Effects of this Liquid Fire.

And when theſe Evils in Public Houſes are corrected, Hops, illegal Aſſemblies and Gaming Houſes ſuppreſſed, the next Care of the

the Magiſtrate ſhould be to put in vigorous Execution thoſe Laws calculated to remove the Evils and Nuſances in our Streets, *viz.* Beggars, the Inſolence of Coachmen, Carmen, Porters, *&c.* Carters riding on their Carts; Obſtructions by Carriages, Caſks, Goods, Stalls, Bulks, *&c.* and laſtly Street-Walkers.

This will be the Means of making theſe Laws known to the common People; and every good Subject ought to be aſhamed to offend againſt the Laws of his Country. And it is certain that by ſuppreſſing the ſmaller Evils in Society you will prevent the greater; for it is much eaſier to check Diſorders in their infant State, than to conquer them when they are ſuffered to riſe to a troubleſome Height; and Prevention muſt always be a more eligible Object of the Mind than Puniſhment or Severity.

THE HISTORY and EFFECTS Of the Late HENRY FIELDING'S POLICE,

From the latter End of the Year 1753, to this present Time.

ABOUT the latter End of the Year 1753, a moſt notorious Gang of Street-Robbers, in Number about fourteen, who divided themſelves in Parties, committed ſuch daring Robberies, and at the ſame Time ſuch Barbarities, by cutting and wounding thoſe they robbed, in every Part of this Metropolis, as ſpread a general Alarm through the Town, and deterred his Majeſty's Subjects from paſſing and repaſſing on their lawful Occaſions after Night. Theſe Outrages induced his Majeſty to iſſue a Proclamation,

clamation, and offer a hundred Pounds Reward for apprehending each of theſe Violaters of the public Peace. And though this was humanely intended as a Remedy for this dreadful Evil, inſtead of anſwering the End propoſed, it ſoon begat a greater, by inducing a Set of Villains to decoy unwary and ignorant Wretches to commit Robberies, and then to make a Sacrifice of them for the Sake of the Reward; while the real Offenders not only eſcaped Juſtice, but encreaſed their Barbarities even to Murder. Upon which his Grace the Duke of *Newcaſtle* ſent to the late *Henry Fielding* to deſire him to form ſome Plan in Order to bring theſe deſperate Villains to Juſtice. A Plan was immediately formed, approved of, and encouraged by his Grace, which being put in vigorous Execution, very ſoon brought this Gang to condign Puniſhment. But it did not deter others from following the ſame wicked Practices; and a freſh Gang, as deſperate, tho' not ſo numerous as the former, ſoon made its Appearance.

About this Time the late *Henry Fielding*'s want of Health totally diſqualified him from continuing the fatiguing Office of Acting Magiſtrate in this Metropolis; he therefore reſigned the Office to his Brother *John*

Fielding, who had been an aſſiſting Magiſtrate to him for three or four Years.

Upon this Plan the following Reſolutions were formed, *viz.*

1ſt, To break the great Gang of Robbers which then infeſted the Streets, and ſpread Terror throughout this Metropolis.

2dly, To bring to Juſtice the ſeveral Gangs of Houſe-breakers, Lead-ſtealers, *&c.* which conſiſted chiefly of young Fellows who were Thieves from their Cradles, and were at this Time about eighteen or nineteen Years of Age, and very numerous.

3dly, It was propoſed to remove the Shoals of Shop-lifters, Pilferers, and Pick-pockets, who, being the deſerted Children of Porters, Chairmen, and low Mechanics, were obliged to ſteal for their Subſiſtance.

4thly, The Gamblers and common Cheats were to be the next Object of Attention, which were likewiſe very numerous.

5thly, It was propoſed to put down Hops, illegal Muſic-Meetings, and to prevent Gaming in Public Houſes.

6thly, To remove the Nusance of common Beggars; to prevent Street-walking, by keeping the Whores within Doors; and several other Disorders committed by insolent Carmen, which were punishable by Law.

And how far this extensive Plan has been successful the following Review will shew.

1st, About the Beginning of the Year 1754, the then reigning Gangs of desperate Street-robbers were attacked, and in the Space of three Months no less than nine Capital Offenders were brought to Justice, though not without Bloodshed, for one of Mr. *Fielding*'s People was killed, and one of the Robbers cut to Pieces; among which were the famous *Birk*, *Gill*, *Armstrong*, and *Courtney*: nor has any considerable Gang of Street-robbers appeared since, till lately, when a Gang of Journeymen and Apprentices were brought to Justice.

2dly, The next Set of Villains, *viz.* the Highwaymen that robbed near Town, were by this new Method of Persuit brought to Justice in such a Manner, that scarce one has escaped from that Time to this.

3dly, The numerous Gangs of Houſe-breakers, Lead and Iron ſtealers were perſued and harraſſed till they were totally diſperſed and ſent to *Tyburn* and to the Colonies abroad. The Numbers of theſe may be ſeen in the Seſſions Papers of the Years 1754 and 1755.

4thly, Theſe more conſiderable Objects being removed, the vaſt Shoals of Shoplifters, Pilferers, and Pickpockets appeared diſtinct, and were every Day taken up in Numbers; many of whom were tranſported. Theſe conſiſted chiefly of Boys from twelve to ſixteen Years of Age, either the Children of Thieves or the deſerted Offspring of idle and profligate Parents; many of whom, eſpecially Mothers, ſhamefully ſubſiſted from their Robberies: And what was very remarkable, four infant Thieves, the oldeſt of which was but five Years of Age, were brought before *John Fielding*, which appeared to be Children of different Perſons, collected together by one Woman to beg and ſteal to furniſh that Beaſt with Gin.

At this Time, which was about the latter End of the Year fifty-five, there was no leſs than 300 of theſe wretched Boys, ragged as

Colts, abandoned, Strangers to Beds, and who lay about under Bulks and in ruinous empty Houſes. This Evil ſeemed at firſt inſuperable, until Heaven inſpired the Thought of their Preſervation by ſending them to Sea, and cloathing them by public Subſcription; which has not only remedied the Miſchief, but will remain an everlaſting Proviſion for ſuch Objects.

And as this Scheme may in future Times be again made uſe of as an immediate Reſource for ſupplying the Navy with Boys in Time of War, I ſhall here ſtop a Moment in order to give a ſuccinct Account of the Origin and Utility of the Scheme itſelf. And as to the Sanction it met with, let the Honourable Names printed at the End of theſe Sheets teſtify.

In the Month of *January*, 1756, his Majeſty's Ship the *Barfleur* of 90 Guns, being in want of Captains Servants, that is to ſay, Boys; for every Man of War is allowed four Boys to every hundred Men on Board, whoſe Pay the Captain receives, allowing them forty Shillings a Year for Cloaths; ſo that the Boys Pay is abſolutely a Part of the Captain's Pay, and was intended to be ſo, in Order that the Captains might take Care to

have

have ſuch a Number of Boys on Board, by Way of Nurſery for Seamen; and theſe Boys are therefore called Captains Servants: Beſides which, every other Officer on board is allowed one or more of theſe Boys, according to his Rank, on the ſame Footing with thoſe belonging to the Captain. And as long as this Regulation is duly regarded there never will be wanting a Succeſſion of Seamen to ſupply the Navy. The *Barfleur* was at this Time commanded by Lord *Harry Pawlett*, who wrote to Mr. *Fielding* to procure him thirty Boys, which his Lordſhip cloathed at his own Expence. And as Mr. *Fielding* had been at Sea himſelf, and was well acquainted with the Station of Captains Servants abovementioned, he began to think that this would be an excellent Proviſion for the numberleſs miſerable, deſerted, ragged, and iniquitous pilfering Boys that at this Time ſhamefully infeſted the Streets of London: But the great Difficulty was to get them cloathed and cured of the various Diſtempers which are the conſtant Conſequences of Poverty and Naſtineſs. To effect this, Mr. *Fielding* put a Paragraph into the Papers, which ſtruck ſo ſtrongly on the ſenſible Minds and generous Hearts of the *Engliſh*, that in the Space of ſix Months the Sum of 600*l.* and upwards was paid into the Hands of that Magiſtrate, by Perſons whoſe Names are hereunto annexed, for the above Purpose; by which Means the Navy was at once supplied with near four hundred young Recruits from fourteen to eighteen Years of Age, and our Streets were cleared from Swarms of Boys whose Situations made them Thieves from Necessity; though many of them were unhappy enough in Parents, who subsisted from the Felonies their Children committed, not only by their Consent, but, what is still more shocking, by their Tuition.

About *July*, 1756, the ingenious Mr. *Hanway*, struck with the great Utility of this Scheme for providing for Boys, collected a Number of Merchants and other Persons of Rank together, and, to use his own Expression, adopted this Plan under the Name and Title of the Marine Society, with Intention to cloath Men and Boys for the Sea.

This Society soon increased in its Members and in its Subscriptions. And Mr. *Fielding*'s Subscriptions being now exhausted in this Service, and there being still a great Demand for Boys for the Navy, he applied to the Marine Society for Assistance, and was immediately most nobly supplied with the

the Sum of fixty Pounds. And from that Time all the little Intereft Mr. *Fielding* had with his Friends, Acquaintance, or the Public, he employed to promote the Succefs of thofe worthy Gentlemen's Endeavours who were engaged in this valuable Undertaking; which foon became fo much the Object of univerfal Attention and Encouragement, that from *February* 1756, to *December* 1757, there has not been lefs Money fubfcribed, including the 610*l.* Mr. *Fielding* received while he carried on the Scheme of Boys himfelf, than 12110*l.* 2*s.* by Means of which generous Subfcriptions no lefs than 2405 Boys, including the 400 firft fent by Mr. *Fielding*, have been cloathed and fent on Board his Majefty's Ships. Befides which they have cloathed 3072 young Fellows to go on Board the Fleet.

Who can behold this Supply, and not be pleafed with the Profpect of this everlafting Fountain the Marine Society? which, fo long as it is fupported by Generofity, and managed with Honour and Oeconomy, promifes Strength to our Fleets, Security to our Country, and Protection to our Commerce.

Having thus fhipped a Number of Recruits on Board our Fleet, and thrown many

Boys into a new Station of Life, the next Confideration of the Father fhould be to make them fully anfwer the End propofed, as well to their Country as to themfelves; and to preferve them from Diftrefs in Cafe of a fudden Peace. Nor can I do this better than by mentioning a Thing which I hope has been duly attended to on Board our Ships of War; I mean a School-mafter to inftruct the Youths in Navigation: For in large Ships where there are many Boys, moft of whom perhaps may have had fome Education, a good School might be framed; out of which in procefs of Time, the Navy might be furnifhed with fkilful Navigators, as well as good Sailors, to fupply the Places of Mates, Mafters, and Pilots.

And as it is the Schoolmafter's Province to inftruct thefe Boys in Navigation, the Boatfwain in his Turn might make them good Seamen, and teach them the Art of Rigging. And if the Chaplain were to take a little Pains on a *Sunday* Afternoon, to inculcate the firft Principles of Chriftianity into thefe Boys, by expounding the Catechifm to them, it would have a Tendency to improve their Morals, and be no Difadvantage to their Courage, as it might teach them where to place Dependence for Succefs.

And

And as it was obſerved by an Officer of high Rank in the Navy, that in Caſe of a ſudden Peace many of theſe Boys would fall into Diſtreſs, Mr. *Fielding* was deſired to form ſome Plan that might prevent this Evil; and the following Obſervations are ſubmitted to the Public on that Account; which may, with ſuch Improvements as they may meet with, be productive of a Plan which may fully anſwer the End propoſed.

Whereas a great Number of Boys are diſcharged whenever any of his Majeſty's Ships are paid off, and returned to their Parents, who are generally poor, after they have been one, two, or more Years on board Ship, and have then no viſible Way of getting a Livelihood, and are rejected as Apprentices or domeſtic Servants, merely becauſe they have been at Sea; by which Means they are too often drove, if not to wicked, to the meaneſt Courſes of Life; and thereby Numbers of good Sailors are loſt.

In order therefore to continue them long enough at Sea, or in that kind of Occupation till they become Sailors, it is propoſed, that whenever any of his Majeſty's Ships are paid off, all the Boys belonging to the ſaid Ships,

Ships, under the Age of eighteen, ſhould be continued on Board, when in ordinary, on the common Allowance, under the Direction of the Commiſſioners of the Yard or Dock where the ſaid Ships ſhall be paid off; to whom any Maſter or Owner of any Ship, Veſſel, Lighter, Fiſhing-boat, *&c.* may, by applying, have one or more of the ſaid Boys (the Whale-fiſhery eſpecially ought to be conſidered, as it will take a Number of Boys and certainly make them good Sea-men) on entering into a Covenant with the ſaid Commiſſioners, to employ in the Seafaring Way, cloath, and maintain ſuch Boy or Boys, until they arrive at the Age of Twenty, and allow them forty Shillings a Year, to be paid at the Expiration of the ſaid Time; when they ſhall be diſcharged, unleſs the ſaid Maſter or Owner chuſe to give them Seamens Wages.

It is preſumed that this Propoſal will be equally agreeable to both Parties; for the one may, by this Means, obtain ſeveral uſeful Hands at an eaſy Rate, and the other will have the Advantage of becoming eſtabliſhed Sailors, inſtead of Vagrants, to their own Happineſs and the Benefit of their Country.

And

And if this Scheme ſhould not be thought extenſive enough to provide for ſuch a Number of Boys as will be diſcharged ſhould our Ships be paid off, it might be uſeful to oblige every Waterman who has either Badge or Protection to take one of theſe Boys on the Terms above-mentioned; though, I muſt confeſs, the Plan that ſtrikes me moſt is what follows, *viz.*

Suppoſe our Merchants, who are both benevolent and beneficent, were to receive all Boys thus diſcharged from his Majeſty's Ships into one common Yard, ſupported by a general Subſcription of their own, by Way of a rigging Academy, ſettled under proper Regulations, where they would be conſtantly and uſefully employed in making Ropes, *&c.* and might be tranſplanted from thence into their Ships as they were wanted; (this might perhaps be a very proper Object for the Marine Society:) and as, even in Times of Peace, there are ſome Men of War in Commiſſion, many of theſe Boys, that are eighteen Years of Age, and have ſerved faithfully during the War, might be admitted on Board theſe Ships as ordinary Seamen, by Way of Encouragement.

It is certain that if the preſent Fleets were to be diſcharged, above two thouſand Boys would be upon their own Hands. The material Point therefore ſeems to me to be the ſelecting and keeping together theſe Boys when diſcharged.

5thly, Acts of Violence, Theft, and Robbery being thus reduced, a Body of artful, deſigning Men, called Gamblers, ſtood in Need of Reformation. The firſt Step towards which, was the ſeparating of them from the Nobility, with whom, by Means of rich, hired Dreſſes, they had inſolently mixed themſelves. And this was done by the following Plan: A Man perfectly well acquainted with all their Perſons agreed with Mr. *Fielding* to point them out to the Peace Officers. He was therefore furniſhed with a rich Suit of Cloaths hired from the ſame Shop that had ſupplied moſt of theſe Gamblers with their rich Dreſſes, and being thus equipped with Dreſs and Ticket, he went to the Ridotto; by which Stratagem nine of theſe ſham Gentlemen were apprehended, and ſo expoſed to public View as to prevent their ever appearing again in public Aſſemblies without being known.

The

The Gamblers being thus prevented from preying on the Nobility and Gentry, they fell immediately on Tradeſmen and Shopkeepers, many of whom they ruined by obtaining great Quantities of their Goods under falſe Colours and Pretences.

Trade being alarmed, complained to the above Magiſtrate, who apprehended many of theſe Cheats. But as the Laws then in Being were inſufficient to bring them to Juſtice, they moſtly eſcaped Puniſhment; and the Tradeſmen, beſides the Loſs of their Goods, were put to additional, fruitleſs Expences. In order therefore to prevent theſe Miſchiefs in ſome Meaſure, till a new and more effectual Law could be made for their Puniſhment, Mr. *Fielding* publiſhed, in a large Sheet of Paper, the numberleſs Artifices uſed by theſe Cheats to impoſe on Tradeſmen, and gave them away to Shopkeepers as Cautions to themſelves and Servants, to avoid the Inroads of theſe Harpies. But in order to eradicate the Evil, he framed a Bill to ſupply the Deficiencies of former Laws, which has ſince paſſed into an Act, and muſt inevitably bring every Cheat to Juſtice, and prevent ſome other

great

great Evils provided for in the ſaid Bill; eſpecially Gaming in Public Houſes.

Felonies and Frauds being thus retrench'd, Diſorders and Irregularities, as they are the Sources of them both, became the particular Objects of Attention, as the next neceſſary Step for the Completion of this Plan.

Laſtly, therefore, he ſet about that Work, and ſoon found that it was more difficult to diſcover where theſe Diſorders were carried on, than to ſuppreſs them when diſcover'd.

To remove therefore this Difficulty, he ſettled an anonymous Correſpondence with the Public; inviting all Perſons who knew of any Gaming-houſe, Hops, Dancing-bouts, illegal Muſic-meetings, and other illegal Aſſemblies, to give immediate Notice by penny-poſt Letter, without Name, mentioning only the Place where the Diſorder was carried on, and leave the Magiſtrate to inquire into the Truth of the ſame by proper Peace-officers, and to ſuppreſs it by legal Means.

This was ſo effectual that, by Virtue of theſe Notices, many of theſe Diſorders have been reduced with the greateſt Eaſe, and Notice from the Magiſtrate has generally

been

been ſufficient to remove the Evil, without the Execution of any penal Law; and by this Means it is hoped Numbers of young Women have preſerved their Characters, and young Men their Morals. Apprentices and Servants of both Sexes, together with Whores, uſually made up theſe Balls and Aſſemblies: And ſuch an Attention is now paid to this Correſpondence (as every Writer finds his End immediately anſwer'd) that the Moment the Neighbour, Father, Maſter, or Miſtreſs, diſcover the Haunts of their Children, Servants, or Apprentices, a Letter immediately goes to the Juſtice, and they are taken in Surprize. Theſe Offences are puniſhable by penal Statutes, all of which make an Informer neceſſary to execute them. The Name of an Informer is odious. Theſe anonymous Letters take away this Odium, as it is not neceſſary to know from whence the Letter comes; ſo that the moſt delicate Lady may with Safety give Notice to the Juſtice of any Hop, Gaming-Houſe, *&c.* where her Servants waſte their Time, loſe their Money, and debauch their Morals.

Frauds, Felonies and Diſorders being thus conſider'd, Nuſances, which without Attention, muſt ariſe in this populous City, came next in Order to be redreſſed, the principal

cipal of which, that fall under the Power of the Magiſtrate, are Beggars, Carmen, Coachmen, Swearers, and Throwers of Squibs.

As for the firſt of theſe, *viz.* Beggars, Mr. *Fielding* has lately formed and executed a Plan in Conjunction with the Juſtices of *St. Clements*, *St. Mary le Strand*, *St. Paul's Covent-Garden*, and *St. Martin's in the Fields*, which effectually anſwers the End to thoſe Pariſhes; for within the Space of ſix Weeks, no more than five Beggars could be found in one whole Week together in the four Pariſhes; and if the Juſtices of the other Pariſhes were to do the ſame, it would be as uncommon to ſee a Beggar in this Town in the Streets as a wild Beaſt.

Tho' perhaps the Execution of this Plan throughout this Metropolis would at firſt create a conſiderable Expence to the County of *Middleſex*; yet as this Expence would leſſen with the Evil, it would, in my Opinion, be Money extremely well laid out; but unleſs the Scheme be generally and diligently executed by all the Magiſtrates, it would anſwer no other End, than driving a Nuſance from one Part of the Town to another; and when one conſiders how diſagreeable it is to be attack'd at every Corner of the

the Streets by Beggars, moſt of whom make a Trade of it; and how diſadvantageous it is to Shop-keepers to have every Cuſtomer that ſtops in a Coach at their Door, to be importuned by theſe artful Petitioners; one ſhould imagine they would all cry out with one Voice, Free us from the Nuſance of Beggars. But what ſhocks one more, is, that ſuch Numbers of frightful Objects ſhould be ſuffered to infeſt the Streets, ſo diſmember'd and disfigur'd, as muſt often occaſion the moſt irretriveable Injuries to Ladies, when in the tender and delicate Situation of Pregnancy.

The Removal of the remaining Nuſances above-mentioned, muſt depend on the Vigilance of the acting Magiſtrate, and the Diligence of the Peace-Officers under him: Tho' any Perſon may apprehend a Man for riding on his Cart, for ſwearing, and begging, and carry them before a Juſtice of the Peace without a Warrant.

If this Police ſhould ſurpriſe the Reader, he cannot be leſs pleaſed, when he hears the the annual Expence of it to the Government, by the Execution of all the above Plans and Purſuits, has never exceeded four hundred Pounds. Indeed double this Sum would be a Trifle, ſhould it leſſen the Payment of of Rewards given by Act of Parliament for apprehending Highwaymen, Houſe-breakers, *&c.* and the Object of the Expence would be moſt agreeably changed from the deſtroying to the preſerving of his Majeſty's Subjects.

From the above Tranſactions, which are moſt ſtrictly true, and ſo very recent, that it is ſcarce poſſible to call any indifferent Perſon from the mix'd Multitude in this Town who could not give full Teſtimony of the Truth hereof, it appears that the Public has the greateſt Share in the Execution of this Police; for without its hearty Concurrence and conſtant Aſſiſtance, little Progreſs could be made towards the Peace and good Order of this Metropolis: For what Good can the moſt active Magiſtrate do, unleſs he receives Informations? In Frauds and Felonies, which are Attacks on our Lives and Properties, not a Moment's Time ſhould be loſt in giving Notice to the Magiſtrate. Theſe are Evils of a violent Nature, their Increaſe quick and dangerous, and require immediate Remedy.

In this Caſe the Morals are already corrupted and the Mind abandoned; ſo that if this corrup-

corrupted Member is not inſtantaneouſly ſeparated from the Body, it gathers Strength every Minute ; and Succeſs and Impunity in Villainy never fail to increaſe Villains.

As to other Offences, which have a Tendency to corrupt the Morals, ſuch as Gaming, Hops, *&c.* they ought equally to be complain'd of to the Magiſtrate, but require not that quick Notice as higher Offences do. A Letter, therefore, will anſwer this Purpoſe : But even here Delays are dangerous ; for the Omiſſion of one Day may ruin many ; at Gaming eſpecially, where one Quarter of an Hour may deſtroy more than the Induſtry of a Year, nay, a whole Life, can gain.

And ſuch indeed is the abſolute Neceſſity of the Countenance and Aſſiſtance of the Public to the acting Magiſtrate, that it is the chief Motive of expoſing theſe Sheets to their View : Hoping that the Advantages that have already accrued to this Town from the Execution of this Police, will be a ſufficient Encouragement to every Perſon that ſhall be injured for the future to complain early ; for ſure it is much better to prevent even one Man from being a Rogue, than from apprehending and bringing forty to Juſtice.

On the other hand, it is apprehended, that the Government will ever find it uſeful to encourage ſome principal acting Magiſtrate, to take this laborious Taſk upon him; and if ſuch a one be bred to the Bar the better; for he ought to have a competent Knowledge as well of the common, as the Crown Law: The former to aſſiſt the Poor with his Advice, and the latter to bring Offenders to Juſtice, to give Notice to the Legiſlature of the Defects of any penal Law (which is eaſier to be diſcovered in the Execution than in the framing that Law) and prevent himſelf and Officers from falling a Prey to that ſwarm of low and hungry Sollicitors who are always laying wait to take an Advantage of their Errors; and the more Knowledge he has of human Nature the better, as it will enable him to detect Art and unravel the dark Clues of Guilt.

His being handſomely ſubſiſted will take away the Temptation of making Gain of the paltry Quarrels of the Poor, and thereby encreaſing the Poor's Rates. And indeed it ought to remove every Temptation that diſhonours Magiſtracy, and muſt in Time free ſuch Men from the ſcandalous Imputation of *Trading Juſtice*, raiſe the Dignity of the

Em-

Employment, and make it an Object worthy the Acceptance, nay, meriting the Study of the beſt of Men. For to root out Fraud, prevent Violence and Oppreſſion, and to preſerve Peace and good Order, are the moſt grateful Purſuits of a good Heart and an ingenuous Mind.

He ſhould keep the civil Power alive; that is to ſay, the Conſtables; conſtantly inſtructing them in their Duty, and paying them for extraordinary and dangerous Enterprizes; and above all, promote Harmony amongſt them; for when the civil Power is divided it is nothing; but when Conſtables are collected together, known to each other, and bound by the Connections of good Fellowſhip, Friendſhip, and the Bonds of Society, they become ſenſible of their Office, ſtand by one another, and are a formidable Body.

And that the Public may know how they are likely to be aſſiſted when they complain, I take this Opportunity of informing them, that there are two Purſuit-Horſes, and proper Purſuers paid by the Government, and always ready to purſue and protect their Fellow-Subjects; which is of excellent Uſe in Robberies on the Highway near *London*, where the Notice is quick.

2dly, There is always one or more orderly Men on Duty to enquire into the Truth of Informations.

3dly, A Regiſter-Clerk to keep an exact Regiſter of all Robberies committed; Deſcriptions of all Goods loſt; the Names and Deſcriptions of all Perſons brought before the ſaid Magiſtrate who ſtand accuſed either of Fraud or Felony, or ſuſpected of either; of the Houſes that harbour them and receive their ſtolen Goods.

Beſides theſe Methods there are many others that ought to be known to none but the Juſtice himſelf, as the Publication of them would defeat their Effects. But with the above it was neceſſary the Public ſhould be acquainted.

And if all Informations of this kind be brought to this Point by his Regiſter, he will ſoon be able to fix on the Offender; and by quick Perſuit ſeldom fail to apprehend him.

This

This Plan honeſtly, actively, and carefully executed, tho' it cannot intirely prevent Frauds and Felonies, muſt neceſſarily produce ſuch good Order in this Town as has yet never been known, and tend greatly to the Safety of the State; as no dangerous Aſſemblies or Conſpiracies can be carried on without the Knowledge of this uſeful Officer of Police.

And as there is no Evil in this Town of any Size, for which there is not ſome wholſome Law provided, the Continuation of that Evil muſt be owing either to the Silence of the Sufferer or the Neglect of the Magiſtrate, not the Legiſlature.

And what adds much to the Efficacy of this Police, there is a Correſpondence ſettled with many of the active Magiſtrates in the Country, at all Diſtances, who conſtantly give Notice to Mr. *Fielding* when they have committed any deſperate Rogue, or ſuſpicious Man, eſpecially, if a Stranger in that Country; by which Means they are often furniſhed with Materials to bring ſuch Offenders to Juſtice.

Having now mentioned every Thing that appeared to me uſeful to be known for the

 Con-

Continuation and Execution of the Police above described (which I flatter myself the Public will receive with Candour as my Motive is good, however erroneous my Opinion may be) I cannot conclude without taking this public Opportunity of returning my sincere Thanks to all those Magistrates who have from Time to Time afforded me Leisure and Refreshment, by their kind Attendance for me on public Business; nor must I forget to acknowledge myself greatly indebted to the general good Behaviour, Diligence, and Activity of the Constables of the County of *Middlesex*, and City and Liberty of *Westminster*, who have never been backward in their Duty, however hazardous the Occasion.

INTRO-

INTRODUCTION

TO THE

PLAN for preſerving deſerted GIRLS.

WHoever has long acted as a Magiſtrate in this Metropolis, muſt have obſerved, that the Body of the neglected Sons of the Poor, Gaming in Public-Houſes, and the very low Bawdy-Houſes are the conſtant Fountains that furniſh the Courts of Juſtice with Offenders, and the Place of Execution with Victims.

Enough has been ſaid of the former of theſe, and the Evil being conſiderably leſſened, the latter is propoſed to be the Subject of what follows; as it ſeems to be as material an Object of the Police as any whatever; for, in theſe Brothels, the Apprentice and Journeyman firſt broach their Morals, and are ſoon taught to change their Fidelity and Integrity for Fraud and Felony; here the Tradeſman, overcome with Liquor, is decoyed into a Snare, injurious to his Property, fatal to his Conſtitution, deſtructive to his Family, and which frequently puts a Period to his Peace of Mind.

Re-

Relieving Induſtry in Diſtreſs, preſerving the Deſerted, and reforming the Wicked and the Penitent, are the acceptable Employments, the favourite and advantageous Delights of thoſe Minds, which are happy enough to have a good Heart for their Prompter. There is indeed abundant Reaſon to believe, that theſe Pleaſures have been fully enjoyed by thoſe who have ſubſcribed towards cloathing friendleſs and deſerted Boys to go to Sea. And it is to be hoped, that the Public in general, as well as the particular Objects of that Charity, have reaped ſome Advantages from thoſe Subſcriptions.

And I ſhall now beg Leave to preſent to the Public a Body of Fellow-Creatures, equally diſtreſſed with thoſe who have been the Objects of the abovementioned Benevolence; and which may, and will, I hope, be made of equal Uſe to their Country.

The Preſervation of the common People, in all States, is highly deſerving Attention; for, from this Fountain, your Manufactures, Fleets, Armies, and domeſtic Servants, are ſupplied: And in Country Villages this Taſk is eaſy, as Temptations to Vice are more rare, and moſt Pariſhes employ their Inhabitants.

bitants. But in ſuch a populous City as is the Metropolis of this Kingdom, numbers of Perſons may be idle, numbers of Children may be deſerted who are capable of Employment, without ever being perceived by the Public, till their Crimes have made them the unhappy Objects of public Juſtice.

For the Truth of which Aſſertion I refer to the Seſſions-Paper, and Kalendars for the Years 1755, and 1756, when Gangs of friendleſs Boys, from 14 to 18 Years of Age, were tranſported, indeed, I may ſay by wholeſale, for picking of Pockets and pilfering from Shops.

And as theſe deſerted Boys were Thieves from Neceſſity, their Siſters are Whores from the ſame Cauſe; and, having the ſame Education with their wretched Brothers, generally join the Thief to the Proſtitute.

This brings me to that completely wretched, diſtempered, deſerted, pitiable Body of whom I mean to ſpeak; whoſe Sufferings have ſo often made my Heart ach, and whoſe Preſervation I now ſo ardently wiſh to accompliſh. And indeed, I think, I have great Reaſon to indulge theſe my Wiſhes, as I flatter myſelf I have hit upon a Plan that will

as

as effectually preserve these deserted Girls from Infamy and Distress, and make them happy in themselves and useful Subjects at Home, as that which has preserved so many of their Brothers, and made them useful Abroad.

But before I speak of my Plan I will endeavour to shew from what Fountain it is, our low and infamous Bawdy-Houses, which furnish our Streets with thieving, distempered Prostitutes, are supplied.

Infinite are the Number of Chairmen, Porters, Labourers, and drunken Mechanics in this Town, whose Families are generally too large to receive even Maintenance, much less Education from the Labour of their Parents; and the Lives of their Fathers being often shortened by their Intemperance, a Mother is left with many helpless Children, to be supplied by her Industry; whose Resource for Maintenance is either the Wash-Tub, Green-Stall, or Barrow. What must then become of the Daughters of such Women, where Poverty and Illiterateness conspire to expose them to every Temptation? And they often become Prostitutes from Necessity, even before their Passions can have any Share in their Guilt.

And as Beauty is not the particular Lot of the Rich more than the Poor, many of the abovementioned Girls have often great Advantages of Perſon; and whoever will look amongſt them will frequently ſee the ſweeteſt Features diſguiſed by Filth and Dirt.

Theſe are the Girls that the Bawds clean and cloath for their wicked Purpoſes. And this is done to ſuch a Degree, that on a ſearch Night, when the Conſtables have taken up near forty Proſtitutes, it has appeared on their Examination, that the major Part of them have been of this Kind, under the Age of Eighteen, many not more than Twelve, and thoſe, though ſo young, half eat up with the foul Diſtemper.

Who can ſay that one of theſe poor Children had been Proſtitutes through Viciouſneſs? No. They are young, unprotected, and of the female Sex; therefore become the Prey of the Bawd and Debauchee.

Here I cannot help mentioning a Misfortune; nay, I may ſay, a Cruelty, that often happens to theſe deſerted Children, and I believe the Offenders as often go unpuniſhed; for the maternal Tenderneſs of their Mothers either ſtarved by their Neceſſities, or drowned in Gin; and, for a Trifle, conceal and forgive an Offence which our Laws have made Capital. And I have ſometimes ſeen Mothers, but indeed they ill deſerve that Name, who have trepanned their Children into Bawdy-Houſes, and ſhared with the Bawd the Gain of their own Infant's Proſtitutions. And ſcarce a Seſſions paſſes without Indictments being found againſt Porters, and ſuch low Sort of Men, for raviſhing the Infants of the Poor. But, as I ſaid before, I am afraid more of theſe Offences are concealed from the Magiſtrate than are brought to light. Who can behold this Havock on Youth and Innocence, and not be ſhocked with their pitiable Caſe? And who can feel for them without being warmed with a Deſire of affording them Protection, and reſcuing theſe helpleſs Lambs from the hungry Jaws of ſuch ravenous Wolves?

To preſerve theſe Objects, and to reform others, who having been decoyed into Vice, and from the Miſeries they ſuffer, are deſirous to withdraw from that dreadful State, is my principal View in what I ſhall hereafter propoſe; though I am perſuaded, if I can ſucceed in the former, there will be at leaſt fewer to repent; for Evils of all Kinds in pub-

publick Societies are only to be cured by being prevented: Remove the Cause, and the Effect must cease. The skilful Surgeon, indeed, when applied to too late, finds Amputation of a Limb absolutely necessary to preserve the whole Body; which very Limb might itself have been preserved, had the same Skill been earlier applied: and *Venienti occurrite Morbo*, is as good a Maxim in Politics as in Physic.

The only Difficulty I see in putting this Plan in Execution, is, the first Expence; for, I hope, in a very few Years, it will not only support itself, but prove a constant Nursery for a Body of useful Domestics, much wanted in this Town.

And as the Evil it proposes to remedy, is grown to a most obnoxious Height, and the Wretches that occasion it are the Objects of universal Compassion, I doubt not, but it will receive an Encouragement proportionable to the Public's Opinion of its Utility; nor do I fear, but that in these my Endeavours, I shall be honoured with the kind Attention, the friendly Approbation, and the generous Assistance of the Ladies, whose tender Feelings will give them a much juster

Idea

Idea of the Sufferings of theſe poor Creatures than any thing the warmeſt Imagination can ſuggeſt; for really ſome of their Caſes, as *Shakeſpeare* ſays, beggar all Deſcription.

A

PLAN

OF THE

Preſervatory and Reformatory.

Being a public Laundry, intended to employ, breed up, and preſerve the deſerted Girls of the Poor of this Metropolis; and alſo to reform thoſe Proſtitutes whom Neceſſity has drove into the Streets, and who are willing to return to Virtue and obtain an honeſt Livelihood by ſevere Induſtry.

I. The Situation and Building.

THE Building for the Public Laundry ſhould be ſituated as near as poſſible to the Centre of the Town, but in the Fields; and ſhould conſiſt of one large Quadrangle; the front Building of which ſhould have a large Lodge in the Centre, divided into two Rooms; one for the *receiving* Secretary, and the other for the *receiving* Matron. Over theſe two Rooms ſhould be a ſpacious Committee-Room, for the Meeting of the Fathers of this Charity. The remaining Part of the Front, on each Side, ſhould be wall'd. The two Sides of the Quadrangle ſhould be divided into Schools, and Bedchambers over them. The Bottom of the Building to be divided into Waſhing Rooms and Ironing Rooms over them. In the Centre, the Kitchen, Brewhouſe, &c. Over it a Chapel. Behind this Quadrangle ſhould be a large Piece of Ground or Outlet, walled round for the Conveniency of drying Cloaths, Exerciſe, &c. In one Part of which ſhould be built a ſmall Infirmary.

II. The Objects to be taken in.

Thoſe Girls that are to be received in this Laundry, ought to be the Daughters of the induſtrious Poor, viz. Porters, Labourers, Servants, low Mechanics, Soldiers, Sailors, &c. from ſeven Years of Age to fifteen, *uncorrupted*, and free from Blemiſh of Conſtitution and Intellects.

Proſtitutes to be reformed, to be taken in to the Age of Twenty-three, and recoverable as to Conſtitution.

Poor Girls put out Apprentice by Pariſh-Officers from Workhouſes, may be received in this Laundry, as they are generally placed in the worſt of Families, and ſeldom eſcape Deſtruction.

III. The Manner of taking them in.

The Girls all to be bound Apprentice either for ſeven Years, or 'till they are twenty-one, to the grand Matron.

The Indentures of the Proſtitutes to be dated back, ſo that they might remain about three or four Years in the Laundry.

IV. The Manner of their being employed.

All the Girls, under twelve Years of Age, to be employed in the Reading-School, under a Head-Matron, and proper Aſſiſtants, for that immediate Purpoſe; who are to teach them to read and learn them the firſt Principles of Plain-work; ſuch as Hemming, &c. and Knitting.

The Girls from twelve to ſixteen Years of Age, to be in the real plain-work School, under a Matron, and proper Aſſiſtants, for that immediate Purpoſe; who are to complete them in the plain and houſwifely Knowledge of Plain-work, Knitting, and every other Uſe of the Needle, that may be neceſſary in a common uſeful Servant; teaching them ſtill to read, and inſtructing them in the Principles of Religion.

From Sixteen, to the Expiration of their Apprenticeſhips, to be employed in the waſhing and ironing Schools, under Matrons and Aſſiſtants for that immediate Purpoſe.

Out of theſe Schools, a Number of Girls are daily to attend in the Kitchen, under Matrons and proper Aſſiſtants for that Purpoſe, to inſtruct them in the Knowledge of plain Cookery; to roaſt, boil, brew and bake.

The reformed Proſtitutes to be employed, ſeparate from the reſt, according to their Ages, in the ſeverer Offices of the Houſehold.

And when any of theſe Girls have ſerved their Time, to be cloathed and fixed in reputable Families, as domeſtic Servants; and reformed Proſtitutes, in more inferior Families.

V. The Manner of furniſhing this Laundry with Work.

As many Families have not the Convenience of waſhing their Linen at Home, it is to be hoped they will ſend it to the public Laundry; where it will be got up in the greateſt Perfection, at a reaſonable Price, and returned with Safety and Regularity.

Linen, likewiſe to be made up, may be done with the ſame Degree of Care and Exactneſs; for which Purpoſe there muſt be a receiving Secretary, and a receiving Matron;

the

he latter to take in the Linen, and the former to take an exact Account of it according to a Method to be fixed on.

VI. The Method of putting this Scheme in Execution.

A Number of Perſons of Rank and Fortune to be fixed on, and to be called *Fathers*; under whoſe Patronage, a Subſcription ſhould be raiſed, to build a proper Place for this Undertaking.

The Subſcriptions to be paid into the Hands of one or more Bankers to be fixed on; and to be ſubject to the Draughts only of ſuch a Number of Fathers as ſhall be appointed *Treaſurer* by the reſt.

And as this public Laundry, if encouraged, will, in all Probability, more than maintain itſelf, an Intereſt, after a certain Time, may be paid for the Money firſt ſubſcribed to raiſe the Building; and the ſaid Subſcriptions made transferable, until it ſucceeds ſo far as to pay the Principal.

VII. Proper Viſitors.

Twenty-ſix Ladies of Rank to be appointed yearly Viſitors. Two to viſit every Week by Rotation; to make the Reports in Writing, and to leave them in the Secretary's Office to the Committee, ſealed up, and directed to the Committee of the Fathers of the public Laundry, propoſing any Amendment or Alteration that their reſpective Viſits ſhall ſuggeſt. The Number of the Committee to be fixed on, and no Subſcriber to be admitted to the Committee, but on the Death or Removal of one of the firſt appointed.

The Chairman of the Committee to be by Rotation; and thoſe who are abſent to loſe their Turn till it comes round again.

Notice always to be ſent to the Perſon whoſe Turn it is to be in the Chair.

The firſt Committee to appoint Officers, Matrons, and Aſſiſtants; and to fix Rules and Orders for the receiving of Objects, and other Things neceſſary for the Execution of this Plan; by which, it is to be hoped, the numberleſs deſerted Wretches that now ſhock the Eye of the Benevolent with their Diſtreſſes, and wound the Ear of the Decent by their abandoned Behaviour, may be put in a Method of gaining a uſeful Education, obtaining an honeſt Livelihood by their own Hand-Labour, preſerving their own Innocence, and become uſeful Members to Society, without really putting the Public to one Shilling Expence.

Servants bred in this Laundry muſt exceed all others, as they will have a general Know-

ledge

edge of Houſewifery, and will ſet out in the World free from the Prejudices of evil Habits.

And who will not rejoice to ſee this happy Change of Barrow Women, miſerable Proſtitutes, &c. converted into modeſt, decent, happy Women, and uſeful domeſtic Servants.

I ſhall now conclude theſe Sheets with the Words of an ingenious Gentleman on another Occaſion; *Si quid recte dixi, hoc eſt quod volui; ſi non, hoc eſt quod potui.*

HAVING mentioned the Want of Employment for poor Boys and Girls, and Gaming in Public-Houſes, as the Sources of moſt of the Diſorders in this Town; I cannot better conclude theſe Sheets, than by taking Notice of a uſeful Body of Men, the Regulation of whom, would, perhaps, more effectually conduce to the perfecting the Police of this Town, than any other; I mean the Pawnbroker's; a Sett of men, who have it infinitely in their Power to prevent the higher Offences of Fraud and Felony. The Laws have laid them under certain Reſtrictions for this Purpoſe; and the following Rules have alſo been very ſtrongly recommended to their Practice, as a farther Aſſiſtance to thoſe Laws. And I muſt here do them the

Juſtice to acknowledge, that a ſelect Number of the principal among them, unanimouſly approved of the ſaid Rules, and chearfully ſubſcribed their Names to the Obſervance of them, as being ſenſible, that they have a direct Tendency to promote the Eaſe and Security of their Trade, and the Safety of the Public. I ſhall therefore, without farther Apology, annex them to this Pamphlet, not doubing, but that theſe Cautions will meet with univerſal Approbation, as they are intended to prevent all Perſons from pawning, exchanging, or otherwiſe unlawfully diſpoſing of the Property of others, without their Conſent or Authority.

RULES propoſed by Mr. Fielding, and unanimouſly aſſented to by a ſelect Body of PAWNBROKERS, for their future Obſervance, as a farther Prevention of Frauds and Felonies.

I. SOME one Public News Paper to be fixed on by them, to be taken in, and publick Notice to be given of the ſame. This will ſave Expences to the Pawnbrokers of different Papers; and ſhew the Publick where to advertiſe Things loſt, ſtolen, or fraudulently obtained.

II. A correct Liſt of the Pawnbroker's Names and Places of abode, to be given to Mr. Fielding, and Hand-bills may be ſent; which as they make no noiſe, may often detect in Caſes of Conſequence. Theſe Bills may be numbered; ſo, that if any Pawnbroker finds himſelf neglected by their not being brought regularly, he may complain to that Magiſtrate.

III. It would be uſeful to diſtinguiſh the time of Day, in which every Pledge is received. Ex. gr. For the Morning write M. for the Afternoon, A. for this may often prove material Evidence.

IV.

IV. To advertiſe at the Pawnbroker's Expence, the Clauſes relating to the Puniſhment of Perſons pawning Goods without the Conſent of the Owners; and the Pawnbroker's Power of ſtopping Perſons ſuſpected with impunity.

V. Pawnbrokers to ſhut up Shop at nine, from Michaelmas to Lady-Day, and at ten from Lady-Day to Michaelmas, Saturday excepted: and to exclude them from their ſelect Society, that will not comply therewith.

VI. This ſelect Body to uſe their beſt Endeavours to convict Offenders againſt the Sabbath; and likewiſe, to convict Perſons offending againſt the late Act of Parliament, in not making proper Inquiries, and ſuch Entries in their Book or Books as is thereby required. This vigorouſly executed, will deſtroy Petty-Pawnbrokers, who keep Chandler's Shops and Ale-houſes.

VII. To take nothing in of a ſtrange Meſſenger, that may not be ſuppoſed to be their own, unleſs you take down the Name of the real Owner, their Place of abode, &c. and in Pledges of Conſequence, ſuch as Plate, Jewels, &c. to ſend to the Owner.

VIII. To keep a Book on purpoſe for Watches; in which all Watches advertiſed to be loſt or ſtolen, ſhould be entered.

IX. To take no Goods whatſoever of any Soldier in his Regimentals.

X. No Perſon to be admitted a Member of the Select Body, who has not ſerved a regular Apprenticeſhip to the Buſineſs; unleſs ballotted in by the Society.

XI. Never to ſend a Boy before a Magiſtrate, or Court of Juſtice, when the Maſter can attend, and give the ſame Evidence.

XII. To be particularly careful in receiving Piece Goods; as an Error or Miſtake of that Kind may bring a ſtronger Imputation.

XIII. To receive no Pledges from Children, unleſs their Parents or Maſters or Miſtreſſes are well known to the Pawnbroker; and in general, to avoid ſo doing as much as poſſible.

XIV. Great Care ſhould be taken to keep Books with the utmoſt Regularity; as they may come under the Cognizance of the Magiſtrates.

XV. That every Member of the Society ſhould have the Name of the neareſt Conſtable to him; and that his Servants ſhould know the ſame, and to have a By-word to his Servants to go for the Conſtable.

A

L I S T

OF THE

ORIGINAL SUBSCRIBERS

Towards Cloathing friendless and deserted Boys to go on Board his Majesty's Ships; begun *Feb.* 1756.

	l.	s.	d.
FROM the Right Hon. the Lords of the Admiralty	15	15	0
From the Nobility at the *Cocoa Tree*, by the Hands of Lord Windsor - -	100	00	0
From the Nobility at *Arthur*'s	210	10	0
From the Nobility at *George*'s Coffee House, *Pall Mall*, by the Hands of Lord Windsor	29	6	0
The Right Hon. the Earl of Hardwicke - -	5	5	0
The Right Hon. Lord Royston	6	6	0
The Hon. Charles Stanhope, Esq;	10	10	0
Sir Thomas Drury -	1	1	0
—— Nettleton, Esq; -	2	2	0
—— Wogan, Esq; -	1	1	0

Sam.

	l.	s.	d.
Sam. Vandewall, Efq; -	1	1	0
Thomas Wood, Efq; -	5	5	0
The Rev. Mr. Payne -	4	1	0
Mr. Fielding -	1	1	0
—— Hall, Efq; -	1	0	0
Lewis Mendez, Thomas Brown } Efqrs. -	10	10	0
— Windham, Efq; -	1	11	6
Capt. Moore -	2	2	0
Meff. Johnfon and Browne -	1	1	0
Sir John Heathcote -	5	5	0
—— Heathcote, Efq; his Son	3	3	0
—— Ray, Efq; -	1	1	0
John Simonds, Efq; -	2	2	0
Richard Weddle, Efq; -	5	5	0
William Lloyd, Efq; -	5	5	0
Wm. Henry Bernard, Efq; -	2	2	0
William Fitzherbert, Efq; -	1	1	0
Capt. Townfend -	1	1	0
The Rev. Mr. Young -	0	10	6
Peter Delme, Efq; -	2	2	0
William Fellows, Efq; -	1	1	0
—— Whifton, Efq; -	1	1	0
Charles Crockatt, John Nutt } Efqrs. -	3	3	0
Col. Rich - -	3	3	0
Mrs. Mead - -	6	6	0
Thomas Vaffal, Efq; -	1	1	0
Mrs. Emerley -	0	5	0

John

	l.	*s.*	*d.*
John Delme, Efq; -	1	1	0
Sir Jofeph Hankey -	1	1	0
Sir Thomas Hankey -	1	1	0
Mr. Minett -	1	1	0
Thomas Trueman, Efq; -	1	1	0
John Bland, jun. Efq; -	1	1	0
Philip Devifme, Efq; -	1	1	0
Henry Shiffney, Efq; -	1	1	0
Mrs. Fuller -	1	1	0
John Shiffney -	1	1	0
John Cornwall, Efq; -	1	1	0
William Thornton, Efq; -	1	1	0
Edward Hunt, Efq; -	1	1	0
S. Smith, Efq; -	1	1	0
Jonas Hanway, Efq; -	1	1	0
John Scrimfhire, Efq; -	1	1	0
Hugh Rofs, Efq; -	1	1	0
——Pierce, Efq; -	1	16	0
—— Legg, Efq; -	1	1	0
—— Haines, Efq; -	1	1	0
The Rev Mr. Clark -	1	11	6
Capt. Ogilvie -	1	10	0
Peter Motteaux, Efq; -	3	12	0
Dr. Hay -	1	1	0
Dr. Schomberg -	1	1	0
Henry Gould, Efq; -	1	1	0
Capt. Clark -	3	3	0
Dr. Smallbrook -	1	1	0
From a Society of Antigallicans	30	0	0

Mr.

	l.	s.	d.
Mr. Mawhood -	1	1	0
Mr. Nobbs - -	1	1	0
From a Society of Gentlemen at the *Crown* Tavern -	15	15	0
—— Bridges, Eſq; -	10	10	0
Robert Nettleton, Eſq; -	5	5	0
—- Hale, Eſq; -	5	5	0
James Taylor, Eſq; -	5	5	0
Thomas Carew, Eſq; -	1	1	0
Received from a Clergyman unknown -	20	0	0
Mr. Barnes -	0	10	6
Mr. Carne -	0	10	6
Mrs. Philips -	0	5	0
Mrs. Reading -	0	10	6
Mrs. Jourdan -	0	5	0
Mrs. Clayton -	0	5	0
H. and C. - -	1	1	0
W. H. - -	0	10	6
H. J. -	0	10	6
A Member of the Commonwealth -	2	2	0
From a Perſon unknown -	0	5	0
A. B. 121 -	1	1	0
From the Bedford Coffeehouſe	2	12	6
A. B -	1	1	0
S. W. Eſq; -	1	11	6
J. Y. Eſq; -	1	1	0
G. M. Eſq; -	1	1	0

	l.	s.	d.
A. B. -	0	10	6
From a Perſon unknown, by the Hands of Mrs. Redman -	0	10	6
M. - -	0	10	6
From a Perſon unknown -	3	3	0
Z. X. - -	0	10	6
S. W. - -	2	2	0
T. W. at Bedford Coffeehouſe	1	1	0
From the Gentlemen at Mr. Goring's - -	1	1	6
From Ditto. - - -	0	10	0

F I N I S.

AN ACCOUNT OF THE

RISE, PROGRESS, and PRESENT STATE

OF THE

MAGDALEN HOSPITAL,

FOR THE RECEPTION OF

PENITENT PROSTITUTES.

TOGETHER WITH

Dr. DODD'S SERMONS.

TO WHICH ARE ADDED,

THE ADVICE TO THE MAGDALENS;

WITH THE

PSALMS, HYMNS, PRAYERS, RULES,

AND

LIST of SUBSCRIBERS.

THE FIFTH EDITION.

LONDON:

Printed by W. FADEN, for the CHARITY.
And ſold at the HOSPITAL, St. George's-Fields.

MDCCLXXVI

[Price 3s. 6d.]

CHAPEL

PREFACE

TO THE

FIFTH EDITION.

IN a ſhort Preface to the Fourth Edition of this Work, the Reader was thus briefly informed of what was done in it.

" At the End of the original *Letters*, we have ſubjoined " *An authentic Narrative of a Magdalen*," which we hope will be acceptable to the Friends of the Inſtitution: and we have the Pleaſure to ſay, that many Narratives of this ſort, no leſs intereſting, might eaſily be added.

"An *additional Sermon* is printed, which was preached in the Chapel, and intended to obviate an Objection which ſome have thrown out againſt the Undertaking*.

"The *Hymns* have been carefully reviſed, and ſuch only are printed in this Edition, as are uſed in the Chapel: and as a Collection of *Pſalms* has been lately made

* I cannot omit to add here, and I do it with infinite Satisfaction, that ſince the laſt Publication of this Work (in 1769) the Hint reſpecting "*An Aſylum for the Blind*," which I ventured to throw out in p. 148, of the Third Sermon, has in a great meaſure been compleated; and that by the liberal Beneficence of one Gentleman, the Rev. Mr. *Hetherington:* whoſe great Example and extenſive Beneficence yet want farther Aſſiſtance, as I am informed many more of theſe unfortunate Perſons apply than can be relieved.

for

for the Uſe of the Chapel, they alſo are added.

" The *Rules* and *Regulations* printed in the preceding Editions of this Book, were thoſe formed on the *Inſtitution* of the Charity. Several of them having grown obſolete, and others being introduced into practice; a careful reviſal of them hath been made by the *Committee:* and thoſe which are here publiſhed, are the *Rules and Regulations* of the Houſe, as reviſed by that Committee, and as now in Practice.

" No Addition is made to the *Prayers*, &c. as proper Books of Devotion are, and will continue to be, put into the Hands of the Women, by the care of the Chaplain: Nor, on that account, is any thing ſaid reſpecting the *Sacrament*, as this alſo is is the peculiar office of the Chaplain, and there ſeemed no need to interfere with him in that neceſſary department.

" The *Liſt of Subſcribers* having ſwelled to an immoderate ſize, from the particulariſing every Benefaction, however ſmall, it hath been found impracticable to print it in the ſame way as before; and therefore a *new Liſt* hath been formed, and is here added, of *Governors* only." Thus far that Preface.—

To which we have only to add, with regard to the preſent Edition, that to make it as perfect as poſſible, the Sermon preached " on laying the firſt Stone of our new Building, and then publiſhed, is now printed here, to render the Collection compleat: and the whole Work has been carefully reviſed and corrected. Nor have I, as its Editor, any thing farther

ther to ſubjoin, but my beſt wiſhes, and moſt fervent prayers for the ſucceſs of this my favourite Charity!—now by the bleſſing of Providence, and through the benevolent Care of its Friends, eſtabliſhed to the extent of my moſt ſanguine wiſhes. May it long continue to diffuſe its comforts and bleſſings, when my poor unfortunate breath is yielded up to him that gave it! And when I am no more, and the memory of my cruel treatment is forgot, yet at leaſt may this Work live to be ſweet in the grateful remembrance of thoſe, to whom it communicates good!

Conſcious of the Rectitude of my Intentions, and delighting in nothing ſo truly, as imparting Felicity and Conſolation, may God enable me to impart it more and more, ſo long as he thinks fit to continue me here below! and may he render the pleaſing conſciouſneſs of doing ſo, a counterbalance

terbalance to the evils and ſufferings under which, through the cruelty of the mercileſs, I muſt go mourning all the days of my life!

W. D.

June, 1776.

TABLE OF CONTENTS.

PRAYERS

CONTENTS.

PSALMS

CONTENTS.

VIII. Of

CONTENTS

AN

ACCOUNT

OF THE

RISE, PROGRESS, and PRESENT STATE

OF THE

MAGDALEN CHARITY.

THAT in the present disordered state of things, there will always be *Brothels* and *Prostitutes*, is a fact but too indisputable, however unpleasing. Any attempt to prevent this evil, would be no less impossible than impolitic, in the opinion of many; absurd in itself, and productive of the worst consequences. Now, though we should subscribe to this reasoning, and allow this necessity; yet surely there is no *necessity*, that the wretched instruments of passion, the unhappy women assigned to this base service, should endure all the extremities of misery, and perish in troops, unpitied, and unregarded, as if they were not fellow-creatures, and fellow-heirs of eternity. This hath long been the voice of humanity. And as the exquisite distresses of deluded young women, *have* not, *could* not escape observation; many benevolent wishes have been vented, both from the lips and from the pens of different persons *, that some method might be thought of, some humane scheme devised, for the relief of those pitiable sufferers; for their rescue from calamities, of all others most severe, because, *then*, without remedy.

But, from whatever cause, the good design rested only in wishes; and no man had either magnanimity, virtue, influence or address enough to carry it into execution; till Mr. DINGLEY rose superior to mean and popular prejudices; and, depending on the goodness of his cause, and the integrity of his intentions, offered to the public in the year MDCCLVIII, a *plan*; to which the following *Introduction* was prefixed, which does great honour to that gentleman, and well deserves the reader's attention.

"Noble and extensive are the charities already established in this Metropolis; unfortunate Females seem the only objects who have not yet catched the attention of public benevolence: but we doubt not, it will appear on reflection,

* Among the rest, see the *Gentleman's Magazine* for *April* 1751; and the *Rambler*, No. 107.

flection, a taſk of as great compaſſion and conſequence, neceſſity and advantage, to provide a place of reception for them, as for any under the protection of the public.

"Humanity, with its utmoſt efforts, pleads their cauſe more powerfully than any thing which can be offered on the ſubject; and it is obvious to every mind, from its own experience, that there cannot be greater objects of compaſſion, than poor, young, thoughtleſs Females, plunged into ruin by thoſe temptations, to which their very youth and perſonal advantages expoſe them, no leſs than thoſe paſſions implanted in our nature for wiſe and good ends. Surrounded by ſnares, the moſt artfully and induſtriouſly laid; ſnares, laid by thoſe endowed with ſuperior faculties, and all the advantages of education and fortune; what virtue can be proof againſt ſuch formidable ſeducers, who offer to commonly, and too profuſely promiſe, to tranſport the thoughtleſs girls from want, confinement, and reſtraint of paſſions, to luxury, liberty, gaiety, and joy? And when once ſeduced, how ſoon their golden dreams vaniſh! Abandoned by the ſeducer, deſerted by their friends, contemned by the world, they are left to ſtruggle with want, deſpair, and ſcorn; and even in their own defence to plunge deeper and deeper in ſin, till diſeaſe and death conclude a miſerable being.

" It is too well known, that this is the cafe with moft of the Proftitutes in their feveral degrees, fooner or later, from thofe pampered in private ftews, to the common dregs infefting our ftreets: and that far the greateft part of thofe who have taken to this dreadful life, are thus feeking difeafe, death, and eternal deftruction, not through choice, but neceffity. The feeds of virtue would exert themfelves; but, alas! the poffibility is removed. The fame neceffity obliging them to prey on the unwary, diffufes the contagion; propagating profligacy, and fpreading ruin, difeafe, and death, almoft through the whole human fpecies.

" What act of benevolence, then, can be greater, than to give thefe real objects of compaffion an opportunity to reclaim, and recover themfelves from their otherwife loft ftate; an opportunity to become, of pefts, ufeful members of fociety, as it is not doubted many of them may and will?

" Numbers, it is hoped, amongft our countrymen, famed through every nation for their humanity, will readily and gladly bear a part in fo benevolent a defign, and rejoice to promote an undertaking, which will at once be a bleffing to the community, and an honour to human nature."

Happy

Happy in the approbation of the public, Mr. DINGLEY, with the concurrence of ſome worthy friends *, (whoſe names deſerve to be had in remembrance, and whoſe characters would do honour to any undertaking) began the generous ſubſcription. Theſe gentlemen made themſelves accountable for whatever money ſhould be ſubſcribed; which very ſoon amounted to three thouſand pounds and upwards: —— ſufficient proof of the good diſpoſitions of mankind to ſo humane an undertaking, and a ſucceſs, we believe, unparallelled by any charitable propoſal. A commodious place in *Preſcot-Street* was immediately engaged for the charity; and, after ſeveral previous meetings of the *Subſcribers*, to conſider the plan, to chooſe proper officers, and to ſettle all requiſite preliminaries, THE HOUSE was opened on the 10th of *Auguſt*, 1758, when *eight* unhappy objects were admitted †.

* ROBERT NETTLETON, GEORGE WOMBWELL, JOHN DORRIEN, Eſqrs. | JOHN THORNTON, THOMAS PRESTON, CHARLES DINGLEY, Eſqrs.

† For the Method of *Admiſſion*, ſee the *Rules*—"Of *Admiſſion*."

From that time to Chriſhmas 1775, there have been received into the houſe,	1637

Of theſe ſeveral were very young: ſhocking to think, even under fourteen years of age! and ſeveral, objects of ſuch complicated diſtreſs, that no man could hear their piteous complaints, or behold their deplorable miſeries, without the tendereſt emotions of compaſſion!

The conductors of the charity have had the happineſs to ſee of theſe, reconciled to, and received by their friends, or placed in ſervices in reputable families, and to trades,	943
Proved lunatics, and afflicted with incurable fits, who have been ſent to *St. Luke's* hoſpital, or their own pariſhes,	44
Died with all the marks of unfeigned contrition,	43
Diſmiſſed, at their own requeſt, and upon reaſonable views of advantage, or uneaſy under confinement, though otherwiſe not blameable in their conduct,	204
Never returned from hoſpitals, to which they were ſent to be cured,	52
Diſmiſſed for irregularities, amongſt which want of temper has been the common evil,	255
In the houſe,	96
In the Whole —	1637

With

With reſpect to thoſe who have *left the houſe with credit*, we have had the pleaſure to hear the moſt favourable accounts in general: they turn out good ſervants, and have approved themſelves to the families in which they are placed, and in which we have the ſatisfaction to find that they continue; a very ſmall number only excepted.

For thoſe who have been *diſmiſſed the houſe*, for *irregularities*, it is but juſtice to ſay, that though doubtleſs ſome of them have been turned out for *crimes*, yet the far greater part have been diſmiſſed for *falſe* and *imprudences*; little petulance of temper, and refractorineſs of behaviour, which could not by any means be allowed. And who can wonder at this, in a ſociety of above an hundred young women, who have lived ſo much at large; have had, many of them, ſo few advantages from education or example; and been ſo little accuſtomed to the decency of regular and amiable conduct? Nay, we are perſuaded, that they who conſider the nature of the *inſtitution*, and that the preſent is an account of its firſt *eſſay*, will rather be ſurpriſed to find, that ſo few out of the large number admitted, have been diſmiſſed for irregular conduct—At the firſt opening of the houſe, before experience had yet given in her aid, compaſſion, it is to be ſuppoſed, might perhaps have too great prevalence; and from a reluctance to reject the miſerable petitioners, ſome not altogether proper gained admiſſion. This was one ſource of more frequent diſmiſſions at firſt. And as in the firſt inſtitution one *Matron* only was provided, the multiplicity of whoſe neceſſary attendance upon the other buſineſs of the houſe, prevented her conſtant preſence with the women; a proper check upon them was wanting, to ſtifle little quarrels, correct refractory tempers, and diſcourage petulant and opprobrious language. But ſince an *aſſiſting Matron* has been choſen, whoſe buſineſs it is conſtantly to be preſent with, and to influence the conduct and diſcourſe of the women; thro' her good care, and the exemplary management of the *ſuperior Matron*, we have had much leſs cauſe of complaint: and the diſmiſſions for irregular behaviour, have been far leſs frequent.

But we deſire particularly to inform the reader, — what hath given us the higheſt ſatisfaction, — that even of thoſe who have been diſmiſſed, *many* have never returned to their former deteſted way of life; but have ſought to maintain themſelves, in the moſt laborious ſervices; declaring, they would rather endure any extremities, than plunge again into guilt and ſhame. Nay, and ſome have applied to the *Lord Mayor*

to

to be ſent abroad, that ſo they might avoid the fatal neceſſity of returning to vice through mere want of ſuſtenance.

As no man could ever ſuppoſe, that each individual admitted within the walls of the *Magdalen-houſe*, would prove a real penitent, and reap all the benefits there propoſed to them: ſo, certainly, it muſt be confeſt, that theſe are as happy conſequences as the moſt ſanguine eſpouſers of this charitable deſign could expect; conſequences, which muſt delight the heart of every humane and ſincere Chriſtian; who can never fail to hear with pleaſure of the reſtoration and recovery of ſo many young and helpleſs fellow-creatures from a ſtate the moſt pitiable; from fearful deſtruction of body and ſoul, apparently inevitable, without this hoſpitable ſuccour. Were we allowed to mention the particular circumſtances of diſtreſs, and all the mournful ſtory of the woe which many of them have ſuffered, as well as the innate goodneſs of mind which hath diſcovered itſelf in many, the compaſſion of the public would be much moved towards them; and they would rejoice with us, in having ſaved from diſtreſs, far beyond deſcription, many truly deſerving, though moſt unfortunate young women.

For the *women now in the house*, we have the pleasure to assure the public, that they behave themselves with all imaginable propriety. Nay, the *public* are themselves, in some measure, judges, by seeing their decent and commendable deportment in the *Chapel*, which has dispelled the doubts, and dissipated the scruples of many hesitating objectors to this design. Their conduct, in other respects, is conformable to that in the Chapel; as unexceptionable as could be expected; nay, and much more so than might generally be imagined, considering their former state and circumstances.—Several of them constantly attend the Sacrament; more, we hope, in due time, and after proper instructions, will follow the good example; and, if from external marks we may be allowed to infer the sincerity of the soul, we have every proof which could be desired. They express the greatest gratitude to their benefactors, and the most affectionate sentiments towards their friends: In proof of which, we are permitted to subjoin a few *original Letters*. Nor is their regard for each other less conspicuous: solicitous as they shew themselves to serve and to recommend each other, according to their abilities, to proper places and employments. A tender zeal for the welfare of their Sister-Magdalens hath frequently

shewn

ſhewn itſelf in thoſe who have left the houſe *; and the delicacy of many to keep ſecret their connections, has been truly commendable. Senſible of the happineſs of their ſituation, they are truly thankful for the *comfort* they enjoy, ſuperior, as many of them frankly declare, to whatever they enjoyed in any part of their lives. And what wonder? when they are treated with the utmoſt humanity; are ſupplied with all things neceſſary to the well-being of ſoul and body; have an opportunity to attend a regular courſe of divine worſhip; and in ſickneſs want neither the beſt aids of phyſic, nor the beſt conſolations of a ſpiritual inſtructor? While ſolicitous for their future welfare, the *Conductors* of the charity, with a truly paternal regard, uſe all their kind endeavours to

* The following ſhort extract of a *Letter* from one of the *women* to another, for whom ſhe had procured a place, may ſerve as a proof of the aſſertion. After directing her to her ſervice, ſhe proceeds, "Now, my dear *Nancy*, as Providence has put it in my power to help you to this place, I hope and doubt not that you will be cautious in your behaviour, as my own character will ſo much depend upon it. I hope in God it will be in my power to provide for more of my dear ſiſters in time; till when I remain, dear *Nancy*, your ſincere well-wiſher," *&c. &c.*

N. B. They are both now in ſervice, and behave very well.

ſettle them in life with propriety, and to enable them to procure their own bread with decency and reputation.

They are divided, according to the original *plan*, into ſeparate *claſſes*; over each of which a *ſuperior* preſides, who is treated by thoſe in her claſs with becoming reſpect, and is accountable for their work and behaviour. Several, who were totally ignorant on their admiſſion, have been taught to read by their *ſuperiors:* proper books for inſtruction and amuſement are ſupplied them; and every method is taken to ſhew them the excellence of the choice they have made, and to eſtabliſh their minds in that *divine religion*, a ſerious regard to which can alone influence effectually their moral conduct. Now, it is but reaſonable to ſuppoſe, that ſuch women will be found faithful and excellent ſervants, whoſe woeful experience hath taught them the ſad conſequences of a deviation from virtue; whoſe minds have been diligently cultivated with the beſt inſtructions, and whoſe induſtrious way of life in, and attendance upon, the buſineſs of the houſe, muſt neceſſarily qualify them for all menial offices. Nor have we any doubt but the virtuous and humane, nay, and ſuch who perhaps can aſſiſt this charity no other way, will at leaſt endeavour to aſſiſt it by employing

ploying the women in their ſervices; of whom at leaſt they may be aſſured to have a faithful character, and whoſe former way of life may certainly, by proper meaſures, be preſerved an inviolable ſecret.

As an encouragement to the women who have been diſmiſſed reputably, and in order to provide them all decent and proper neceſſaries, a ſum of money hath been uſually given, more or leſs, according to their exigence, merit, or ſituation in life—from two guineas and a half to five guineas—to the amount of 2700 pounds, and upwards: and provided they continue a year and a day in their places, to the ſatisfaction of their maſters and miſtreſſes, they are allowed one guinea. As moſt of the poor objects who have eſcaped from looſe houſes, have come almoſt naked, or with borrowed cloaths to appear in, this too hath been a ſource of large expence: For it hath been neceſſary, on that account, to provide cloaths even for thoſe who have been ignominiouſly diſmiſſed, as they could not be ſuffered to go out in the *Uniform* worn in the houſe. Beſides this, the major part of the young women, in a little time after their admiſſion, have been ill, in conſequence of the great change in the manner of their life, or from the remains of former complaints, imperfect cures, and conſtitutions broken by their fatal irregularities.

Hence

Hence hath arisen a double evil; not only the loss of their time and industry, but the expence of medicine, which hath annually amounted to upwards of 150 pounds, though sparingly administered, and charged very low; and though the Physicians and Surgeons generously *give* their attendance. The necessary repairs, furniture, &c. of the *house* and *chapel*, have, as might be expected, amounted to no inconsiderable height: —But the bounty of the benevolent hath risen above all these great and extraordinary expences; and we have no reason to doubt, nay we have the utmost encouragement to hope, that under the divine blessing, this excellent institution will go on to prosper and *improve*.

That it is capable of *improvement* the Gentlemen who are so kind as to undertake the arduous and painful task of admitting the wretched penitents, are but too feelingly convinced. For arduous and painful indeed it is, to receive the petitions of so many unfortunate and forlorn young creatures, sunk in the deepest woe, and to be able to admit so few! An enlargement of the design would be like opening the doors of heaven to many destitute daughters of affliction, who have no place to fly unto, no eye to pity, and no hand to relieve! And in an age, distinguished for its humanity and compassion, what may they not reasonably hope?—We see already many

many miſerable fellow-creatures, by means of this happy Aſylum, reſcued from ſorrow, to which they had been introduced by all the iniquitous ſtratagems of deceit and ſeduction; in which they had been detained by a kind of horrid neceſſity; from which they had no probable, no poſſible retreat; and in which they muſt, ere now, according to all human chances, have periſhed:—periſhed in the moſt deplorable diſtreſs! We ſee them reſtored to their God;—to their parents;—to their friends;—to their country;—to themſelves;—to health;—to induſtry;—to happineſs! And what ſingle, charitable deſign, can propoſe and effect ſo many valuable ends? What charitable heart, what truly chriſtian hand can refuſe their generous aſſiſtance, or with hold their beſt endeavours from an undertaking ſo laudable and beneficent? Who would not wiſh to add to the number of ſouls preſerved from deepeſt guilt? of bodies reſcued from fouleſt ſhame, and moſt afflicting diſeaſe? Who would not wiſh to wipe away the tear from the aged parent's eye, and to prevent the hoary head from going down to the grave in ſorrow? Who would not wiſh to give life to the drooping and deſponding family? to add to the number of uſeful and induſtrious members of the ſtate?—to add—to the number of the inhabitants of heaven? Happy they, who can bear a part! abundantly happy they, who can bear the largeſt part, in ſo truly

truly godlike and chriſtian a deſign.—But I forbear, that I may not anticipate what I have already urged in the Diſcourſes following.

The *Writer* of this begs leave to add, on his own account, that he thinks himſelf particularly bleſt by providence, in an ability to co-operate with men of ſuch diſtinguiſhed character and undoubted worth, as the *benevolent* Governors of the *Magdalen-houſe*, and to join his little, though imperfect ſervices with theirs, for the promotion of ſo good a work. If they are pleaſed to eſtimate ſuch ſervices as *his*, at any price; how highly muſt the thinking part of mankind rate *their* generous actions, who not only contribute ſo largely of their ſubſtance, but give their important time, thoughts, and unwearied endeavours, with the moſt diſintereſted benevolence, to ſave, reſtore and bleſs their fellow-creatures! If there is a more peculiar reward reſerved for mortals, it muſt certainly be the lot of ſuch exalted philanthropy. *They that turn many to righteouſneſs ſhall ſhine as the ſtars for ever and ever.* Their public virtues muſt win the regard, and obtain the beſt wiſhes of every ſincere chriſtian. But what the ſentiments of an heart towards them muſt be, which hath felt the friendly and particular influence of their private virtues,—I will leave to the determination of the moſt exalted minds.

W. D.

April 1763.
1st Edit.

LET-

LETTER I.

From M. —— *to the Treasurer, upon hearing that a Relation had left her a Legacy..*

Honoured Sir,

AS you have been ſo kind to give yourſelf the trouble of enquiring about that money, and are informed, Sir, that it can be paid immediately; I take the liberty of aſking your advice, in what manner to diſpoſe of it; for as I have, thro' your kind care, no occaſion for it, in my preſent happy ſituation; and being ſenſible how much I have made my dear Mother ſuffer upon my account, not only in regard to the grief my ill conduct brought upon her, but alſo by diſtreſſing her in her circumſtances, think it my duty, as a ſmall amends, to give it to her; hoping it will make her ſomething eaſier than ſhe is at preſent, in her way of living. I ſhall hope, Sir, to be honoured with your advice, as that will be eſteemed the greateſt pleaſure to,

Honoured Sir,

Your much obliged Servant to command,

Jan. 28, 1759. *M.*

LETTER II.

Dear Betſey,

I Do myſelf the pleaſure to enquire after your health, and I hope you keep in the ſame opinion of coming here, as nothing but your company can make me happier than I am. I can't expreſs the comfort I go to bed with, and riſe with in the morning

ing: I often wish you as happy and contented as I am. If any one would give me all that this world could afford to come out to morrow, I would not; and, I am sure, if you have any regard for your future state, you will come here, and quit the way of life you are in, as a blessing will certainly attend you if you do. I know you have no true content, as you may be in debt where you are; and what must you expect but misery! O dear *Betsey*, consider in time, for fear you should repent when it is too late. You know I would not tell you a story in regard to this happy place: but I would have you embrace the opportunity; for the house, I believe, will be shut up on *Thursday* next, and I would fain prevail on you to come: for had I a mother, a sister, or a brother, I would leave them all, to be here. I beg you will let me have the pleasure of seeing you between this and *Monday*, as I can't say so much of my mind for your good in this letter.——You never will be so happy again as long as you live; consider what a comfortable life we live here, every thing provided for us, and the best of provision: Only think what a favour it is to come here; there is many a one would be glad of such an opportunity. Did you but know the satisfaction I have, I am sure you would make no delay: But I am afraid you are persuaded not to come. Believe me, they are your foes who do it. Pray give my humble respects to Mrs. —, and tell them all I am really happy. Last night I had the joy to put on some part

part of my drefs, which gave me great pleafure.* Pray remember me to Mrs. ——. I will not trouble you with any more, but beg you will fhew this to Mrs. —— and Mr. ——, and I return them thanks for all their goodnefs to me. I fhall expect to fee you as foon as you can, which will greatly oblige,

Your fincere friend and well wifher,

Dec. 29, 1758. *A. F.*

Have altered my name.

* This Girl's drefs when fhe came in, was neat and elegant.

LETTER III.

From S—— *to Lady* ——.

Magdalen Houfe, Dec. 12, 1759.

EVERY living creature, my dear Madam, is intitled to offices of humanity; the diftreffes of our enemies fhould reconcile us to them: If they thirft, give them drink; and if they hunger, give them food: Infpired by thefe fentiments, be not led away by prejudices and refentments. This difpofition which, by experience, I know you to be endowed with, I hope you will exercife towards her, who, though unworthy, wifhes once more to regain, if poffible, your favour, and a place in your efteem It is with thefe hopes I muft entreat your acceptance of the enclofed, which is an order to fee one, who after all the various miferies and hardfhips endured juftly by my my own follies and imprudent conduct, (though some you are not insensible have happened through the inadvertencies and rigours of my own family) have at last found a peaceful, happy and blessed refuge; I mean the *Magdalen House*, having that charity afforded me by strangers, which, joined by importunities from abler tongues than mine, had been denied by my own relations, I dare not say friends; and hath given great occasion to the uncharitable censures of the world I have long laboured under. As the chief end of this noble and excellent institution is to regain unhappy women to the favour of God, their parents, and friends, every one but me are happy in that blessing: and must I alone, by the too rigid inflexibility of my relations, be denied that, which even the most abandoned prostitute that ever entered this blessed retreat, hath now the enjoyment of? Here daily do we see people of all ranks coming to visit and congratulate, without the least upbraidings, their new-found children, relations, and friends, which clears them from all anxieties; by which, with the instruction of our worthy chaplain, and a lady who deserves rather the tender appellation of a good mother to all her little family, than that of a mere matron, they are made fit to partake of that happy and blessed Sacrament of the Lord's Supper, which blessing I shall be deprived of by the fixed resolutions, folutions, I find in Mrs. ——— and Mrs. ——— never to forgive me; having done my endeavours by writing to each, without fuccefs of either fide: which makes me intreat the favour of your company next *Tuefday* evening, where I hope you will hear and fee that, which will prevail on you to believe to be true what I have here related, more than all the arguments my mean genius could make ufe of to explain the excellence of it. As an order will admit two, I fhould efteem it as an honour if you would bring mifs *P*——— if convenient; if not, whom you pleafe; and you will much oblige, moft amiable lady,

Your moft refpectful humble fervant,

S. ———

LETTER IV.

From *M.* ——— to her Father.

Magdalen-Houfe, Prefcot-Street, Goodman's Fields,
Dec. 27, 1759.

Moft affectionate Parent,

I HAVE finned againft heaven and before you, and am no more worthy to be called your child; but with a heart full of grief I have once more attempted to addrefs myfelf to you, imploring your pardon and forgivenefs of all my former follies and tranfgreffions; for although I have been abandoned and difobedient to your commands, I am now in great hopes that you will have the pleafure of faying by me, as the Pro-

Prodigal's father ſaid by him, *For this my child was dead, and is alive; ſhe was loſt, and is found.*

I am now almoſt ready to think with the Pſalmiſt, that it is good for me that I have been in trouble, that I may learn the ſtatutes of my Creator; for in this bleſſed Aſylum, I have the beſt opportunity I ever had of improving myſelf in the principles of religion, which is an advantage of a moſt weighty importance. We have in this manſion two ſermons preached every *Sunday*, and prayers twice a day in the week, beſides private prayers read every night by our moſt worthy matron and governeſs, whoſe good example and œconomy have been of infinite ſervice both to me and others; and I make no doubt but that her conduct will prove to be of great help towards the converſion of many of us unhappy women. Here is in this houſe upwards of 130 unfortunate young women, the greateſt part of which, ſince they have been here, have had the good ſucceſs of obtaining the pardon and reconciliation of their friends: but, for my part, I am quite forlorn and forſaken by you and all my relations; though indeed, when I look back on my paſt ill-ſpent life, I cannot help reflecting greatly on my own miſconduct, and I almoſt deſpair of ever being admitted any more into your favour. But when I conſider that you are my father, it gives me encouragement to hope, that

that you will exert that affection to me, which is due from a parent to a child, though I own I am unworthy of the leaſt of your favours, by reaſon that I have offended you in ſeveral reſpects in the worſt manner that a child could do; and I am ſincerely ſorry for the ſame, and I ſhould be glad if it was in my power to call the time back, which is paſt: but that is an impoſſibility; therefore, all that remains now in my power to do, is to bewail my follies, and to be penitent and ſorrowful for my ſins; which I am, from my very heart; and there is nothing wanting to compleat my happineſs, but your pardon and forgiveneſs, without which I ſhall be the moſt unhappy creature in the world; therefore I entreat you, my dear father, to take my caſe into conſideration, as you are ſenſible how uncertain a thing life is: Think with yourſelf what a melancholy thing it would be, if it ſhould pleaſe God to take either of us out of the world before we are reconciled to each other; for I am very ſenſible, that was I to hear of your death, it would prove of fatal conſequence to me. I ſhould not have refrained ſo long from writing to you, but that about three months ago Mr. —— was here to ſee me, and told me that he would write to you, and that he would call of me again, as ſoon as he had received an anſwer from you: but I have not ſeen or heard any thing of him ſince, which

which has given me an inexpressible concern and uneasiness; therefore I hope you will excuse my long silence, and not stile me ungrateful in not writing to you sooner. Pray be so good as to communicate the contents of this letter to my dear aunt ——; and at the same time inform her, that these are the true sentiments of a reformed and contrite heart: and I conclude with my prayers to the Almighty to instil into your heart a sincere pardon and forgiveness for all my former misdoings and offences; which Pardon, when once obtained, will be the means of compleating my happiness in this world, and of giving me a satisfactory and quiet mind to prepare myself for the world to come. I should be extremely glad if you would send some person of reputation to see me, and to inspect into my character; and I hope my present and future behaviour will encourage you once more to contract a correspondence with your only child. And I remain, between hopes and despair, with my most submissive duty to you and my aunt,

Your much reformed, truly penitent
And dutiful daughter.

P. S. I hope you will not make any delay in writing to me, as I shall not be easy until I have heard from you.

L E T-

LETTER V.

From C. ——— *to a Friend.*

Madam,

EMboldened by the kind notice you was pleas'd to take of me, when Mrs. —— favoured me laſt with a viſit, I venture to attempt a taſk I am much unworthy to perform, that of paying my reſpects to you. When I reflect how great the contraſt between the perſon wrote to, and the unworthy writer, it fills me with horror; I could wiſh to bury in everlaſting oblivion my paſt unhappy year, and dedicate my future to atone, if poſſible, for the ills my unhappy conduct has occaſioned in my family, in giving ſo much pain unto my near and dear relatives; which is the reſolution of a heart truly ſenſible (I hope I may ſay) of my paſt errors. But words are too faint to expreſs the praiſe the Gentleman deſerves, who was the firſt author of this retirement, for protection of the unhappy. I have a great favour to beg of you, which is to intercede for me, to calm the angry brow of that friend to whoſe care my dear child is intruſted, and beg it as the greateſt boon they can grant me, to ſuffer me to be acquainted, by your means, how the dear little innocent does; that would greatly add to my content in this voluntary retirement; I know, dear Madam, one of your good ſenſe is not at a loſs to judge of the tender ties of nature; therefore, oh Madam, think what I muſt feel in my recollected hour!—But I muſt quit this ſubject, finding myſelf unequal to the taſk, and all the unhappy mother is riſing in my heart. It is you muſt ſpeak my ſentiments, and breathe for me my ſighs, in hopes to ſoften. I hope, dear Madam, you will favour me with an anſwer; but I don't dare to diſpute your goodneſs, and beg you will accept me as one who will, with God's grace, ſtudy to be all you can wiſh me to be in my future conduct, and beg leave to ſubſcribe myſelf,

Your moſt obedient and

Obliged humble Servant.

LETTER VI.

From M—— to the Treaſurer, on her diſmiſſion, being received home by her Mother.

Honoured Sir,

HAving frequently experienced your good nature, I flatter myſelf you'll pardon this intruſion, when I aſſure you, it is with the higheſt ſenſe of gratitude I return you my moſt ſincere thanks for the many favours I have received through your exemplary goodneſs, and the kind indulgence of all my worthy benefactors, during two years ſecluſion from the world; which has been the happy means of bringing me to a reconciliation with my ever honoured Mother, and to a juſt ſtate of mind, and a true ſenſe of my

duty

duty to my too much offended God, for which I am at a loſs for words to pay back the gratitude I owe you. All I can ſay is, may the all-gracious God grant you a long continuance of happy years, and when you quit the ſtage of this mortal life, may your ſoul enter into a happy bliſsful eternity: which will always be the conſtant prayers of, honoured Sir,

Your much obliged, and ever dutiful

Aug. 14, 1760, Humble ſervant.

LETTER VII.

From the Brother of one of the Women.

To the worthy Treaſurer, Governors, and Matron of the Magdalen Houſe in Goodman's Fields.

The humble and ſincere thanks of —— are hereby addreſſed.

THanks are the only return he can make you, and prayers for your preſent and everlaſting felicity; theſe, ſo long as he lives, will be offered to, and for you. You have been, I humbly truſt, the beneficent inſtruments of preſerving a Siſter of mine from eternal ruin. I dwell not upon the deplorable ſituation ſhe was reduced to with regard to this life, though when ſhe ſolicited the favour of your protection, nothing ſurely could be more miſerable; pardon a brother's ſilence on that head, whoſe ſoul, once covered with ſhame, now rejoices, that by your goodneſs, Gentlemen, and the care, pains, and tenderneſs of you, Madam,

dam, he can view a ſiſter with ſuch delight, as did the father his diſtreſt returning prodigal; ſhe is now reſtored (I pray heaven the conviction may be real, and its influence laſting) to a ſenſe of her paſt miſery, a thankfulneſs of heart to you and heaven, to the affection of her friends, and may, through divine grace, become an uſeful member of ſociety, an honour to that inſtitution, by which ſhe has been reclaimed, and (God grant it!) an inhabitant of heaven. I am, with the deepeſt ſenſe of gratitude, Gentlemen and Madam,

Your moſt obliged and
moſt obedient ſervant.

LETTER VIII.

From ——— to her Huſband.

THE taſk I am going to attempt is ſo difficult, that with trembling heart and pen I begin, well knowing how juſtly I have deſerved your diſpleaſure; but beg you'll be kind enough to permit me to implore your forgiveneſs, and to unload a heart, torn with anxiety ever ſince— I may, with the greateſt truth, juſtly ſay, the unfortunate moment I became an alien to your affection, my child, and long lamented home: a ſevere trial, although I with ſhame and ſorrow acknowledge but too juſt a puniſhment for my faults. But, if ever gentle pity dwelt in your breaſt; if ever affectionate regard for this wretched unfortunate had place in your heart, as I once

once had reafon to believe it had !——oh ! that *once*, would I could but fay *now !*——it would be like precious balm to this unhappy breaft, fo long inured to woe. Let my Uncle bring me the kind affurance of your forgivenefs. Diftreffed on every fide, both in body and mind, a wretched out-caft and forlorn wanderer, I fought this heavenly hofpitable afylum to hide myfelf and my forrows, where I enjoy every bleffing I could wifh or hope, but peace of mind ; which is for ever loft, unlefs reftored by you. When amidft all the kind indulgence I meet with here, when I reflect I am a childlefs mother, and a widowed wife, what tongue or pen can exprefs the agonies I feel ! therefore let me beg it once more, that you'll fend to me by my uncle, and give me leave to know how my child does ; aud that I may be indulged in hearing of you and him, will greatly add to my fatisfaction. The hopes of being reftored to you again, though it would crown my utmoft wifhes, I dare not think of ; but leave to you the decifion of my fate, and can only wifh that fome affectionate fpark may yet re-kindle in your breaft for her, who will ever remain the future part of my life,

Magdalen-Houfe,
Oct. 19, 1760.

Moft affectionately and
Faithfully yours.

LETTER IX.

From the Mother of one of the young Women, to a Governor.

SIR,

THE favour of your moſt kind letter I received, which filled me with joy at the confirmation of my once unhappy daughter's being under ſuch good hands, and with gratitude to you for the trouble you have taken in informing me to whom I am obliged for my daughter's preſervation from utter ruin; and I ſhall take care to obſerve your kind inſtruction, and to ſhew my gratitude to the good lady; and be pleaſed to accept of my heartieſt and beſt thanks for your ſpecial care of, and kindneſs to the diſtreſſed daughter of her, who never can ſufficiently acknowledge it, but who ſhall ever pray for the happineſs of her benefactors. And am,

Good Sir,

Your moſt obliged and obedient Servant.

April 8, 1760.

LETTER X.

Honoured Sir,

YOUR goodneſs demands my hearty thanks; and as I have not an opportunity of ſeeing you, I hope you will pardon my writing to you, to return you my thanks for adviſing me to this happy retreat. I can't help ſtanding to admire how good God has been to me, to raiſe me

ſuch

ſuch friends: I muſt not forget to tell you, the kindneſs I received from our good Matron, and that ſhe ſtudies to make us all happy.

When I reflect what inward happineſs I loſt for ſome years, it is a great trouble to me; but now I hope, Sir, you will pardon my aſking you to join thanks with me that am ſo ſoon called out of it, and I can truly ſay, heartily ſorry for what is paſt: and now with ſubmiſſion muſt conclude,

Your moſt obedient humble ſervant.

LETTER XI.

From H. —— *to two young Girls, her former Companions.*

Dear P. *and* B.

I Was thinking it would be right to let you know of my welfare in this bleſſed place, where I hope I ſhall ſtay my life time. When I look back, and think of the ſad way of life which you know I was in a great while, the reflection grieves me to the heart; for there is nothing but miſery attends it at the long run, and ſo you will find. Dear *P.* and *B.* think of what I ſay, for now I have nothing to think of but happineſs, and to repent of my former ſins, which I am now aſhamed of, and ſo you will both, with the grace of God. I may bleſs the hour that I came to this houſe, for now I am reconciled to all my friends, and I hope I ſhall with God.

Only *think what a bleſſing it is to go to bed with God in your heart, inſtead of tearing about all night with the devil's inſtructions in that way of life*; for you are always troubled in your minds, unleſs you are in liquor. It is a great favour to get admitted into our houſe; but if you have a mind to come, I hope you will both get in. Don't think our houſe a place of confinement, for our benefactors won't keep any body againſt their will, nor detain them a minute.

From your ſincere friend and well-wiſher.

AN AUTHENTIC NARRATIVE OF A MAGDALEN.

BEFORE the Inftitution of the MAGDALEN CHARITY, the cafe of unhappy young Women in a ftate of Proftitution was frequently deplored. Miferable beyond redemption, they had no place to fly unto, and however well difpofed to forfake their abandoned courfe of life, they found every door of hope clofed againft them. The voice of humanity prevailed. The MAGDALEN HOUSE was opened; and in proof of the good will of the Public towards fuch an inftitution; of the readinefs of the objects to accept the relief it propofed; liberal contributions were fpeedily made; numbers of unhappy young Women immediately applied for admiffion.

Benevolent and humane Chriftians felt a fenfible delight in the Charity: they flocked in numbers to behold the good work, and bountifully bleffed it with their gifts; while it was faid—truly and humanely faid, "that if half, if a quarter, if a fmall portion only of thofe who fled to this houſe of repentance, ſhould truly and properly improve the bleſſing; the work was great and good; demanding all ſuccour, deſerving all applauſe."

After near eight years experience, and amidſt all the difficulties under which every infant inſtitution labours, it may be ſaid with truth, that theſe good hopes and wiſhes of the benevolent have been accompliſhed. A large proportion of thoſe unfortunate young creatures, who, under the burden of every miſery, have ſought this ſole retreat from their wretchedneſs, have, by the bleſſing of God, and to the great comfort of the friends of this Charity, being reſtored to all things valuable upon earth; and what is of moſt importance, to the probable expectation of eternal happineſs in Heaven.

There cannot be a greater ſatisfaction than to know, and be aſſured of the felicity of thoſe whom Providence hath made us the bleſſed inſtruments of reſcuing from extreme diſtreſs. But, however deſireable, this is a pleaſure which the friends of the MAGDALEN CHARITY muſt in a great meaſure be denied: for except in ſome particular caſes, it is impoſſible, it would be cruel, to mark out thoſe, who, reſtored to life by the interpoſition of the Charity, maintain a good reputation, and

fill

fill up their ſphere with propriety. However conſcious and concerned ſuch may be for their paſt miſdeeds, they would wiſh, doubtleſs, to ſteal through the world ſilent and unknown; born again, as it were, to new life, and redeeming the paſt, by their preſent good conduct*. Let, therefore, ſuch remain in that decent privacy which they deſire: And, may the bleſſing of God concur with their good reſolutions, and enable them to perſevere ſteadfaſt and unblameable unto the end!

But, when the laſt act is finiſhed; when the ſcene is cloſed; when all the hopes and fears of life are over, we may be allowed briefly to ſpeak of thoſe, whoſe deaths have been honourable; cancelling, through redeeming grace, all the errors of their paſt behaviour.

* The judicious will eaſily diſcern that this Charity muſt always lie under ſome peculiar difficulties, and conſequently will need much candour, on account of thoſe women who return to vice; whether they have been ignominiouſly or otherwiſe diſmiſſed from it. Theſe will neceſſarily be public; and indeed every bad woman will bring, or attempt to bring an opprobrium upon the Houſe; while no counterbalance can be had from the public and becoming conduct of thoſe, who perſevere in the paths of virtue, and whoſe caſe will be ſimilar to that here related.

Of this number was *A. F.* an haplefs young woman, of about fixteen years of age, admitted into the MAGDALEN HOUSE under a load of infamy and horror, in *December* 1761. She was the favourite daughter of her father, a perfon of a decent and refpectable character in life, who, though he had feveral children, regarded this with eyes of peculiar tendernefs and affection. Pleafing and delicate in her perfon, fhe had always hitherto fhewn an equally amiable mind, and returned her father's regard with becoming attention. But alas! an infidious feducer foon found the way to her heart; and under the delufive pretenfions of courtfhip and marriage, in an unguarded hour, ruined and withdrew her from her father's houfe. He, in all the frantic rage of diftrefs, fought the child of his tendereft affection. He found, forgave, and brought her home. But, whether through an infatuation for her feducer, (which, however ftrange, is found but too often the cafe) whether through the admonitions of her afflicted parent too repeatedly urged, or through reftraint, not known before; once more, in an evil hour, fhe left her father's houfe, and foon, abandoned by her

feducer

ſeducer, plunged into total licentiouſneſs and debauchery.

Her father, who felt ſuch anguiſh as none but the parental heart can in any degree conceive, now gave up his child as irretrievably loſt. Happening, however, ſome time after, to paſs along the ſtreet, he ſaw a young creature, highly dreſſed, throw herſelf into a chair, which waited at the door of one of thoſe many infamous houſes in this city, to convey her to her lodgings, after the debaucheries of the place. Let the parent gueſs what He muſt have felt, when he perceived this gay victim of licentiouſneſs to be — his child, his favourite child—his daughter! He ſtood ſtruck with horror and amazement, whilſt ſhe—pierced no doubt to the heart, yet unwilling to humble herſelf, and confeſs her guilt turned from him, and by her immediate order was carried off, leaving the parent who had paſſed ſo many ſollicitous hours for her, almoſt petrified with grief, and unable to move!

There is great reaſon to believe that this occaſional but affecting interview touched her to the quick, and was the foundation of that reſolve which ſhe ſoon after put into practice. For, the fury of unbridled paſſion beginning to abate, and the diſtreſſes of her deteſted courſe of of life daily increaſing; the early impreſſions of parental tenderneſs naturally coincided with theſe to awaken reflection, and to ſhew her herſelf.

Alarmed at the view, ſhe wiſhed, ſhe determined to return, and try what repentance could do. For which purpoſe ſhe applied to the MAGDALEN HOUSE, and found a ready admiſſion. For how could admiſſion be refuſed to one ſo young, labouring under ſuch a burden of miſery, and with ſuch probable expectations of ſincere amendment?

Thoſe expectations were not diſappointed: ſhe continued three years in the Houſe; during the whole of which her behaviour was decent, conſiſtent, and commendable. But, though reconciled to God, though conſcious of the ſincerity of her heart, ſhe could find no ſolid ſatisfaction, till reconciled to the father whom ſhe had ſo much injured, and to whoſe ſoul ſhe had given ſuch unſpeakable anguiſh. The father, however, was now deaf to all her ſollicitations. In vain ſhe wrote, in vain ſhe pleaded: every effort proved ineffectual to procure that pardon, without which her heart can never know peace.

A perſon who deeply intereſts himſelf in favour of the Objects of the Charity, wrote to

her

her father. The following was the anſwer he received.

"*SIR,*

"I Had the honour of yours, and with it a "renewal of my ſorrow of heart; which "proceeded, not from your relation of an "amendment of life in a long loſt and aban- "doned child, but from the remembrance of "her unhappy fall. Did you but know, Sir, "with what care and induſtry an affectionate "father and mother (poſſeſſed of but little, "perhaps worthy of more,) have diſcharged "their duty, there is nothing but your great "goodneſs of heart could induce you to be ſo "generous an advocate for one, that has for- "feited ſo much. But what can I ſay on this "afflicting ſubject, with any degree of pro- "priety, to keep clear of offending the fathers "of an unhappy many; whilſt my indigna- "tion for the conduct of one, cauſes ſuch per- "turbation of body and mind, as renders me "defenceleſs both in words and actions.

"Un-neglected by precept and example, "unprovoked by want or ill uſage, ſhe ſacri- "ficed all that was binding, to a lawleſs "unruly paſſion, and plunged herſelf into "that long ſcene of miſery, which muſt have

"been

" been longer ſtill, were ſhe not reſcued by the " humane hands of this noble Charity. Happy " is it for her, that you, Sir, have conde- " ſcended to ſay, ſhe has approved herſelf " worthy of it; and happier ſtill will ſhe be, " if ſhe continues to deſerve, from thoſe boun- " tiful hands which protect, and have led her " back to thoſe paths of virtue from whence " ſhe ſtrayed.

" Pardon me, Sir, that I detain you ſo " long on a melancholy ſubject, perſuaded as " I am, that your tenderneſs of heart has ſuf- " fered by many ſuch doleful tales; and I hope " you will forgive me when I ſay, that I am " not ſufficiently prepared for the ſorrowful " interview your deſire, with my once moſt " tenderly beloved daughter. But, as your " kind and fatherly letter has conveyed ſome " conſolation to a long diſturbed and afflicted " heart, by telling me that her repentance " has begot compaſſion in you, and the reſt " of the worthy Governors of that bleſſed " Charity; I will not appear ſo obdurate and " unrelenting to ſay, that I will never ſee her; " but, in time, on her perſevering in good " works, and finiſhing her reformation, agree- " able to the time inſtituted by that excellent " Charity; I may not only ſee her, but alſo

" have

"have pity, and reſtore her to that care and "protection, which never departed from me, "until ſhe departed from them.

"Thus far, and no further, am I capable, "overflowed with ſorrow, to determine at pre- "ſent; and, as virtue is its own reward, I "know you expect no more than the thanks "and prayers of a grateful heart, which ſhall, "publicly and privately, be paid by me, for the "proſperity and advancement of that beſt and "moſt humane of Charities; for the preſer- "vation of all its Members; and particularly "for you, Sir, to whom I have the honour to "be, *&c.*"

Thoſe who are acquainted with the human heart, will not be ſurprized to hear that the heart which dictated this letter was afterwards reconciled to a daughter, once ſo much beloved, and returning, like the Prodigal, with true contrition, both to her earthly and her heavenly parent. This happy event ſoon after taking place, the daughter wrote with joy to the ſame Gentleman to whom the father's letter was directed; and we ſubjoin a part of her letter, as it demonſtrates the goodneſs of her mind.

"*SIR*,

" *S I R*,

" THE inclosed will shew that the happy
" reconciliation with my dear father
" is, to my unspeakable joy, at last effected:
" and as you, Sir, have been the kind instru-
" ment of bringing it about, I should be guilty
" of the greatest ingratitude, were I to omit the
" first opportunity of returning you the thanks
" that such an important service merits: and
" believe me, Sir, that in whatever station it
" shall please the Almighty hereafter to place
" me, I shall retain the deepest sense of the
" many mercies I have had vouchsafed me,
" while life remains, *&c.*"

She did not forfeit these promises. Her heart was sincere, and her reformation real. Received home with joy, she proved by her whole behaviour the truth of her repentance, and conducted herself in every manner suitable to her circumstances, and agreeable to her parent.

Sollicitous for her welfare, he soon after gained her an establishment in a family of worth and distinction, where getting an unfortunate scratch upon the leg, and through attention to her duty neglecting it, bad consequences ensued; a mortification speedily came on, and an amputation of her leg was found unavoidable.

She

She bore the dreadful tidings with great composure and resignation, sent to the Chapel of the *Magdalen Hospital*, earnestly requesting the prayers of all her sister penitents for her, and underwent the cruel operation with a patience and resolution which surprized those who performed it.

It is easy to conceive, from a habit of body so wretched as that which rendered the amputation necessary, what must have been the consequences of such an expedient: a total mortification came on; and in a few days after she expired: expired with blessings on the Charity, as the great means of her salvation; expired with all that serenity of soul, with all that humility, yet confidence of hope, which nothing but true christian principles can inspire; but which those principles will always inspire into the breast of the real Penitent.

Upon this Narrative, which is in every particular conformable to truth, I would only beg leave to make one or two observations. The *first*, and most natural one is, the great utility of the MAGDALEN INSTITUTION, without which, this young creature, thus preserved, and now, we trust, amongst the blessed, in all human probability would have been lost; lost in early youth, before she had seen her

her twentieth year; loft in the extremity of fuffering here, and loft to all the rewards and comforts of futurity: and not only herfelf thus deplorably undone, but her wretched father would have been left to mourn with bittereft forrow the temporal and the everlafting mifery of his beloved child. Who can be infenfible to the value, the importance of an inftitution, which thus prevents the direft woe; which not only in the prefent cafe, but in a variety of others, we have all poffible reafon to believe, hath faved, and will continue to fave, many fouls from eternal lofs!

Let a *fecond* obfervation from this mournful Narrative, be carried home to the hearts of thofe daughters, who are bleffed with worthy and affectionate parents. Let them learn from hence what horrid confequences——confequences, in a great degree, irremediable in this life, however their ill effects may be totally cancelled in the next,——attend a deviation from filial duty. Let them fettle it in their hearts, that no love can be equal to the parental; and that whenever the fyren-voice of feduction wooes them to forfake a tender father's roof, however fweet the found, however alluring the promifes, Deftruction awaits the fatal ftep, and Ruin ftands ready to clofe her gloomy doors upon them!

A SER-

A

SERMON,

Preached before the

PRESIDENT, VICE - PRESIDENTS, TREASURER and GOVERNORS

OF THE

MAGDALEN-HOUSE,

By *WILLIAM DODD,* M. A.

Publiſhed at the Requeſt of the Preſident, *&c.*

HE THAT IS WITHOUT SIN AMONG YOU, LET HIM FIRST CAST A STONE AT HER.

JOHN viii. 7.

The EIGHTH EDITION.

To the Right Honourable

The Earl of HERTFORD, PRESIDENT.

The Right Hon. Lord *Romney*, Sir *George Savile*, Bart. Sir *Alexander Grant*, Bart. Sir *Samuel Fludyer*, Bart. and Alderman, } Vice-Presidents.

Robert Dingley, Esq; Treasurer.

John Barker, *Edmund Boehm*, *James Crockatt*, *Charles Dingley*, *Edward Dixon*, *John Dorrien*, *John Dupré*, *Isaac Eeles*, *Jonas Hanway*, *Fraser Honywood*, *Thomas Light*, } Esqrs.

Robert Nettleton, *Thomas Preston*, *William Reynolds*, *Hugh Ross*, *Thomas Spencer*, *John Tozer*, *John Thornton*, *Saunders Welch*, *George Wombwell*, *John Weyland*, } Esqrs.

The Annual COMMITTEE,
And all the other Worthy Governors and Subscribers to this Excellent and Useful Institution;

THIS

DISCOURSE,

Preached at their Request,
And published by their Order,
Is, with all due Respect and Esteem,
Dedicated and Inscribed,

BY

The AUTHOR.

Plaistow,
April 28, 1759.

PREFACE.

IN an age, when vice is, in ſome reſpects, become faſhionable, and that of Lewdneſs eſpecially treated with ſmiles, not degraded with due indignation; it cannot ſeem ſtrange, that an attempt like the preſent ſhould meet with ſome ridicule, and be liable to ſome objections, as well from the gay, as the grave; from the thinking as the thoughtleſs. And as there is a variety of motives which may induce men to give to charitable inſtitutions, ſo are there motives no leſs various, which may withhold them from giving; and of conſequence, lead them to decry a deſign, ſolely becauſe they mean not to ſupport it.

But as we hold not, with a noble Lord *, *ridicule* to be any *teſt* of the truth; and conceive that light mirth is as indecent as weak, where the life and ſalvation of fellow-creatures are concerned; we ſhall not be diſcouraged from any good purpoſe by its random ſhafts, or diverted from any benevolent deſign, by its loud and unmeaning madneſs.

The ſucceſs and encouragement, which the preſent inſtitution hath met with, in the

* Lord *Shafteſbury*.

ſhort time ſince its commencement, from the Great and the Good, abundantly ſpeak its utility; and we are pleaſed to obſerve, that very few, if any charitable propoſals, have made a more rapid progreſs in the ſame compaſs of time *.

As the purpoſe of the worthy Patrons and Managers of this Charity is only to do good, and to render an important ſervice to *Religion* and their *Country*; they will never be inattentive to any obſervations of the wiſe and well-meaning; never be backward to conſider any objections, which ſpeculation may propoſe; or to admit any uſeful hints, which ſerìouſneſs and ſobriety may urge, for the advancement of the good work, and the furtherance of its utility.

We remember, that when the *Plan* for this inſtitution was laid before the world, ſome,—either ignorant, as it ſhould ſeem, of human nature, or averſe to the benevolent deſign,—urged that "it was chimerical and abſurd; that no objects would ever preſent themſelves; or, if they did, that the reformation of ſuch was impoſſible."

The doors of the *houſe* were no ſooner opened, than this objection was powerfully

* For this we refer to the general printed account of the charity.

removed

removed indeed, by the *number* of pitiable ſufferers who flew joyfully to the firſt harbour where they could be admitted; and where, in full proof that the reformation of ſuch is nothing *ideal*, their behaviour, in the general, hath been excellent and exemplary; and all the ſigns and fruits of reformation, which could be fancied or formed, have and continue to ſhew themſelves.

Surely they who have talked of this deſign, as of "a ſcheme to waſh *Ethiopians* white," muſt have been very inattentive obſervers of human nature; muſt have conſidered but very ſuperficially the end and deſign of the religion of *Chriſt*.

For all the world knows the miſery and diſtreſs of theſe objects: every man who reflects on the true condition of humanity, muſt know, that the life of a common proſtitute, is as contrary to the nature and condition of the female ſex, as darkneſs to light: and however ſome may be compelled to the ſlavery of it, yet we can never imagine every line of right and virtue obliterated in the minds of all of them. And indeed, as the *voluntary* entrance of thoſe who are now in the *houſe* is a ſufficient proof of their wearineſs, and deteſtation of this way of life, and a ſtrong recommendation in their favour; ſo from many letters *, and many affecting incidents which have already happened in the houſe, it appears, beyond all contradiction, that the nobleneſs of virtue, and the delicacy of ſentiment, have been rather covered over with defilement, than wholly blotted out; which, upon the firſt removal of the filth, have ſhewn themſelves in particulars, which would do honour to the moſt amiable characters.

When the ſucceſs of the inſtitution rendered theſe objections no longer poſſible; then,—as nothing is ſo inconſiſtent as the ſpirit of oppoſition and malevolence,—it was ſaid on the one hand, 1. "That the deſign of the promoters of this charity was wholly to prevent the Vice of Fornication;"—And on the other, 2. "That their purpoſe was favourable to the vice; and if not meant to encourage and recommend laſciviouſneſs, yet evidently productive of theſe conſequences."

* Concerning theſe a more ſatisfactory account may be had from Mr. *Dingley*, who is in poſſeſſion of the manuſcript letters referred to.

For

For the *first*; surely the objectors must have had a low opinion of the proposers of this institution, and supposed them men of very mean understandings, to fancy they could think of stemming the torrent of such an overflowing vice, by providing a receptacle for a small number of the thousand victims, which are annually offered up in this metropolis to lust and destruction! In truth, they are not so sanguine as to conceive, or so ignorant of human nature as to imagine, that a retreat for the few who may be willing to retrieve and repent, will diminish the dominion of this all-ruling passion. The corruption of human nature must first be totally eradicated; and the favourers of this vice need be under no apprehensions, nor join the infamous *bawds* and *panders* in the cry, as if their craft was in danger *. But if they will not

 unite

* While such execrable methods are pursued, to entrap innocent and unwary girls, as are publicly avowed; and while infamous bawds are suffered so to *ruin* and *enslave*, no prevention can ever be thought of. These arts are in general well known, except to such as it most concerns not to be ignorant of them. But one

unite in the good deſign, nor, in juſt retribution, aſſiſt in providing an aſylum for ſuch as may be called upon, by their bodies or minds, to forſake the paths of death; let them be entreated to curb their own evil propenſities; let them be intreated not to add to the number of theſe miſerable objects, already too great: let them be intreated to conſider the innumerable fatal conſequences to public, private, and domeſtic happineſs, which ariſe from unbridled luſt, and a promiſcuous commerce; and, at leaſt, for their own ſakes, learn the practice of that virtue, which never

leaves

one of this infernal crew, with an impudence which is ſcarce to be parallelled, hath lately hired the venal quill of ſome hackney writer to proclaim publicly to mankind his ſcandalous and horrid proceedings; and hath laid open ſome of thoſe artifices, which may perhaps tend to another purpoſe than the ſpirit of that pamphlet proves it written with. It will not be long doubted, that I refer to "The remonſtrances of the *Pimp-general:* "—Honourable Title!—And, poſſibly, it is the ſame infamous, and malevolent pen, which lately, in language the moſt virulent and ſhocking, hath poured forth its deteſtable venom againſt

this,

leaves her votaries to diſeaſe and diſtraction, to anguiſh of conſcience, and future condemnation.

For the *ſecond* objection; the characters of the worthy Gentlemen who are concerned in this deſign, are too public, and too well known for the amiable practice eſpecially of all domeſtic virtues, to dread any prejudice from the loudeſt voice of ſuch ſlander. But, acquitting them of the *purpoſe*; Let any man only conſider the *progreſs* which this vice hath made in our nation; its general and fatal prevalence; the many thouſand women yearly periſhing, in all the extremities of diſeaſe and

this, and all other *Public Charities!* Poor man! what a horrid mind muſt he poſſeſs, and what a puniſhment muſt he ſhare hereafter, unleſs he repent! For, not to ſpeak of the univerſal deteſtation in which ſuch a being muſt be held; can we conceive any crime more complicated than *his*, who endeavours to prevent the workings of benevolence, the nobleſt and firſt of virtues; and who takes as much ſavage delight in doing evil, in calumniating and abuſing, as the virtuous take in doing good to, and bleſſing their fellow-creatures? Wretched writer! what a black and pitiable mind is thine!

diſtreſs, by means of it: let them only conſider how many capital ſtreets, for many years paſt, have been thronged, and every corner of our *metropolis* infeſted by the miſerable wretches, to the ſhame of good order, decency, and religion: and then let them never fancy, that ſuch a deſign can encourage; then let them be glad, that here — but here only — an opportunity preſents itſelf, to ſave ſome of theſe poor ſufferers from almoſt inſtant perdition.

In truth, this objection might as well be urged againſt every other charitable inſtitution; nay indeed, I have heard it urged againſt ſome, which ſeem leaſt liable to its force. And you might, with as much reaſon ſuppoſe, that a maſon would be careleſs how he mounted the ladder, and indifferent whether he fell down or not, and broke a leg, becauſe there is an *hoſpital* ready to receive him; as that a woman ſhould *commence* * proſtitute, becauſe there is

* The reader will obſerve that I ſay *commence*: That ſome of the miſerable wretches who are obliged to that hardeſt of all ſervice, the walking nightly in the ſtreets, may ſometimes, in their *diſſem-*

is a houſe of *penitence* and *induſtry* to receive her in woe and diſtreſs.

Different, far different, are the motives which are urged, and the proſpects which are preſented, when the ſeducer ſpreads his toils againſt artleſs unſuſpecting innocence. Golden dreams, and gay delights, lull her fancy and her conſcience ; and ſhe thinks of nothing elſe, — till ſhe awakens from her ſleep, and finds herſelf undone !

But, ſuppoſing the preſent deſign well planned, the purpoſe good, and the effects more admirable than could have been expected, even by the moſt ſanguine favourer of this charity : Some will yet object again (and we would wiſh every objection removed) "that they are doubtful what may become of theſe women, and whether they may not return to the ſame courſe of life, when removed from the houſe."

diſſembled jollity, boaſt of the *Magdalen-houſe*, no man can wonder ; and the leſs ſo, as they are ſo frequently reminded of it by paſſengers of every ſort. But the diſcerning and judicious will perceive, that this can be no objection to the *houſe* itſelf.

 We

We muſt be allowed here to rejoin, that inſiſting too much on this point, in the preſent infant ſtate of this deſign, is rather unkind; and eſpecially, if it be ſo inſiſted on, as to be made an objection againſt it. Let thoſe, who raiſe it, rather employ their time and their thoughts,—as they would wiſh to unite in the good of their fellow-creatures,—how beſt to remove it, and propoſe whatever may ſeem reaſonable to themſelves on this head; and I believe I may take upon me to ſay, that all ſuch propoſals will be received with due deference and eſteem.

But ſurely, they muſt not have reflected ſeriouſly on the influence of religious principles, who lay too much ſtreſs on this objection. All parents and friends ſuppoſe the advantages of education great, and the bias of religious principles ſuch, that it is ſufficient to preſerve the mind from deviating into the paths of error and folly. If not, why are we ſo ſolicitous for giving our children good education, and an early tincture of virtue? And why ſhould we not preſume the ſame in regard to theſe women, many of whom have entered the houſe utterly ignorant of and uninſtructed

in

in the religion of their country; ſtrangers, too much to their God and their Saviour, the glad tidings of whoſe mercy is like refreſhing balm to their ſouls? Now, as the Chriſtian Religion, in ſuch circumſtances, is a perfectly new thing, great and admirable are the effects which may reaſonably be expected from it: and as the moſt diligent care is taken to inſtruct them in the ſound principles of the faith, no friend to that faith can doubt the good effects of ſuch inſtruction.

Beſides, after the time of their probation, which will be more or leſs, as proper behaviour may dictate, and opportunity offer; it is not to be doubted, but that many friends will be reconciled to and receive them; (ſome have already been reconciled:) — that upon the exacteſt knowledge of their characters, — which may be had here without the leaſt deception, many worthy perſons will employ them as ſervants, which will be but an act of ordinary juſtice: Some may become uſeful and faithful wives; and as being habituated to induſtry, and taught many uſeful branches of employment in the houſe, they will moreover be enabled to procure their own bread; and that more especially, as it will be the care of the Directors of this Charity, so to fix those in future life who shall gain their esteem by proper conduct, and so to occupy the little Sums they may gain * during their stay in the house, as to enable them the better to procure an honourable subsistance. For it is well known, that many of these unhappy women, who have once lost their character, have no possible opportunity to get their own bread, however able and desirous they may be, thro' the natural reluctancy there is in the generality of people to employ them; nay, indeed, we might say, through the almost unavoidable impossibility of employing them. So that when they leave the house, stored with good principles, and with an habit of industry, and are put into a way to procure a livelihood, there can be no doubt but they will do so. And should some miscarry out of the number, yet if *some*, if *half* only, are

* Every woman is entitled to a part of what she gains by her labour in the house. See the Rules of *Employment*, Numb. 1. *&c.*

restored

reſtored and ſaved; certainly it will well repay all the trouble: And I cannot but remark, in juſtice to the women now in the houſe, that they are truly ſenſible of the neceſſity of induſtry. The account of what they have already gained, which hath been publiſhed *, is a ſufficient proof that they have not been, that they are not idle. And this account may ſerve alſo to corroborate another remark, which was made when the Plan was firſt laid before the world; that greater good may be done, at a leſs expence, in this undertaking, than in almoſt any other charitable ſcheme; ſince it is to be ſuppoſed, that when the whole is duly regulated, the women will nearly maintain themſelves.

This may ſerve as an anſwer to the objection under view: but I muſt add beſides, that a due attention will be had to

* It appears from this account, that from the commencement of the charity, *Auguſt* 10, 1758, to *April* 12, 1759, the work done by the Women, as ſpinning, making caps, ſhirts, winding ſilk, embroidering of gloves, *&c.* —— amounted to 168*l.* 19*s.* 11*d.*

the

the demands of our colonies abroad; where ſuch as are willing, upon the beſt advantages and propoſals, will be transferred, at the diſcretion and direction of the Governors. *

The great decreaſe of our people is a ſubject of common obſervation, and doubtleſs one ſource of it is that abominable luſt, and prevalent promiſcuous commerce of the ſexes, which, to the prejudice of honourable matrimony, ſo notoriouſly abounds. As very many of the objects in the *Magdalen Houſe* are extremely young, the preſerving them from that immediate deſtruction into which they muſt otherwiſe have fallen, it is hoped, is an object not unworthy men who love their country, and wiſh to promote its happineſs. And as many of them have been deluded, in the moſt *ſcandalous* manner, ſome, I may ſay, without a figure, almoſt in their *hanging ſleeves*, and have been kept purpoſely in black and total ignorance of the crime, to which they were unwittingly introduced; ſurely, it is but a debt we owe to ſuch,

* This is now more immediately under conſideration

to give them the means of inſtruction, and *one* chance at leaſt for eternal life, which they could otherwiſe never have found.

If, as ſome have fondly advanced, an attempt of this kind be *methodiſtical*; let thoſe perſons be told, it would well become us all to be *ſuch* Methodiſts. Indeed this little wild bolt of weakneſs ſcarce deſerves to be mentioned; except to remark the abſurdity of ſome ſort of people, who think it ſufficient to decry a good man, or a good work, if they brand them with the name of *Methodiſt*. This ſurely is moſt injudicious; ſince it is giving the higheſt honour to the people, whom they mean to condemn, by ſuppoſing that real virtue, and ſubſtantial piety, is only to be met with amongſt them. However, be it known, that nothing of *Methodiſm* or *Enthuſiaſm* hath, or ever will have place, we truſt, in this Deſign. The Gentlemen concerned in it have knowledge too real, and piety too ſolid, to countenance or encourage any thing weak, wild, and blaſphemous: and though they are not aſhamed to think the doctrines of the Chriſtian Religion eſſentially neceſſary to be taught in all their plainneſs to the *Penitents*, with whom deepneſs of learning, or vaſt

vaſt reach of thought, is by no means neceſſary; yet they will always take care ſo to provide, that imputations of this ſort may be only the blaſts of calumny, or the inane effuſions of ignorance and inattention.

Noble minds are always the moſt free from envy: this is a baneful plant, which grows moſt luxuriantly in the worſt ſoils. But it is well that the preſent undertaking can never be affected by the malevolence of the lower ſort; who may regret ſuch a proviſion for their miſerable, and by *them* judged, utterly unworthy fellow-creatures, but will never be able to prevent it. Sometimes too, there is a ſtern ſeverity even in virtue, which knows not to forgive failings, whereto itſelf is a ſtranger: and full often we find, that men can be extremely rigid to faults of which they themſelves are guiltleſs; while they harbour ſins equally odious and deſtructive in their boſoms, and can very readily pardon and paſs over them;—quick-ſighted to the mote in their brother's, very dim to the beam in their own eye. To the latter of theſe we would wiſh to recommend our Saviour's conduct in the caſe of the wo-

man

man caught in adultery, and advise such *as are without sin* themselves *to cast the first stone.* To the former, with all the winning mildness of the father to the *eldest son* in the parable, we would reply, *It is meet that we should make merry and be glad: for this thy brother*, thy fellow creature, and fellow Christian, *was dead, and is alive again; was lost, and is found!*

Thus much seemed requisite to urge, over and above what follows in the *Sermon*, and which it was not so convenient to add there. And I have only to request my reader's favourable regard, which I shall not doubt to obtain, when the novelty and niceness of my subject is considered. I must not, however, with-hold my acknowledgments from the noble and worthy Supporters of this Charity, for the kind opinion they were pleased to express of this my endeavour to forward their useful design: And could I presume, that the discourse might meet with a reception near as favourable from the *Press*, as from the *Pulpit*, I should be happy. "But the ear is a favourable

favourable judge: a reader, we know, is ſevere and inexorable *."

Satisfied however in the ſincerity of my intention; aſſured, that to give the leaſt offence is at the utmoſt diſtance from my deſign; and deſirous to be as inſtrumental as my ſtation will admit, in the great work of benevolence and love; I commit it to the world, and to the patronage eſpecially of the *Friends* and *Governors* of this Charity, at whoſe requeſt it was *preached*: (an office, which, they can bear me witneſs, I ſtrove much and long to commend to one of ſuperior ſtation and ability), and at whoſe command and deſire I now *publiſh* it: heartily praying, that the Divine Grace may accompany it, and this good work, and crown all the generous inſtruments of it with length of days, riches, and honour here below, and with immortality and glory in the world to come!

* A remark from *Lawſon's uſeful* lectures concerinng *Oratory*, page 100.

St.

St. MATT. ix. 12, 13.

AND WHEN JESUS HEARD THAT, HE SAID, THEY THAT ARE WHOLE NEED NOT A PHYSYCIAN; BUT THEY THAT ARE SICK. — BUT GO YE AND LEARN WHAT THAT MEANETH, I WILL HAVE MERCY, AND NOT SACRIFICE: FOR I AM NOT COME TO CALL THE RIGHTEOUS, BUT SINNERS TO REPENTANCE.

NOTHING can be conceived more amiable than the character, nothing more benevolent than the design, of the great Redeemer of the world. The religion he hath instituted is the most agreeable and correspondent to the necessities of mankind: the example he hath set, the most conducive to that perfecting our nature, which is the end of our Being, and the foundation of our felicity.

That

That Virtue is preferable to Vice; that, if there be a God, he muſt delight in virtue; that what he delights in, may reaſonably expect to be happy; was the general perſuaſion of the beſt and wiſeſt Heathens. But theſe opinions left them only in ſad diſquietude and uneaſy ſuſpenſe; ſince the prevalent corruption of human Nature permitted very little ſatisfaction to ariſe from the contemplation of Virtues defiled with innumerable blemiſhes, for which they were utterly ignorant whether pardon might be obtained at all; or if obtained, in what manner the Deity could be atoned, and made placable. This held them, as it were, all their life time ſubject to bondage; and made death, as one of the ableſt of them calls it, "of all dreadful things the moſt horribly dreadful."

Theſe clouds are removed, and this darkneſs diſpelled, by that life and immortality which is brought to light by the Goſpel. And, to the unſpeakable comfort of our ſouls, we perceive the Son of God himſelf moved by the moſt affecting benevolence to eſpouſe our cauſe, to purchaſe our ſalvation, to proclaim our pardon; and making

ing a Revelation of the ſovereign Will, compleatly adapted to our wants, perfectly diſperſing our doubts and our fears, and inſpiring us at once with the moſt pleaſing confidence, and the warmeſt love.

The words of the text ſerve well to ſhew us the admirable Diſpoſition of our Saviour, and the important End of his appearance amongſt us: And as that Diſpoſition was the moſt amiably benevolent and compaſſionate, and that End the ſalvation of repenting ſinners; there ſurely can be nothing more proper to engage our attention at preſent, when we are aſſembled to promote and encourage an undertaking, of which BENEVOLENCE and COMPASSION are the noble *Foundations*: of which the SALVATION of LOST and RUINED SOULS is the glorious *End*.

I ſhall take occaſion, therefore, from the words of the text,

I. Briefly to ſet forth the *End* and *Excellence* of the Chriſtian Religion; And,

II. To ſhew the exact and pleaſing conformity of our preſent *inſtitution* to it: the Utility whereof, and the many motives which ſhould urge us to a generous aſſiſtance

ſtance of it, will conclude the preſent addreſs. Wherein I ſhall need all that candor and favourable attention, which a ſubject ſo new and ſo delicate may juſtly claim. And permit me to hope, that as I tread firſt, by your appointment, in this trackleſs path, you will make the more indulgent allowances.

Iſt then, let us take a general view of the *end* and *excellence* of the Chriſtian Religion.

And certainly that *end* is the moſt noble that can be fancied, the moſt commendable that can be conceived. It is nothing leſs than the recovery of mankind from ruin and wretchedneſs: than the reſtoration of a fallen world to favour and felicity, with the author of their exiſtence, and the fountain of all good.

The Scriptures ſet this end before us in terms the moſt expreſſive, and the moſt pleaſing. We are told in them, that *God ſo loved the world, that he gave his only begotten Son, that whoſoever believeth in him, ſhould not periſh, but have everlaſting life.* We are told that this divine and only begotten Son, *came into the world to ſave ſinners.*

sinners. Nay, and he himself, throughout the course of his ministry, uttered only pathetic invitations to the *weary* and *heavy-laden* to come to him, and find mercy and *life* ;—to take his *easy yoke*, and receive *rest* and tranquility. And in the words of the text, you perceive what kind encouragement fell from his blessed lips, fully expressing his benevolent design, and engaging the humble penitent to access and confidence. *They that are whole*, (said he to the malevolent Pharisees, who objected to him, because they saw him eat with Publicans and Sinners,) *they that are whole need not a physician* ; *but they that are sick*. " Murmur not therefore, ye Scribes and Pharisees, that I eat and converse with Publicans and Sinners : My business is with such : and the end of my coming into the world was the salvation of these. I converse not with them to lull them in fatal security amidst their vices, or to contract any taint from the contagion of their impurities ; but, as the *physician* visits the chamber of the sick, and is occupied amidst the couches of the languishing and distrest ; so do I, as the great

great physician of the soul, seek out the sick and diseas'd in mind; and offer health and salvation to the children of men, suffering under a malady the most mortal and inveterate, the malady of *sin*. — And what physician, in cases of distress and danger, stands upon the niceties of forms, or the exactness of punctilio? Why then do ye marvel and murmur that I, in the like extremities, act in the like manner? *Go ye, and learn what that meaneth*, which God delivered by his prophet of old, * *I will have mercy, and not sacrifice*; I will have mercy, RATHER THAN sacrifice: Where the one or the other must be omitted, let MERCY, by all means, let the work of compassion, beneficence and love be preferred to SACRIFICE,—to instituted forms, and merely external ordinances; which, though necessary in themselves, and highly useful, as ordained of God, and as means to an important end, must yet never destroy that end, but give place and preference to it: for of all things *mercy*, acts of humanity and benevolence, are most pleasing to the God of love; and of all acts, as being the most humane and bene-

* *Hosea* vi. 6.

ficent

ficent, the salvation of lost sinners from destruction and death. And this is the great work for which I came into the world; this is the great end I have in view to accomplish. *I am not come to call the righteous, but sinners to repentance* *."

There is one remark, which from a review of this apology of our Saviour to the Pharisees, naturally ariseth in the human mind; and the more naturally, as daily experience gives us unpleasing proofs of it; which is, the much greater readiness and willingness (if I may so say) in the sovereign Lord of the world to pardon offences, and to blot out the remembrance of them from his book, than is but too commonly found amongst fellow-creatures. Great offences, and deep blots in life are frequently treasured up in the tables of human memory; and however repentance and a thorough change of conduct may witness a renewed life, and a pardoned state, we find men but too apt to recollect the old grievance, and too backward to forget and to cancel

* See Dr. *Whitby*, and the other commentators for a full explication of this passage.

what God hath forgotten, and long since freely forgiven.

The sense of our own frailty, the knowledge of the Almighty's ready pardon, and the consideration of the great end which brought the Saviour into the world, should teach us another conduct, and inspire us with mutual forbearance, and that feeling compassion, which above all things dignifies and distinguishes *human nature.*

And surely a brighter example we cannot have before our eyes, than in that *incarnate* GOD, who hath set us the pattern, and whom it is our duty, as it will be our happiness, to imitate.

Moved with tender pity towards the children of men, he disrobed himself of his glory, and assumed human nature in its lowest form: *Glory to God in the highest, peace on earth, and good will towards men,* was the gladsome song which the heavenly chorus echoed at his birth: *Good will* towards men influenced his whole life, and shone beautifully displayed in his every action. When the children of affliction surrounded him, and he beheld the tears of distress, his generous heart was moved at the call

of

of compaffion: He faw; he pitied; he relieved. None ever requefted his aid, and found a repulfe: none ever implored his mercy, and were rejected in their fuit. He refufed no company, he declined no fatigue, he fhrunk from no danger, whenever he might adminifter relief to the fouls or the bodies of men. Unwearied in love, he went about diffufing peace and bleffing: and as he came into the world to fave finners, fo he left no means untried, no motives unurged, to call them to repentance and pardon: And, at the end, after having done all to gain and reftore a loft world, he crowned his mighty benevolence, by an act fuperior to all praife.——He *died* for finners!

Of the *excellence* of a religion like this, whofe *end* is fo eminently noble, whofe *author* is fo great and fo good, the only begotten and eternal Son of God, the perfect pattern of every laudable and heavenly affection;—of the *excellence* of fuch a religion why need we fpeak? We muft all feel it: and to be happy, we muft experience it. But who can help remarking, from the flighteft view of it, the great importance of human fouls,

 and

and the high value, which the God who made us, is pleaſed to ſet upon his rational creatures? Rather than they ſhall periſh, his own Son ſhall become one of them, ſuffer for, ranſom, and redeem them. A thouſand and a thouſand pathetic calls and invitations ſhall be given them: nay, and the ever bleſſed Spirit itſelf ſhall be commiſſioned to awaken and inhabit, to comfort and to guide them. Even the holy angels are introduced as intereſted in their welfare; and heaven itſelf, with its ſupreme inhabitant, repreſented as partaking in the joy of ſouls reſtored: *There is joy in heaven, and before the angels of God, over one ſinner that repenteth*; one ſheep that is found, one ſon that is reſtored to life. And can we conceive a higher notion of the value which the Father puts on the leaſt of his reaſonable creatures? His higheſt angels have charge of them; his only begotten Son lives and dies to ſave them: and himſelf condeſcends to ſhare in the joy with which the heavenly beings are filled on their recovery! Need I then ſay, how amiable and honourable, nay, how neceſſary it is, that we ſhould labour

labour to increaſe this celeſtial joy, by an attention to our own, by a benevolent concern for the *ſalvation* of others?

I would juſt make one remark more on the *excellence* of the Chriſtian Religion; which is, that though it affords abundant conſolation to the *returning* ſinner; yet it gives not the leaſt countenance conceivable to ſin itſelf. Our Saviour came, he tells us, as a phyſician to *heal* the ſick; as a ſhepherd to *ſeek* and to *ſave* that which was loſt; as an almighty Redeemer to call ſinners to *repentance*. *Repentance* can alone admit to, or render us capable of his favour: while we continue in the practice of Vice, we have no room to hope for, we have no ground to expect, his pardon and grace: Of which would we partake, undiſſembled contrition muſt lead us to his throne, and a perfect reformation, in a renewed life, witneſs the ſincerity of our minds, and the reality of our profeſſion. And they, be aſſured, who lead you to hope for *pardon* without *penitence*, and to depend on an enthuſiaſtic *faith* without *fruits*, or a *righteouſneſs without works* (a doctrine we have heard but too

 lately

lately enforced *) lead you to depend on that which hath no exiſtence, and to deceive yourſelves with a deluſion, which is of all others moſt dangerous.

So

* In a weak and obnoxious Sermon preached by the Rev. Mr. *Elliot*, then Chaplain of St. *George*'s Hoſpital, intitled *Encouragement for Sinners; or, Righteouſneſs attainable without Works*. When St. *Paul* in his epiſtle to the *Romans*, chap. iv. ver. 9. ſpeaks of *Righteouſneſs without Works*, it is evident to any man, who underſtands the language in which he writes, or who attends to the context, that he means only *juſtification* or *pardon* of *paſt* ſins, upon *Faith* and *Repentance*. For in the 7th verſe he ſays, (quoting the *Pſalmiſt*) *Bleſſed are they whoſe iniquities are forgiven, and whoſe ſins are covered.* Δικαιοσυνη ſhould properly have been rendered *juſtification*, in agreement with εδικαιώθη, &c. which our tranſlators have rendered *juſtified*, *juſtifieth*, &c. in ver. 2, 5, &c, And it is much to be wiſhed, that this accuracy had been preſerved throughout our Tranſlation; that the ſame word in the *original* always had been rendered by the *ſame* word in the *Engliſh*. By this means many objections and controverſies agitated with no ſmall fury, had been prevented. *Righteouſneſs without Works*, is a contradiction in terms, in

So that you may obſerve with great pleaſure, that the Religion of Chriſt propoſeth, with the moſt winning benevolence, conſolation to ſinners the moſt afflicted, and to ſouls the moſt depreſſed; while it encourageth not the leaſt appearance of iniquity, but recommends the moſt ſolid and rational piety, in a ſyſtem of laws the moſt pure and the moſt perfect that the earth ever ſaw; upon motives, the moſt affecting and perſuaſive, and under ſanctions the moſt holy, awful, and formidable.

This may ſuffice to ſhew the *end*, and the *excellence* of the Chriſtian inſtitution: which might indeed be conſidered in various

in our language; for *Righteouſneſs* is only a complex word for all moral virtues, or good works. To ſay that it means the *Righteouſneſs* of Chriſt in this place betrays great inattention; ſince the apoſtle is evidently ſpeaking only of *juſtification* or *pardon* of paſt offences, through *faith*; and *faith*, ſays he, *was reckoned to Abraham for righteouſneſs*, ver. 9. ηλογισθη τω Αϐρααμ η πιςις εις Δικαιοσυνην: that is, He was looked upon by God as a *juſtified perſon*, as in a ſtate of pardon, on account of that *Faith*, which the Apoſtle deſcribes in the following verſes. See alſo ver. 5. and 22.

other inimitable parts, did not the time, and the design we are met to encourage, render it the less seasonable. I cannot however fail to observe, that so striking is the beauty of the Religion we profess, that it hath extorted, as it were, unwilling praises from the pen of a late noble writer *, who applied all his wit and his parts to oppose and degrade it. For *HE* acknowledgeth that it is *a most amiable and useful institution; whose natural tendency is directed to promote the peace and happiness of mankind*; that it *contains all the duties* of *natural Religion, and teacheth them in the most plain and simple manner*; that it *is one continued lesson of the strictest Morality, of Justice, of Benevolence, and of universal Charity*: That, *as its moral precepts are excellent; so its positive institutions are not only innocent, but profitable, and extremely proper to keep up the spirit of Religion*; that *it is a most simple and intelligible rule of belief, worship, and practice*, &c.

* Lord *Bolingbroke*, from different parts of the fourth volume of whose works the passages following are extracted.

Now

Now, if even an *enemy* could bear ſuch a teſtimony to it, how much doth it behove *Us* to bear a more uſeful teſtimony to it, by the integrity of our lives, and the exemplarineſs of our practice?

II. And YOU, worthy hearers, are ready to bear that teſtimony, I am perſuaded, by your appearance in this place, for the promotion of a charitable deſign, ſurely of all others moſt conformable to the nature and end of the Chriſtian Religion.

That *end*, you have heard from the mouth of the benevolent author of this religion himſelf, is "the ſalvation of ſinners:" that ſalvation you perceive is to be effected "by bringing ſinners to repentance:" and your great Lord and Maſter hath ſhewn you a pattern, and left you to imitate an example of the moſt tender compaſſion and unwearied benevolence in this important work. Your preſent laudable Deſign is a noble copy after his example: Tender compaſſion, and the moſt diſintereſted benevolence have moved you to provide the means of repentance, and ſo the means of ſalvation for many miſerable ſouls; who, without this proviſion, muſt periſh in inevitable deftruction. Thus are you happy in treading in the fteps, and being fellow-workers together, with the God of your falvation.

'Tis true, that to common and fuperficial obfervers of things nothing feems a more deteftable object, more worthy our hatred and fcorn, than a common and peftilent Proftitute. And indeed were thofe in that miferable condition, either placed in it by their own choice, or detained in it by their own free will: had a vicious inclination at firft introduced, or did the fame vicious inclination continue them in it, amidft repeated opportunities to retrieve and return; we would then grant they were utterly unworthy the leaft compaffion, and more beneath humanity than the beaft that perifheth. But when we are fully convinced, that different, far different is the truth of the cafe; compaffion pleads their caufe, and humanity urgeth us to their fuccour and redrefs.

For, though the great author of our being hath, for wife and good ends, implanted the fame paffions in either fex, and therefore

fore tranfgreffion is as poffible, and of confequence as excufeable on the weaker fide, as it is on the ftronger; yet fact abundantly demonftrates to us, that men, for the moft part, are the Seducers; and the generality of thofe who now claim our aid, have been introduced to their mifery by the complicated arts of feduction, and by every unjuftifiable method which cruel and brutifh luft fuggefts to the crafty feducer.

And it is well known how much harder the cafe, in this particular, is with the female fex, than with our own.—One falfe ftep for ever ruins their fair fame; blafts the fragrance of virgin innocence, and configns them to contempt and difgrace! while the author of their diftrefs may triumph in his villainy! and—fhame to human nature—not be branded with one mark of reproach for the ruin of a fellow-creature!

And when once, by whatever unhappy means undone, the wretched out-caft hath no refource, no redrefs: but muft fall from fhame to fhame; from forrow to forrow: fall lower and lower in the pit of foul miſery, and drudge in the labour of odious proſtitution, to preſerve a burthenſome Being from famine and death.

Thus ſoul and body are loſt at once; and an uſeful member is cut off from the community, in early youth, having done no good, nay, having diffuſed much evil amongſt her fellow-creatures. In *early youth* indeed;—very many of the unhappy objects now in the *houſe*, being under fourteen years of age, and a great part debauched and introduced into this wretched way of life, before that age *, and of courſe, before nature and inclination could have any part in their crime: And it is greatly more than probable, that of theſe objects, *ſixty* in an *hundred*, or more would have been dead in leſs than two years; that many of them, who are *now* healthy and

* In a paper of our worthy Treaſurer's before me, and written ſome time ſince, I read, "Out of an *hundred girls*, now in the *Magdalen* Houſe, above a ſeventh part have not yet ſeen their fifteenth year; ſeveral are under fourteen; and one third of the whole have been betrayed before that age!"

happy

happy in the houſe, would have been *now* ſuffering in the miſeries of future condemnation!

To prevent this, as far as you may, and to provide ſome relief for ſufferers ſo truly pitiable, is the benevolent and humane motive, which hath engaged you, my worthy Friends, and Brethren, the GOVERNORS and PROMOTERS of this deſign, to unite your generous efforts, and to join hand and heart in the good cauſe.

And what cauſe can more deſerve encouragement, what charitable inſtitution be calculated to do greater good? for this extends itſelf to the *ſouls* as well as the *bodies* of our fellow-creatures: and as much more noble and excellent as an immortal ſoul is, than a periſhing body; ſo much more noble every inſtitution which extends to the welfare of the former, than thoſe which extend only to the welfare of the latter. The great ſucceſs this charity hath hitherto met with, abundantly confirms this opinion.

Permit me ſincerely to congratulate you on that ſucceſs, which hath thus far crowned your commendable undertaking. If they, who turn one ſoul to light and to righte-

ouſneſs,

ousnefs, caufe joy in heaven, and fhall *fhine as the ftars for ever and ever*; what may they reafonably expect, who, mov'd by the jufteft motives, actuated by a fincere love to Chrift, and a true compaffion to their fellow-creatures, are happily inftrumental in the falvation of many fouls, are happily inftrumental in faving numbers from that death eternal, which, without their kindly affiftance, they could never, humanly fpeaking, have avoided?

And fuch, we have the utmoft reafon to hope, will be,—already is, the confequence of your charitable provifion for thefe unhappy daughters of woe and diftrefs. I doubt not, it delights *your* hearts—for it muft delight every heart—to behold and obferve the ftriking contraft, when you vifit the dwelling and the Houfe of God, where thefe rejoicing Penitents fhare the bleffings of your mercy. To behold the decent and orderly behaviour of fo many fellow-creatures, late abandoned to every calamity, who of their own *free-will* have fought this retreat, and thus fhew their difapprobation of Vice, by the only method in their power;

power;——to fee them cloathed in health and neatnefs, who but now were languifhing under difeafe, and covered with foulnefs and filth; to hear the tongues fweetly tuning forth the praifes of the Redeemer, which late were hoarfe with oaths, and empoifoned with lafciviousnefs; to hear from their mouths earneft prayers and joyful thankfgivings; to fee from their eyes the flowing tears of penitence and remorfe; and to behold in their hands the inftruments of chearful induftry and labour; inftruments of induftry in hands, which were wantoning in pernicious indolence, and impelled perhaps to the extremities of theft. To fee thefe things, muft convince you of the great utility of your defign, and chear you with this comfortable reflection, "that already you reap fome fruits of your beneficence." May thofe fruits be increafed ten-fold here and hereafter!

Nothing great and good can be carried on without fome oppofition: nothing great and good was ever attempted in any age, but malevolence would find fomething to object, and Envy, with her jaundiced eyes, would

would ſpy out ſomething to caluminate and cenſure. But this, ſo far from cooling our ardour in honourable purſuits, ſhould enkindle and enſlave it. And I am perſuaded, that you, *Gentlemen*, have too much fortitude and true elevation of heart, to be moved from any good purpoſe by the weak ſounding of calumnious breath.

In truth, human works are ſo imperfect, and the very beſt inſtitutions ſo liable to ſome defects and abuſes, that nothing can be attempted or propoſed, wherein ſome evil may not probably mix itſelf with much good: and whoever ſhould refuſe to enter upon any excellent work, till every poſſible objection was removed, wound hang in the heſitancy of doubt all the days of his life, and waſte uſeful time and talents in fruitleſs enquiries and empty ſpeculations. We muſt advance to action with all reaſonable precaution; proceed with all imaginable activity and care; and obviate with all wiſdom and ſagacity every objection, which experience may find prejudicial to the progreſs of the purpoſed inſtitution.

The

The objections * indeed raifed againft this undertaking have been, and are fo flight and infignificant, that they deferve not to be mention'd. Its utility and prefent great advancement, above all other arguments, anfwer every cavil. And whoever are yet but ill convinced of its advantage, will be far more ftrikingly, far more feelingly convinced of it, by a fight of the comely order, and decent appearance found in the public worfhip, at the *Chapel* of the Houfe, (where many have *loft* their objections, and *felt* its utility) far more than from any thing I can urge on its behalf. Yet, furely, if any thing be ufeful, if any thing be excellent; if any thing be praife-worthy; if any thing becomes us as men; if any thing becomes us as members of civil fociety; if any thing becomes us as Chriftians; it is, to fave from utter and inevitable mifery, the fouls of poor, abandoned, wretched fellow-Chriftians, who have no other refource, no other means of relief: It is to preferve from prefent and afflictive

* Thefe, however trifling, it hath been thought proper not to pafs over entirely; and therefore they are obviated in the *Preface*;—to which the reader is referred.

death,

death, the bodies of many young and periſhing fellow-creatures; it is to take from our ſtreets the ſhame of our community, the inſtruments of fouleſt pollution, and moſt poiſonous contagion: it is to reſtore to the ſtate many uſeleſs members; and to introduce to health and to induſtry, to happineſs and to heaven, many, who could otherwiſe neither ever have been employed, nor ever reſtored.

Let me not doubt then, that all of You who hear me this day, will readily and chearfully join in the beneficent work, and contribute as much as you can towards the perfection and ſupport of ſo uſeful a deſign. At leaſt, if you mean not to promote, do not injure it, and endeavour to prevent its ſalutary effects, by futile objections and uſeleſs inſinuations: For as, beyond all controverſy, the intention of the worthy perſons, who have engaged in it, is excellent, and deſerving the higheſt applauſe; as their characters are the moſt reſpectable, and, permit me to ſay, not only an ornament to this noble undertaking, but to this *Metropolis* alſo, which is itſelf an ornament, in its public charities eſpecially, to human na-

ture,

ture, and to Chriſtianity ; as theſe things are ſo, every good and generous heart ſhould tenderly conſider their motives, and wiſh well to their deſign ; and with a candour, which is always pleaſing, and will ever be acceptable, ſhould labour to promote, far as they may, and think of means to further, not of objections to diſcourage, ſo benevolent an undertaking.

Were you to behold a poor harmleſs animal, fallen into diſtreſs, and ſuffering in miſery, and were able to reach out your hand, and to help it ; there is, I am ſure, ſo much compaſſion in the human mind, that few could ſuffer themſelves to paſs by it unregarding. How much rather then ſhould we reach out our hands to the relief of many of our fellow-creatures, many of the ſofter and more defenceleſs ſex, fallen into the pit of extreme diſtreſs, without any hand to relieve, and with but few hearts to compaſſionate ; and, if unrelieved, ſpeedily to periſh in the utmoſt miſery, and to breathe out from polluted bodies more polluted ſouls, into a world of utter and everlaſting woe ! who then would not exert all their efforts to ſave ſuch bodies,

to

to ſnatch ſuch ſouls from horror unſpeakable!

This, we are convinced, will be the amiable conduct and proceeding of thoſe of the SAME SEX, for whom we now plead; and who, we are ſatisfied, can never be inattentive to the welfare, never unaffected by the calamities, of their fellow-creatures. You, who have happily perſevered in the pleaſing paths of virtue, can beſt tell the comforts ariſing from ſo delightful a conduct, and may eaſily gueſs the miſeries of a different ſtate. You, who have known the fatal pleadings of paſſion, can more eaſily pity them, whom thoſe pleadings have ſeduced and deſtroyed. And you, who are poſſeſſed of all the ſweetneſſes and delicacies of the tender mind, and happier ſtate, can more eaſily gueſs the extreme miſery which muſt ariſe to a female heart, from the foulneſs and horror of promiſcuous proſtitution; and will, on theſe accounts, be the more ready to reach out your pitying hand, and ſave from diſtreſs beyond the reach of deſcription, many of your own ſex, for whom, till this happy opportunity, no redreſs was provided.

And

And while many of you feel the foft yearnings of the mother for the child that was fuckled at her breaft; while many of you glow with the tender warmth of a fifter's love and the generous affection of a beloved friend and companion; think, oh think of thofe unhappy mothers, who late were weeping over the daughters, dear to them as the right eye, and nearer than the ftrings that hold the heart; of thofe fifters, thofe friends, who were lamenting over their friends and their fifters, loft, as it feemed, beyond all poffibility of hope: Oh, think of the joy, which many of them now feel, many have lately felt, many, we truft, will hereafter feel, on the recovery of the child, of the friend, that was *dead*, that was *loft*: And as you wifh to diffufe fuch bleffednefs, for your beloved offspring's fake, join in the good work, ahd do all you can, to wipe the tears from thefe aged and afflicted eyes, and approve yourfelves at once compaffionate to your fellow creatures, and grateful to your Saviour and your God.

Your concurrence, MY BRETHREN, in this beneficent defign, may reafonably be expected

expected to the utmoſt. For *generoſity* alone would not ſuffer Us to be wanting in any endeavours for the advantage of that ſex, to which life owes ſo much of its ſweetneſs and felicity: to which we are indebted for the greateſt and choiceſt of earthly comforts, from the cradle to the grave: from whoſe tender and virtuous endearments, this world, otherwiſe lonely and afflicting, gathers what of ſweetneſs and ſerenity is found in it.

Motives of *honour* too, ſhould certainly much influence many, and thoſe more eſpecially who have been inſtrumental in the undoing, or the means of leading any into the path of deſtructive pleaſures. If ſuch reflect at all, the bitter upbraidings of conſcience will ſoon convince them, that they cannot exert themſelves too much, or too much endeavour to repair the ruin they have wrought. For only, in the ſilent hour, when paſſion is huſhed, and reaſon will hear, ſuppoſe the wretched unfortunate introduced to miſery, to diſeaſe, to death, and now about to periſh in extreme diſtreſs; ſuppoſe you heard her thus expoſtulating; "See to what thy unbridled paſſion, and

"ſeducing luſt, hath brought me! Late
"gay in beauty, and elegant in charms,
"thy heart was captivated, and every art
"was uſed to win, and to deſtroy me.
"Thou didſt prevail; and I was undone!
"and ſoon, unkind and cruel! thy paſ-
"ſion ſated, I was abandoned, and left to
"all the extremity of woe! Now ſee
"the ſad end of thy triumph! Oh look
"upon me, and ſee what cauſe thou haſt
"to exult! Behold theſe wretched tatters,
"which ſcarcely cover my diſeaſed limbs:
"where are the remains of their former
"gracefulneſs? See, my tongue cleaves to
"the roof of my mouth with hunger and
"with anguiſh. But, worſt of all, my ſoul
"is tormented with every ſorrow: dire con-
"ſciouſneſs of my paſt miſdoings torments
"and wracks my heart. Oh ſee me, hope-
"leſs and abandoned:—look and repent, and
"amend thy ways! See body and ſoul in
"early youth conſigned, the one to a ſevere
"temporal; the other, — mercy, mercy
"ſweet Father! —— the other to an eternal
"death."

Oh then, as you are men, and if ever you have been ſo unfortunate as to be the fatal

fatal caufes of fuch forrow, now by fincere repentance, labour to obtain the great Redeemer's pardon; and by a ready affiftance of this Charity, calculated for the relief of fuch deferted fufferers, endeavour to make the beft amends you are able for your fault *.

To conclude; As you are *Chriftians*, unite in the good defign: for it is intended to promote that work, for which your compaffionate Saviour died,—the Salvation of Sinners: and you cannot be Chriftians, if you follow not your mafter's example.

As you are *Parents*, whenever you view the children of your bofom, the daughters like lovely flowers blooming around you; confider how often that very beauty hath proved a fatal fnare to its poffeffor: Oh confider how much feducers throng around, whofe rank paffions have no law, and whofe barbarous lufts have no mercy: And while you are thereby moved to the more

* My meaning in this Paffage, tho' fufficiently plain to the candid reader, will be juftified *even* to thofe of a different Character, if they will take the trouble to refer to *Luke* xix. 8.

diligent

diligent implantation of every virtue in the minds of your own children, let generous fympathy touch your hearts; and join to wipe the tear from the aged father's eye; to prevent the hoary head from going down to the grave in forrow, by liberally aiding this charity; which fo many fathers may have caufe to blefs, and which, I am, pleafed to be able to obferve to you, hath already been the happy means to dry fome aged eyes, and to revive fome languifhing parents' lives.

As you are *members* of the *civil community*, and as you wifh to wipe off any difgrace from the ftate and policy, unite in this laudable undertaking; which we hope may tend, through the zeal of good men, and the vigilance of magiftrates, in due feafon, to wafh away that nuifance of our times, the pollution of our ftreets: in which, furely, and in every undertaking that may *tend* to remove it, we fhould join hand and heart, if we wifh to preferve in innocence and virtue our children, our fervants, our dependants of whatfoever fort; if we wifh to prevent unfpeakable diftrefs, and the moft cruel injury, which too often the virtuous and guiltlefs have found, from the dire contagion of this promifcuous defilement.

And fince, bleffed be God, amidft the many evils too juftly complained of, and the many depravities too notorioufly reigning, benevolence and charity feem yet not to be wanting amongft us; let us endeavour to promote thefe excellent virtues, as much as we may, upon the foundation of Chrift's bleffed gofpel, and in imitation of his compaffionate and heavenly temper. And while, with fincere hearts, each in our generation ftudies to advance the good of mankind; let us always keep in view that great, that important hour, when every thing here below fhall diffolve and vanifh from our fight; and we ourfelves fhall ftand at that aweful judgment-feat, where every external accommodation will be removed; where no regard will be had to place, or to rank; but *they* only will fhine with moft diftinguifhed favour and happinefs, who have moft diftinguifhed themfelves in this fhort ftate of trial, by works of benevolence, humanity, and compaffion, fpringing from an unfeigned affiance on the all-complete and meritorious facrifice of an incarnate GOD.

To

To whoſe praiſe may we all live here below; for whoſe ſake may we be zealous in this, and in every other work; and for whoſe merits may we all finally hear the applauding ſentence:

IN AS MUCH AS YE DID IT UNTO THE LEAST OF THESE, MY BRETHREN, YE DID IT UNTO ME.

COME, YE BLESSED OF MY FATHER! RECEIVE THE KINGDOM PREPARED FOR YOU FROM THE BEGINNING OF THE WORLD!

A

SERMON,

Preached at the Chapel of the

MAGDALEN-HOUSE,

BEFORE

His Royal Highneſs Prince EDWARD.

By *WILLIAM DODD,* M. A.

AND

Publiſhed by the Command of His ROYAL HIGHNESS.

The SEVENTH EDITION.

TO

HIS ROYAL HIGHNESS

Prince EDWARD AUGUSTUS,

DUKE of YORK, &c.

May it pleaſe your Royal Highneſs

GRACIOUSLY to accept the following diſcourse; which owes its publication ſolely to your Highneſs's command. To diſobey this would ill become me; otherwiſe, my former endeavours on this ſubject, might well have pleaded my exemption from another attempt: in which, ſimilarity of ſentiment, in various particulars, muſt be ſuppoſed to prevail; and will need much candid acceptation as well from your Royal Highneſs, as from the public.

We congratulate ourſelves on the favourable opinion your Royal Highneſs was pleaſed to expreſs of our charity: where ſo many young, helpleſs, and truly pitiable objects muſt ſurely move compaſſion in every humane breaſt. We are ſenſible of the honour done us by your Royal Highneſs's preſence; and eſpecially by that condeſcending, yet princely, behaviour, which cannot fail to engage all hearts. Nor could We expect leſs from the SON of a PRINCESS, whoſe amiable conduct hath juſtly rendered her the univerſal object of Britiſh eſteem; From the BROTHER of a PRINCE, whoſe ſhining example and diſtinguiſhed humanity give him a place in every Engliſhman's affection: and of whom we might ſay the higheſt things, without the leaſt ſuſpicion of flattery, as we hope the greateſt things, without the leaſt apprehenſion of diſappointment.

We flatter ourſelves, that your Highneſs's kind repreſentation of the happy ſtate

ſtate of ſo many of our gracious Sovereign's people, reſtored from the moſt conſummate diſtreſs, from idleneſs, vice, and early ruin, to induſtry, virtue, and life, will diffuſe a pleaſure through your Royal Family, but eſpecially through our beloved Monarch's breaſt, anxious as He is, we know, for the preſervation of his people; and will gain his approbation to ſo benevolent a deſign. A deſign, allow me, SIR, with pleaſure to remark, conducted by Gentlemen, perfectly convinced of the happineſs of the preſent glorious Eſtabliſhment; and honoured, peculiarly, by the Preſidency of one, whoſe valuable and excellent qualities, ſo well known to your Royal Highneſs, it would be impertinent in me to mention. As on every other account we think ourſelves happy in Lord HERTFORD's attachment; ſo particularly, for that he was pleaſed to introduce your Royal Highneſs amongſt us.

EDWARD is a renown'd and a favourite name in Britiſh ſtory; no leſs fam'd for martial than for munificent virtue: That your Royal Highneſs may, under the conſtant guidance of Heaven, nobly unite, in yourſelf, both theſe characters, and advance into action, amidſt the concurrence of every favourable circumſtance; and that under the continued protection of your illuſtrious Houſe, our land may long enjoy its preſent great felicities, is the ſincere wiſh and moſt ardent prayer of

SIR,

Your Royal Highneſs's

moſt devoted and

obedient Servant,

Jan. 31, 1760.

WILLIAM DODD.

A

SERMON, &c.

St. LUKE xix. 10.

FOR THE SON OF MAN IS COME TO SEEK AND TO SAVE THAT WHICH WAS LOST.

THE reaſonableneſs of its precepts, and the great agreement of its Doctrine to the neceſſities of mankind, are clear evidences of the Truth of Chriſtianity, and ſatisfactory proofs that it comes from the Father of Wiſdom, and the God of all Mercy. Let every religion, which pretends to divine revelation, be examined in this view;—the *Heathen*, or *Mahometan*, or whatever other oppoſite perſuaſion; and they will be found wanting; offenſive to the beſt reaſon, and inadequate to the moſt preſſing exigency of human nature;—That I mean, of pardon and reconciliation with an offended Deity; of forgiveneſs and peace to the wounded conſcience; of aſſured grace and favour to the repenting and returning Sinner.

This was a diſcòvery, a glorious and heavenly manifeſtation reſerved for, and truly worthy of that Son of God, and Saviour of the world, who came to *ſeek and to ſave that which was loſt*; who came to raiſe the penitent from the gloom of deſpair to the light of enlivening hope; who came to reſcue Sinners from the bondage of ſin; at once to ſet them free from the anguiſh of a wounded conſcience, and to direct their feet under the guidance of gratitude and grace, into the happy paths of Obedience and Virtue.

We will briefly conſider the Chriſtian Religion, in reference to this its great deſign; and then ſhew, how much comfort may be derived from hence, to *YOU* eſpecially, who have ſought the ſhelter of this hoſpitable dwelling; which, like Heaven, opens its friendly doors for the reception of afflicted and returning *Penitence*: and which, of conſequence, well deſerves that regard and protection

tection which it finds, and, we truſt, will continue to find, from the moſt virtuous and the moſt noble: from ſouls moſt enlarged by religion, from hearts moſt tenderly influenced by humanity.

I. With an eye then to this good undertaking, let us conſider the great and leading principle in the revelation of Chriſt: which is amply diſcovered to us by our Saviour, in the words of the Text, who certainly beſt knew himſelf the intent of his coming into the world;—And He came, he aſſures us, *to ſeek and to ſave that which was loſt*; to recover and reſtore loſt ſinners: and to admit them to grace and pardon, on their true repentance and return to God. His revelation therefore is founded upon, and neceſſarily ſuppoſes, the depravity of nature, and the irregularity of practice; as it is immediately calculated to remedy the former, and to provide a ſufficient atonement for the latter. Look upon it, in any other view, and it becomes a thorough contradiction.

For were human nature perfect; and were it poſſible to pay an unerring obedience to the law of conſummate righteouſ-

neſs:

neſs: did virtue continually attend our ſteps; uprightneſs and integrity ever wait upon our doings: did no vices defile, no guilt alarm, no tranſgreſſions bear teſtimony againſt us; there would be no room for penitence or pardon: we could never want the grace of forgiveneſs, as unconſcious of offence; and might, with ſome ſhew of juſtice, demand the Deity's attention, and lay claim to the rewards of his kingdom. The religion of Chriſt upon this view, would be vain and inefficacious: and the names of *Saviour*, *Redeemer*, and *Reſtorer*, would be ſounds without meaning, and words without ſenſe.

But in truth, This hath never been the caſe with mankind: Ever ſince the fall of our firſt parents, time and corruption, depravity and offence have gone on hand in hand: and the hiſtory of every period fully ſatisfies us, that human nature hath been in every period, the ſame; ever alike prone to ſin, ever alike tainted with guilt: *every imagination of the thoughts of man's heart* (in the language of the ſacred volumes, *of man's heart*, when not reſtrained by the grace of God) *hath been only evil continually.* And

And tho' the preference hath in every respect been given to virtue; tho' Philosophers have taught; tho' education from infancy hath exerted its power; nay, tho' the Most High hath revealed his holy will, under the most tremendous sanctions; yet the malady hath still remained unremoved: and to this day we too feelingly lament the prevalence of passions, and the degeneracy of our nature.

The wisdom of philosophy, tho' conscious of the evil, could neither assert the true cause, nor assign the adequate remedy. Virtue, they allowed, they constantly maintained, was infinitely preferable to vice; was the only road to true happiness here; was that alone which could recommend to God, if indeed there was a God who regarded human affairs. But silent was their voice, and unavailing their knowledge, when the heart oppressed with guilt sought to them for relief: when erring virtue, burden'd in conscience, and desirous of comfort, applied for ease to the one, and solid grounds for the other. They could neither assure such of pardon for past offences; nor by any means enable them to walk blameless for the future. Fluctuating

ing in doubt themſelves, they left others equally fluctuating; and the beſt hopes they could dare to entertain, aroſe from ſome uncertain and dark expectations of a mercy whereto they were ſtrangers: even doubting whether ſuch mercy exiſted at all; or if it exiſted, on what foundation they could preſume to expect it.

To remove this uneaſy ſolicitude; to relieve theſe urging neceſſities; and to make the fulleſt and plaineſt diſcovery of divine mercy, reconciliation, and peace; The Son of God aſſumed human nature, and entered upon his bleſſed miniſtry; the grand intent of which, was early diſcovered to *Joſeph*, by the angel, who informed him, *Thou ſhalt call his name JESUS: for he ſhall ſave his people from their ſins.* Accordingly, that Prince of Peace no ſooner made his public appearance, than *Pardon* and *Life* were offered from his gracious lips to *Penitence* and *Faith.* The burdened ſoul, the heart oppreſs'd, the ſtricken conſcience ſought him; — and he removed the burden, gave them comfort, gave them reſt. *Come unto me, all ye that travel, and are heavy laden,* was his royal and acceptable proclamation. That he

came

came to ſeek and to ſave thoſe who were loſt; loſt to their God, loſt to themſelves, loſt to future bleſſedneſs, that he *came not to call the righteous, but ſinners to repentance*; that he came to ſearch for and reſtore the wandering ſheep to the fold; to embrace with fatherly compaſſion the returning prodigal; that his grand buſineſs was the ranſom of Mankind, the reſcue of Sinners, the redemption of Tranſgreſſors, he continually witneſſed by every word, and by every action. But above all, he gave teſtimony to the great, the conſolatory truth, when, good and tender ſhepherd! he laid down his life for his ſheep; when, as the prophet *Iſaiah* finely expreſſes it, he was *wounded for our tranſgreſſions*; *when the chaſtiſement of our peace was upon him*; *when he was oppreſſed, and was afflicted*; *when he poured out his ſoul unto death*; *and the Lord laid on him the iniquity of us all* *.

Under this gracious diſpenſation, we have no longer any cauſe of doubt, diſtreſs, or deſpair: no longer, as in the heathen world, need we wander in the wretched wild of perplexing uncertainty; oppreſſed with the

* See the whole 53d Chapter

con-

consciousness of guilt, which we fear can obtain no pardon, or unacquainted wherewith to come before the Lord, or what sacrifice to offer as an atonement *for the sin of our souls*. Happy for us, though our guilt be complicated, and our offences numerous, we may be assured of forgiveness, through His sufficient merits, who lived, who died, who rose again to save us. *Whosoever cometh to him*, he hath himself declared, *he will in no wise cast out*: he never rejects the petition of the contrite and the humble: *None ever trusted in him, and was confounded: nor did he ever despise any that called upon him* *.

And to perfect his heavenly purpose, not only pardon is freely bestowed upon the penitent, but grace is given to assist, and the spirit of his love never withheld from those, who wish, by future obedience, to win his regard, and to witness their sincere sense of their former misery, and present happiness. For we must never fail to remark, at all times, in testimony of the complete wisdom and excellence of the Christian dispensation, that though it hold

* Eccles. ii. 10.

out

out to the penitent believer the moſt ſubſtantial conſolation, in full and free forgiveneſs; yet *that* forgiveneſs is ever ſuſpended on the condition of future gratitude and obedience: a deficiency in which, will infallibly cancel all former grants of mercy. And thus, while with the moſt beautiful propriety, it affords the wiſhed, the only valuable, relief to the repenting ſinner; it yet adminiſters not the leaſt encouragement to ſin itſelf;—thundering out its threats to the preſumptuous offender; ſweetly tendering its divineſt comforts to the contrite and ſelf-abaſed Chriſtian. This was a point, at which human wiſdom, and the ſchools of antient ſcience could never arrive: they knew no means to ſave the guilty, yet condemn the guilt: they knew no method to preſerve at once the honour of the *Mercy* and of the *Juſtice* of the ſupreme Ruler of mankind *.

Thus

* Dr. *Young*, in his Night-Thoughts, has finely enlarged on this topic:

O'er guilt (how mountainous!) with out-ſtretch'd arms
Stern *Juſtice*, and ſoft ſmiling *love* embrace,

Sup-

Thus we ſee the religion of Chriſt is completely calculated to anſwer the wants of imperfect mortals; to relieve the ſoul from the preſſure of conſcious offence; to wipe the tears from the eye of drooping penitence; to awaken the beſt, and higheſt hopes in the ſoul; and to lead from diſtreſs,

Supporting in full majeſty thy throne,
When ſeem'd its majeſty to need ſupport,
Or *that*, or *man*, inevitably loſt.
What, but the fathomleſs of thought divine,
Cou'd labour ſuch expedient from deſpair,
And reſcue both? both reſcue! both exalt!
O how are both exalted by the *deed!*
The wond'rous deed!—or ſhall I call it more?
A wonder in omnipotence itſelf!
A myſtery, no leſs to gods than men!
Not *thus* our infidels th' *Eternal* draw,
A God all o'er, conſummate, abſolute,
Full-orb'd, in his whole round of rays complete:
They ſet at odds heaven's jarring attributes,
And with one excellence another wound:
Maim heaven's perfection, break its equal beams;
Bid *mercy* triumph over—God himſelf,
Undeify'd by their opprobrious praiſe:
A God ALL *mercy*, is a God *unjuſt*.

Night 4th, page 92.

diſtreſs, anxiety, and deſpair, to comfort and peace; to renewed virtue, gratitude, and God.

II. Can it fail then to fill *Your* ſouls with the moſt ſenſible joy, when you reflect, that all the comforts of this bleſſed religion may be yours? that all the felicities it propoſeth are now within the reach of your future good endeavours? that, led by real penitence and faith to your Saviour and your hope, preſent pardon undoubtedly is yours; future bliſs will be yours, as undoubtedly, if you happily perſevere in the good part you have choſen! And we will not be backward to believe, but that the ſame right inclinations which induced you to ſeek this peaceful haven, from the ſtorm and tempeſt of vice and the world, will, thro' Grace, continue to influence your conduct; * and to preſerve you ſtedfaſt in thoſe

* It is but diſcharging a debt juſtly due to the good conduct of the women in general, to inform the public, that there appears amongſt them every ſign of real penitence, which could have been expected: of many, we could ſpeak with the higheſt com-

those resolutions, which we doubt not you will use all proper means to strengthen; and for which all proper means are in this place provided you.

For, only reflect, had not the mercy of God brought you to this mansion, had not his gracious goodness provided a reception and an asylum for you here; whither must you have fled, and what resource could you have found from your pressing distress? Lost to Virtue, of consequence you were lost to reputation; the most humane and beneficent could only behold and commiserate;

commendation; and when the circumstances of some are considered, who have unhappily never had the advantages of educatien; it will be rather marvellous, that they demean themselves so well, and improve so much, than that they should behave otherwise. The judicious and humane, reflecting upon themselves, and upon human frailty, will never too suddenly expect perfection in any: and till we are perfect ourselves, under superior advantages, let us not be too hasty in condemning others for the want of it, under advantages greatly inferior. For proofs of propriety of sentiment, I refer, as upon a former occasion, to the manuscript papers in the hands of Mr. *Dingley*.

they had no power to relieve. Loſt to Virtue, you were loſt to your friends, even to your beſt and neareſt friends; even to the beloved *parents*, whoſe delight you once were; who, with tender and ſleepleſs anxiety, watched over your infant wants; who, perhaps, with daily toil, ſoftened by the endearments of parental affection, laboured to ſupply your growing neceſſities; and who hung with pleaſure, with anxious, bleeding pleaſure, over the child of their comfort; — little then, oh little ſuſpected the ſad ſource of their future miſery! Loſt to Virtue, you were loſt to yourſelves; — worſt loſs of all! loſt to reflection, and the knowledge of your fearful danger: loſt to your God, and treading, with careleſs terror, on the alarming precipice of utter ruin, and ſpeedy *death!* And that *death*,—introduction to one eternal, irremediable, that dreadful *death* muſt inevitably have been your lot! For where could you have fled to eſcape it? Who would have poured the balm of Chriſtian mercy into your bleeding conſciences, and raiſed you to the hope of pardon and of life? Nay, how could thoſe conſciences,

amidſt

amidſt the defilements of ſin, have admitted it? Whither could you have fled from anguiſh, and from woe unutterable; cut off in the very bloſſom of your ſins; early ſacrifices, young * and unpitied offerings to the remorſeleſs grave? And had your ſorrows ended here, your fate had been leſs to be deplored: but alas! this had been but the beginning of ſorrows †.

'Tis too affecting the review: I urge no more: Only let your converſation be ſuch as becometh this great redemption: only labour to ſhew yourſelves ſenſible of the exquiſite bleſſings vouchſafed you: of that unſpeakable goodneſs of God, which hath reached out the kind hand of preſervation, and received you from the impending deſtruction; the goodneſs of that God, *who is full of compaſſion and mercy, long-ſuffering and very pitiful; who forgiveth ſins, and preſerveth in time of affliction.* Here, ſaved

* For this point, I refer to the Sermon before the *Preſident, &c.*

† For more on this head, I refer to what I have ſaid in the "*Advice to the Magdalens,*" at the concluſion.

from

from the threatening ſtorm, you may look back and contemplate your danger, the more to inſpire you with gratitude and praiſe. And while in ſincere contrition, you lament your paſt miſconduct; remember, to elevate your hopes, that free mercy and forgiveneſs await you, through His divine merits, who came *to ſeek and to ſave that which was loſt*. Happy in the Senſe of which, you will think no time too long, no endeavours too ſevere, to teſtify the grateful ſenſe you have of theſe bleſſings, to ſhew the ſincerity of your repentance and faith: All you can do will ſeem mean and poor, in compariſon of the good things you have received. But all you can do, muſt be exerted: and your beſt endeavours, however frail, will be graciouſly accepted by the Lord whom you ſerve: the kindneſs of your noble and generous friends and benefactors will thus be ſecured; nay, and perhaps you may thus ſerve to keep alive the laſt lingerings of ſome aged parent's breath; to gain from their pale and trembling lips the bleſſing you have forfeited, but muſt rejoice to obtain: filled with the higheſt ſatisfaction, while you enable them to ſay, " Lord, it is enough: Let thy ſervant now depart in peace: my unhappy, but beloved child, is recovered and reſtored: Lord it is enough, that I have thus ſeen her before I die *."

III. Were it only (right noble and illuſtrious hearers) to relieve the diſtreſs, and remove the anguiſh of one ſuch parent, I perſuade myſelf, you would think the preſent deſign moſt worthy your attention: and it is with pleaſure we can obſerve, that this is no imaginary ſuppoſition †. No heart can be unconſcious of, or unaffected by the tenderneſs of parental regard; nor can any earthly affliction be ſuppoſed, ſuperior to that which wounds the affectionate parent's heart, through the offence and ruin of a beloved and unhappy child. By reſtoring them, and recovering ſuch children, the moſt noble and commendable of human affections, the pa-

* See Gen. xiv. 28.

† Several parents have already been reconciled to their children: one, in particular, at an affecting meeting, made uſe of nearly the ſame words with thoſe above.

rental

rental, is comforted and relieved: and not only the child, but the parent too, ſhares in the generous mercy.

But not in this view only, under whatever circumſtances we conſider it, every laudable motive, every ſentiment of religion, of virtue, of humanity, pathetically pleads for this undertaking; and we are ſatisfied will not *now* plead in vain. From the ſurvey we have taken of the grand deſign of Chriſtianity, and the benevolent purpoſe of the Son of God in coming amongſt us, *to ſeek and to ſave that which was loſt*, we have ſeen abundantly, how conformable the preſent inſtitution is to that deſign: founded as it is upon the ſame godlike principle of ſeeking and ſaving thoſe who *were* loſt; who muſt otherwiſe (it is more than probable) have been loſt for ever: loſt in the very beginning of life; loſt in the bitterneſs of diſtreſs. For what greater diſtreſs can even imagination fancy, than that of a wretched female, plunged, by one falſe ſtep, perhaps, into irretrievable ſuffering: deſpoiled by ſickneſs, by ſorrow, and by ſhame, of all that lovelineſs, which, poſſibly, had been the fatal cauſe of her undoing; and ſinking into everlaſting miſery, amidſt want, and cold, and nakedneſs; deſerted by every friend; deprived of every conſolation; and unable to ſupport at once — for, alas! who *can* ſupport? — the inſufferable load of an agonizing body, and a condemning conſcience!

If *Rome* decreed a *Civic* crown, and public honours to him, who ſaved the life of a ſingle citizen; of what honours may not *they* be thought worthy, who ſhall conduce not only to ſave ſo many lives, to their country *; but alſo to reſcue ſouls,

* In this ſingle view,—independant of their parents, families, and their own eternal ſalvation, —that the preſent deſign takes out of the public ſtreets, ſo many objects, who are the peſt and the reproach of the metropolis, who exiſt by making a prey of the thoughtleſs, and unwary, the maudlin huſband, and the unguarded apprentice; and that it renders them happy, healthy, uſeful members of the ſociety;—Surely in this ſingle view, it merits every commendation. "But, ſay ſome, the ſtreets are not leſs peſtered now, than before this inſtitution." This, we are informed, is not quite true; and we apprehend it cannot be true: The *diminution*

souls, the souls of many fellow-creatures and fellow-Christians, from death *everlasting?* If any thing be praise worthy, such benevolence hath the justest claim to that

tion of so many women as are now in the Magdalen-House, cannot fail to be perceived, in some quarters of the town at least, and mischief is indisputably prevented; as they must have been employed in their dire trade, had they not been sheltered there; though alas, poor wretches! *many* of them had certainly been no longer nuisances in this world. But supposing this fact true, we observe, that it reflects not at all upon the charity, nor the worthy supporters of it; who have not the immediate power to cleanse the streets. *They* should look to that, whom it directly concerns; and we have good hope they will do so: exerting all their influence, — which surely every well-wisher to Society should exert, —— to expel this scandalous defilement from the *grand* and most public streets of our city. A defilement, we remark, with concern, not found in any other civilized city upon earth. And, pleased as we are to conceive our own one of the most *civilized*, and the most *Christian*, how can we suffer such a reproach to disgrace at once our *Police*, and our *Christianity?*

 praise;

praiſe; aſſuredly, it is moſt becoming the Chriſtian character, moſt becoming the nobleſt virtue, the beſt and moſt generous humanity. For, ſhall we ſuffer ſuch miſerable unfortunates to periſh unpitied, nor attend to the cries of thoſe, who, in the moſt exquiſite calamity, call aloud for our relief; the cries of that ſofter * and more helpleſs ſex, who ſeem peculiarly to claim *their* protection, to whoſe comforts in life they ſo eminently adminiſter; the affecting cries of thoſe, who have no other means of redreſs, who have no other power of return;—ſhall we ſuffer them to periſh, caſt off, abhorred, and neglected by all; and, ſteeled to pity by their faults, not be melted by their miſery and diſtreſs?

And yet, perhaps, for their faults, (to ſoften the rigour of obdurate *Virtue*; though,

* We hope the poet's remark will be verified in reſpect to theſe poor creatures.

——— When women ſue,
Men give like Gods: but when they weep and kneel,
All their petitions are as truly theirs,
As they themſelves would owe them.

See the Beauties of *Shakeſpear*, vol. 1. p. 41.

indeed,

indeed, *true* virtue lefs requires to be foftened: the moft virtuous are always the moft compaffionate: yet) perhaps, to extenuate their faults, much they might have to plead: nay, much they have to plead;—the complicated arts of feducers; the treachery of perfidious friends; the foftneffes and infirmities of our common nature: Some, the early lofs of parents; others, the deficiency of religious principles and ferious education; and many, too too many, the refiftlefs calls of hunger and of thirft! One falfe ftep too, they might urge, plunged them in a fea of difficulty; barred up every avenue of return *; and left

* It is a fact which hath undeniably been proved fince the eftablifhment of the *Magdalen-Houfe*, (though indeed, I believe, rarely denied) that far the greater part of thefe miferable women have both been introduced by *others* into a ftate of proftitution; and have been unavoidably detained in that courfe of life, fhocking to themfelves, fome by debt, fome by downright defpair, fome merely to fupply their bodily neceffities, and fome by the abfolute impoffibility of procuring a place of reception from their diftrefs, and the means of honeft fupport.

them a ſad prey to inevitable ruin: while the ſource of their miſery felt neither remorſe for their ſeduction, nor found a ſingle ſtain on his reputation; though, theirs unhappily blaſted, every eye beheld them with ſcorn *. O let them then, for honour and

* It is ſaid, that a law formerly prevailed in *Tuſcany*, in order to prevent robberies, that in caſe a man ſhould ſuffer himſelf to be robbed by a ſingle man, (unleſs, we preſume, by ſurpriſe, or manifeſtly ſuperior ſtrength) the perſon robbed ſhould *himſelf* ſuffer the ignominious puniſhment due to a *robber*. However hard and barbarous this cuſtom may appear, there is a ſimilar one, but in a higher degree, which now prevails in one of the moſt civiliſed nations in the known world. Where a man has the privilege of arming himſelf at all points; may uſe every ſtratagem and artifice, nay, and even engage others to aſſiſt him, in order to violate the moſt valuable property of another, however weak and incapable of reſiſtance (with this proviſo only, that a main ruffian force is not abſolutely uſed, though this not unfrequently is the caſe) yet the *plunderer* not only eſcapes unimpeached, but dares to make a boaſt of his act, and values himſelf upon ruining one, whoſe greateſt fault perhaps was only too much

and for compaſſion's ſake, let them experience your beneficent regard! let them have, at leaſt, one chance for life and for pardon! caſt them not utterly away: but ſave ſuch as are willing to be ſaved, from miſery infinitely beyond the power of my pen to paint! reſtore, with the tenderneſs and humanity which ſo diſtinguiſheth *Britain*, thoſe who are deſirous, (as their admiſſion into this houſe ſufficiently demonſtrates; which is at once a pleaſing recommendation in their favour, and the beſt, nay the only proof they can give, of their ſincere deſire to recover their loſt character, and of their diſapprobation of the ways of

much love for him, and too little ſuſpicion of his honour; while the poor bereft object is perſecuted with the utmoſt contempt and miſery; left without any means of ſupporting a wretched exiſtence, but by becoming a peſt cf Society, a burden to herſelf, and an ignominy to her whole family, who are neceſſarily involved in her ruin and diſgrace. Let the reader apply: And then think, in what eſtimation thoſe infamous wretches ſhould be held, who live by theſe arts! Nay, *can they believe,* as the poet finely remarks, *their living is a life, ſo ſtinkingly depending?*

vice) reftore thofe who are defirous to be reftored; reftore them to their God, to their parents, to their country, to themfelves: that fo *the bleffing of thofe, who are ready to perifh, may come upon you,* and you may one day hear, *Come, ye bleffed: I was an hungry, and ye fed me; I was naked, and ye cloathed me; I was a ftranger, and ye took me in.*

But I forbear further to prefs the caufe of thefe unhappy fufferers before the prefent audience: fatisfied of your tender regard and humane difpofition to relieve the afflicted, and to raife the drooping head of mifery and diftrefs.

Befides, the fruits of this good undertaking now before your eyes, will be more prevailing than any arguments that might be urged, and will prove, we doubt not, far more perfuafive. The decent and affecting view of fo many fellow-creatures, refcued from the loweft ebb of forrow, and from the very brink of ruin everlafting, cannot fail to diffufe the moft pleafing fatisfaction through every benevolent breaft; and a moment's reflection on the ftriking contraft between their prefent and their paft paſt ſtate, will not fail to improve that ſatisfaction. With devout and chearful melody thoſe voices now praiſe their God, which late were employed in far different exerciſes: earneſt ſupplications and praiſes, now happily flow from the lips, which were lately prophaned in a contrary ſervice.

For the garments of ſhame, they are cloathed with the robes of decency; for intemperance and defilement they put on ſobriety, meekneſs, and virtue; from the ſervants of Satan and Sin, they are made the ſervants of God and of Holineſs: and from heirs of eternal miſery, are become, through hope, happy candidates for a kingdom of eternal glory.

Who, but muſt rejoice in the reflection! who, that bears a heart, touched at all with the tender feelings of humane good-will, or influenced at all by the nobler ſentiments of divine and Chriſtian love; who, but muſt wiſh good ſucceſs to ſo benevolent a deſign, which may be the means of bringing numbers from the error of their ways, and of turning many from darkneſs and death, to light and to life?

Earthly glories may fade, and the honours of time, and the world *will* leave us; but a subserviency to beneficent attempts like these, will ever comfort us, will attend us beyond the grave: these are imperial works, and such as will survive the proudest pillars and most superb Mausoleums; works, we are assured, which will never want your honourable countenance.

Yet, permit me, ILLUSTRIOUS PRINCE, on behalf of this infant charity, to request *your* favourable and generous attention in particular. Happy in your presence, it would rejoice in your protection: for that protection would serve to dignify the undertaking, already much honoured, and amply encouraged: and that protection would tend to enroll it amidst the distinguished blessings of the present happy æra, which shines no less glorious in the gentler arts of peace, than in the high atchievements of war; and in which it gives every Briton joy to reflect, that while the world around him is in arms, he sits secure beneath his own vine and his own fig-tree; plans, at pleasing leisure, the milder schemes of humanity and benevolence

volence; ſtudious to preſerve life, while war is buſy to deſtroy; and under the auſpices of a beloved ſovereign, gathers the choiceſt ſweets of ſucceſsful union, perfect liberty, and undiſturbed repoſe.

May the favour of heaven, long continue theſe excellent bleſſings to us: may it crown our gracious and venerable monarch with peace, as it hath crowned him with glory; and protect his illuſtrious line from generation to generation! May works of beneficence and humanity abound ſtill more and more amongſt us: and may the preſent eſpecially, bud, bloſſom, and bear fruit abundantly under the dew of princely and right noble favour! May it prove a bleſſing to numberleſs ſouls, in their perfect ſalvation, an advantage to our country in the preſervation of many lives, and an honour to our holy religion in the zeal of its worthy ſupporters! May the ſouls of thoſe who are reſcued by means hereof from ſorrow, ſhame, and death, from preſent and eternal miſery, gratefully unite in conſtant prayers for every generous inſtrument in the good work; and may every

gene-

generous inſtrument be amply bleſt by the Father of mercies with every deſirable bleſſing; peace, and true felicity on earth; eternal peace and unfading felicity in heaven, thro' Jeſus Chriſt our Lord! *Amen:*

A SER-

A

SERMON,

ON

JOB, Chap. xxix. Ver. 11—13.

Preached at the

ANNIVERSARY MEETING

OF THE

GOVERNORS

OF THE

MAGDALEN CHARITY,

On THURSDAY, MARCH 18, 1762.

In the Pariſh Church of

St. GEORGE, HANOVER-SQUARE:

By *WILLIAM DODD*, M.A.

The SEVENTH EDITION.

At a Special General Court of the Governors of the Magdalen Charity, *holden at* Drapers Hall, *the 18th Day of* March, 1762.

Resolved,

THAT the Thanks of this Court be returned to the Rev. Mr. *Dodd*, for his excellent Sermon preached this Day before the President, Vice-Presidents, Treasurer, and Governors of this Charity, at St. *George's* Church, *Hanover Square*; and that he be desired to cause the same to be printed and published,

By Order of the Court,

A. WINTERBOTTOM, Sec.

TO the Right Honourable

The Earl of HERTFORD, PRESIDENT.

The Right Hon. Lord *Romney*,	Vice-Preſidents,
Sir *George Savile*, Bart.	
Sir *Alexander Grant*, Bart.	
Sir *Samuel Fludyer*, Bart.	
Lord Mayor,	

Robert Dingley, Eſq; Treaſurer.

Iſaac Akerman, Eſq;
John Barker, Eſq;
Jonathan Barnard, Eſq;
Mr. *John Barnes*,
Edmund Boehm, Eſq;
Edward Dixon, Eſq;
John Dorrien, Eſq;
Thomas Farrer, Eſq;
Thomas Fletcher, Eſq;
Edward Forſter, Eſq;
T. Edw. Freeman, Eſq;
Steph. Peter Godin, Eſq;
Jonas Hanway, Eſq;
Philip Milloway, Eſq;
George Perrot, Eſq;
George Peters, Eſq;
Thomas Preſton, Eſq;
John Thornton, Eſq;
Rob. Cotton Trefuſis
George Wombwell, Eſq;
Mr. *Charles Way* Eſq;

The Annual COMMITTEE,

And all the other Worthy Governors and Subſcribers to this Excellent and Uſeful Inſtitution;

THIS

DISCOURSE,

Preached at their Requeſt,
And now publiſhed by their Order,
Is, with all proper Eſteem,
Dedicated and Inſcribed
BY

The AUTHOR.

Weſt Ham,
April 22, 1762.

JOB xxix. 11—13.

WHEN THE EAR HEARD ME, THEN IT BLESSED ME; AND WHEN THE EYE SAW ME, IT GAVE WITNESS TO ME: BECAUSE I DELIVERED THE POOR THAT CRIED, AND THE FATHERLESS, AND HIM THAT HAD NONE TO HELP HIM. THE BLESSING OF HIM THAT WAS READY TO PERISH, CAME UPON ME: AND I CAUSED THE WIDOW'S HEART TO SING FOR JOY.

HOW amiable, how uſeful, how excellent is benevolence! which gives ſplendor to the character, and ſerenity to the heart; engages the univerſal affection, and adds to human nature its greateſt merit and dignity! It is the higheſt perfection, not only of men, but of angels; nay, it is the darling attribute of the Deity himſelf: of the almighty and eternal God, who hath ſtiled himſelf LOVE, and is continually manifeſt-

ing

ing the moſt glorious diſplays thereof, through all the various ſyſtems of creation.

Since we were formed in the image of God, it is no wonder that benevolence is deeply rooted in the nature of man: ſince the Son of God, ſolely actuated by this divine principle, humbled himſelf to the infamy and torture of the croſs, it is no wonder, that this gracious ſufferer hath conſtituted benevolence the ſtandard of all excellence, and the ſummit of all moral perfection: that benevolence, to which we are ſo forcibly influenced by the common wants and common weakneſſes of our nature; and to which we are ſtimulated by ſuch irreſiſtible motives of intereſt, of duty, and of happineſs.

The ſubject being conſidered in this view, it can be no ſurpriſe, that the *benevolent Man* immediately acquires the warm approbation of the community: for who can withhold applauſe from a character which every man naturally admires, and every good man labours to obtain? Behold him, (to collect a few rays only of his brightneſs, not to attempt a draught of his full-orbed luſtre) behold him, warmed by the precepts, and

and animated by the pattern of his Redeemer; like that Redeemer, glowing with the love, and anxious for the welfare of his fellow creatures! Large is his heart, and liberal are his hands: with this he feels, he compaſſionates; with thoſe he relieves, and comforts, the wants and grievances of the children of affliction. No narrow prejudices, no diſcriminating circumſtances damp the glow of his compaſſion, or interrupt the current of his beneficence. Even wrongs, repeated wrongs, cannot cauſe him to withdraw his good-will, or to deny his good offices to the injurious, when wretched, and in need of aſſiſtance. He conſiders not ſo much the merit as the neceſſities of the object: human nature and diſtreſs, are always ſufficient titles to his pity and relief.

The higher his ſtation, and the more extenſive his influence, the more he ſtudies to adorn that ſtation, and to employ that influence, whether of wealth, wiſdom, or power, to the great end of bleſſing mankind; and of diffuſing around the enlivening beams of his beneficence; like the

ſun,

ſun, that inferior miniſter of providence, which cheers, invigorates, and ſuſtains the ſurrounding world *. He knows that the beſt prerogative of an exalted ſtation, is to afford ſhelter to inferiors, who repoſe themſelves under ſuch cover and protection: he knows, that only by doing good, a man can truly enjoy the advantages of pre-eminence.

Let

* See *Hume*'s Eſſays, Vol. IV. It is impoſſible to read without approbation, Mr. *Hume*'s Remarks on *Benevolence* in particular; while, at the ſame time, the good heart muſt feel a ſenſible concern, that a man of ſuch abilities, and ſuch ſentiments, ſhould ever employ his pen to ſo unworthy and pernicious a purpoſe, as the unſettling the great principles of that holy and excellent *Religion*, which this writer *muſt* know, bears all the marks of credibility poſſible, and which is the ever-living ſource of light, from whence he hath kindled his taper. An author ſo acute, cannot but be convinced that he is reaſoning againſt truth, when he oppoſes the great principles of Chriſtianity; cannot but perceive, that ſophiſtry guides the pen, when he pleads in the perſon of *Epicurus*, and when he attempts to decry the evidence of *Miracles*.

Let me obſerve too, that the benevolence which thus leads to an active concern for the univerſal welfare, will naturally incline the good man to do all his kind offices in the moſt amiable and engaging manner. He will reverence the afflicted; and with ſo much mildneſs and humanity, adminiſter his comforts, as ſhall never pain or ſhock the generous and ſenſible heart which receives them. Nor will he want ſolicitations to deeds of goodneſs and charity, becauſe ſuch actions are the delight of his ſoul, and the main employment of his life: he is in continual ſearch after them, and

cles. Yet, can the man, who ſpeaks ſuch exquiſite things on the ſubject of *Benevolence*, have a bad heart? I would fain believe not: and do earneſtly wiſh, that he would not act as an enemy to ſociety, and to the moſt pure and refined truth ever revealed to man: that he would engage in a better cauſe, and endeavour to ſet forth in their fine colours, and as he is able, the high precepts of the Goſpel. For, let him only recollect, what muſt be his fate in a *future* world, (and he believes a future world) if the Chriſtian Religion prove true? While the Chriſtian, even upon *his* principles, cannot be wrong, ſhould his religion prove falſe.

ſtudy-

ſtudying every method whereby he may render himſelf ſignally beneficial to his fellow-creatures; ſo that by furniſhing him with occaſions of utility, you coincide with his favourite purſuits, and ſupply him with the moſt refined and exquiſite ſatisfactions. Nay, ſhould his beneficence be miſconſtrued, or ungratefully abuſed; ſhould diſappointment and perverſion thwart and counteract his beſt deſigns; yet will he not grow weary, or be diſcouraged from the diſcharge of his duty. Candid in all his cenſures, and abounding ſtill in the mildeſt conſtructions, he will perſevere in the path of right: and knowing that ſucceſs doth not always attend good deſerts, or good endeavours, he will not be too anxious about the attainment; but ſelf-ſatisfied in the rectitude of his intentions, he will leave the event to the Great Diſpoſer of all things.

Well then may we repeat, even from this imperfect ſketch, "How amiable, how uſeful, how excellent is Benevolence!" Would you ſee it in a clearer exhibition, (as light is moſt diſtinguiſhed by ſhade) Place by the ſide of our good man, the ſelfiſh, ſordid, low-minded being, whoſe grovel-

groveling ſoul is ever bent to earth, and his own miſerable intereſts; who never lifts his louring eye above the ſphere of his own advantage; and whoſe actions are continually directed by the invariable needle of private good: a wretch, who is *never* communicative, but when he expects a greater return; wiſhing to draw all to himſelf, but never willing to diſperſe abroad in bleſſings to others: greedy as the ſea, and barren as the ſhore!

From ſuch a contraſt the benevolent character acquires new luſtre. Nor can it be an unpleaſing reflection, that amidſt the prevalence of ſelfiſhneſs, of diſſipation, and of diſregard to ſerious religion, (too juſtly complained of, I fear, in the preſent day) yet a general philanthropy happily abounds through the nation. Private charity diſpenſes every where her kindly ſuccours. National charity, extended to ſufferers in other climes, hath never been wanting; *Liſbon*, in its overthrow, can witneſs the humanity of *Britain*; and even our enemies, to the particular honour of the preſent times, have baſked in the ſunſhine of our bounty:

We have fed the hungry and cloathed the naked, even of thoſe who are deemed our natural, and our moſt inveterate adverſaries: And public charity rears up her lovely head, and triumphs! *There* ſhe ſhews you Chriſtian knowledge widely ſpread throughout the earth; and thouſands of children inſtructed in the principles of evangelical truth *. *There* ſhe ſhews you the deſolate and afflicted widow, with her orphans round her, forgetting awhile the deprivation of former comforts, and their ſad downfall from a ſtate of plenty and of peace; while the generous hand of pity, by adminiſtering to their ſupport, is ſupplying the loſs of the affectionate huſband, and indulgent father. *There* ſhe ſhews you the ſick, the wounded, and the lame, ſmiling amidſt the anguiſh, and bleſſing the benevolence which affords them ſuch ſeaſonable relief. *There* ſhe ſhews you induſtry and honeſt labour ſheltered under the ravage of a diſeaſe, whoſe contagion ſhuts it out from

* The Societies for propagating and promoting Chriſtian Knowledge, with which the Charity Schools are connected.

mercy;

mercy; or ſcorning the efforts of that diſeaſe, which heaven-taught art no longer ſuffers to walk attended with deſolation and death *. *There* ſhe points to the refuge of indigent pregnant women, awhile unmindful of their pangs, and gratefully acknowledging that goodneſs, which hath conſulted their ſecurity and comfort, at the hour of ſorrow and extremity. *There* ſhe preſents to your ſight the retreats of phrenſy, at lucid intervals thankful in her cells, for thoſe kind edifices, which ſcreen from public view the moſt formidable diſguiſes, and mortifying abaſements of human nature. *There* ſhe ſhews you the chambers of deſerted infants, of little out-caſts, and unfriended orphans, kindly ſheltered from the rude blaſts of infamy, of ignorance, of ruin; and made inſtrumental to the commerce, the defence, and the domeſtic neceſſities of the nation †. And *there* ſhe

* The uſeful Hoſpital for the Small Pox, not only relieves thoſe who have it in a natural way, but alſo *inoculates*.

† The Foundling Hoſpital, the Marine Society, the Aſylum, &c. &c.

ſhews you happy PENITENTS exulting in the goodneſs of their God; and pouring out their tears and thanks to heaven and their benefactors, for reſtoring them to all things dear and valuable to human creatures upon earth *.

* I heartily wiſh, that I was able to enumerate amongſt theſe public and amiable works, "*An* ASYLUM *for the* BLIND." There is no need to expatiate on the misfortune of loſs of ſight; nor to hint how painful it is to the humane and feeling heart, to be ſtruck with the cries of the blind, at almoſt every corner of the ſtreets of our metropolis. Would it not be a work of diſtinguiſhed humanity, to remove all theſe unhappy objects to a proper place; and to employ them in ſuch works as they are capable of executing, (there are many ſuch works) and to allow them a comfortable ſubſiſtence?

I am pleaſed to find, that ſince the publication of this diſcourſe, many worthy and benevolent perſons have thought and talked of "An Aſylum for the Blind," Happy ſhould I be, in ſeeing ſuch an inſtitution; as well as ready, to the utmoſt of my ſmall power, to forward and promote it, by uniting with ſuch as are willing to carry the deſign into execution.

Muſt

Muſt not, oh muſt not a benevolence like this, thus important, large, and univerſal, "which delivers the poor, the fa-"therleſs, and him who hath none to help "him; which is eyes to the blind, and "feet to the lame; which ſaves thoſe who "were ready to periſh, and cauſes the "widow's heart to ſing for joy;—Muſt "not this make our ears, when they hear "it, to bleſs; and our eyes when they "ſee it, to give glad witneſs" to the authors and promoters of ſuch works of love? Can we refuſe them our teſtimony, our eſteem, our gratitude? May we not hope that the prevalence of a virtue, ſo eſtimable in the ſight of God our Saviour, will plead with his goodneſs in behalf of our nation, ſo bleſt, ſo eminently favoured by him? will ſtand in the gap between us and our manifold iniquities; and ſecure to us, through many generations, thoſe high felicities ſo peculiarly our own?

"O may the goodneſs of God not only "crown our land with every bleſſing; not "only pour forth abundantly into every "heart that ſpirit of benevolence, which

" hath already been productive of fo many " laudable undertakings: but may his pro- " vidential care profper and fucceed every " fuch undertaking! May the dew of his " mercy fall richly upon every good defign; " and caufe each one of them to flourifh " abundantly, and bring forth the moft de- " firable fruits; to the encouragement, fatis- " faction, and comfort of the benevolent, the " worthy, and truly honourable promoters of " them!"

But while we are wifhing profperity and good luck in the name of the Lord, to every benevolent inftitution, YOU will allow me to requeft at prefent your more particular attention to that diftinguifhed work of humanity, for which I am appointed to plead, and which furely deferves a far better advocate. But I am engaged: It will therefore avail me little to urge that I am *preft involuntarily* into this fervice; which I fhould have rejoiced to have feen performed by one of abilities, of dignity, of reputation, far fuperior to mine: It will avail me little to urge, that I have not only faid from the pulpit, but the prefs, repeat-

edly

edly and again *, all I had to offer on the ſubject; and what arguments can I now uſe in behalf of this amiable undertaking? All I can truſt to, is the benevolence of your hearts, which your preſence here proves, are already intereſted in favour of our charity.

And ſurely, if ever charitable deſign peculiarly claimed the patronage of the *great* and the *good*; it is this for which we plead. Every chriſtian, every humane, every tender and compaſſionate motive unites to recommend and enforce it.

Mean and deſpicable is the attempt to raiſe the reputation of one work upon the ruin of another; or to think of applauding this, by depreciating the merit of that charity. True benevolence, however it may affect one more than another, will yet rejoice in all: and though it may not be able to lend much help to all, while more immediately attached to one; yet will it cordially approve all, and, as far as it can,

* See my Firſt Sermon before the Preſident, &c. 1759; That before the Duke of *York*: The Advice to the Magdalens: An Account of the Riſe and Progreſs of the Magdalen Charity, &c. &c.

aſſiſt them; ſhining like a good planet, with a benign influence on all within its ſphere; and by the liberality of its ſentiments at leaſt, participating of the merit of every good work.

Theſe, I know, are the generous ideas of the encouragers of our preſent deſign; whoſe bounty is by no means confined to this ſingle work of mercy; but diffuſed, like ſtreams of water, through the dry deſart of neceſſity and ſuffering; and communicated alſo to many other humane and praiſe-worthy inſtitutions*. It will never therefore be judged that we mean to prejudice any one of them; (God forbid that ſuch a thought ſhould ever harbour itſelf in my breaſt!) that we mean to divert the current of benevolence from other objects of pity, from other labours of love; while for our preſent inſtitution we urge, and will endeavour to prove, that it is one of the

* Let me requeſt any perſon to compare the Liſt of the Governors of the Magdalen Charity, with that of the ſeveral others enumerated in a former page; and the recurrence of the ſame benevolent names will abundantly prove my aſſertion.

GREATEST

GREATEST charities in which Men or Chriſtians can be engaged.

Now of human works, that muſt be the beſt and the moſt perfect, which approaches neareſt to the ſtandard of all goodneſs and perfection. Muſt not that then be the higheſt charity, which moſt reſembles the charity of God; of Chriſt; and of good Angels? Muſt not that be the higheſt charity, which provides not only for the bodily diſtreſſes of fellow-creatures, but for all their ſpiritual wants: which not only reſtores to health, to reputation, to peace in this world; but, properly improved, to everlaſting health and peace in the future world? Muſt not that be the higheſt charity, which not only conſults the happineſs of the objects themſelves, but which takes in a large and affecting circle,—all the dear and tender names of parents, brother, ſiſter, friend: and which gives balm and relief to the moſt acute and tormenting of all pains,—the pain of the affectionate parent's wounded heart? Muſt not that be the higheſt charity, which gives hope to the hopeleſs; relieves from unutterable diſtreſs ſouls plunged into the very bitterneſs of woe; teaches the tongue to bleſs, which before in deſpair even blaſphemed its God, and curſed its own exiſtence; teaches the hands to labour, which were wantoning in the moſt pernicious idleneſs: and, at the ſame time, that it removes obnoxious and deſtructive, reſtores uſeful and induſtrious members to the commonweal?

Such is the charity, which we would recommend to your favourable ſuccour: It cannot want that ſuccour; for your hearts not only feel the noble touches of benevolence; but you are deſirous to imitate the pattern of all perfection; to be like your God, and your Saviour; and to ſhare the buſineſs and the bleſſedneſs of angels. This you will ſhare, by communicating to our preſent inſtitution; thus reſtoring to God, to happineſs, and to hope, loſt and ruined ſinners! And ſinners—let me add, further to recommend our inſtitution—who, denied the ſhelter of this hoſpitable charity, what probability, I might ſay, what *poſſibility* have they to avoid the miſeries of utter perdition? No *benevolent* heart would

ſurely

ſurely refuſe them one chance, one ſingle chance for repentance and life! And this is all for which we plead. Nay, certainly, not even the moſt *rigid virtue* could deny one chance, one ſingle chance for ſalvation, when able to give that chance, to any unhappy fellow-creatures; and when morally aſſured, that they muſt for ever be loſt without it!

"But then, ſome may ſay, were it not better to unite all our efforts for the prevention of this evil, which is attended with ſuch dreadful conſequences?"—Yes, doubtleſs, we reply, if it could be prevented: but while human paſſions continue what they are, it is much to be feared that no efforts *can* wholly prevent this evil. Certainly by the increaſed diligence of the magiſtrate, much of the public nuiſance, ſo juſtly complained of, and ſo reproachful to the police, morals, and religion of our metropolis, might be removed *, and it

* Unqueſtionably theſe miſerable wretches might be prevented from plying ſo ſcandalouſly in the great and leading ſtreets of the metropolis: unqueſ-

is hoped, will be removed. But while human nature remains as it is, men will ſeduce, and women will hearken; and there will ever be, as there have ever been, too many deluded objects, to move our commiſeration, and to call for our chriſtian concern.

"But theſe (it may be ſaid again) are moſt worthleſs objects; they have brought themſelves into theſe evils; and conſequently merit no pity." Alas! how ſuperficially do they reflect upon the charity of God and of Chriſt; how little upon the nature of true benevolence; who thus object. For whom doth God diſpenſe his providential bleſſings? upon whom doth his ſun ſhine, and his light ariſe?—only on the juſt? For

unqueſtionably ſo many of the houſes harbouring, notoriouſly harbouring them, might be diſcountenanced: unqueſtionably they might be prevented from ſitting out, to enſnare, in *ſome parts* of the town, even in the *broad light* of the midday! and all this without any *danger* of leſſening the number of ſuch women to that degree, that *worſe vices* would follow!—as hath been the *inſinuation* and *pretence* of ſome, who perhaps, are glad of an excuſe for their neglect of proper exertion in this matter.

whom

whom did God ſend his only begotten into the world? for whom did that only begotten bleed and die on the croſs?—only for the worthy and deſerving? No: for a world of SINNERS; for ALL OF US, whoſe many offences have made us obnoxious to the condemnation of God! and who, therefore, ſhall we ſay, "merit no pity?" Far different is the method of our God's gracious dealings with us! The prodigal ſon in the goſpel brought himſelf into a ſtate of indigence and miſery; yet did not his father utterly reject him. The adulterous woman; the impure Magdalen; the denying Peter, all, all of them were in this reſpect without excuſe; their mouths were ſtopped before God; guilty and ſelf-condemned, they had nothing to plead. Yet did He freely forgive them all their treſpaſſes. "Nay, and all the ſouls, which are, were forfeited once; and he, even he who might beſt have taken the advantage, found out the remedy *."

Beſides, that benevolence cannot be deemed perfect, which diſtinguiſheth only the

* See Shakeſpeare's *Meaſure for Meaſure*.

good

good and deſerving: *they* not only merit our eſteem, but demand our aſſiſtance: it is a kind of debt due to *them*. But we then ſhew true philanthropy, when not the merit alone, but the neceſſities and diſtreſſes of objects move us to their relief, when we are withheld from diſpenſing our ſeaſonable bounty by no narrow and unworthy prejudices: it being ſufficient to engage all our beſt ſervices, with the good *Samaritan*, that a fellow-traveller, though a Jew, ſtands in need of the ſuccour which we are able to beſtow *.

Thus much may be urged in behalf of the objects of our preſent concern, upon the ſuppoſition of their utter unworthineſs.

One would however imagine, that no human beings could be precipitate in their

* Let it here be obſerved, that there can be but two reaſons for puniſhing, or for permitting perſons to continue in a ſtate of ſuffering; namely, for *example* or *reformation*. When theſe ends are anſwered, it is as barbarous as it is uſeleſs, to puniſh: it is abſolutely inhuman not to relieve the ſufferer. When, therefore, unhappy women are deſirous to reform and amend; what can juſtify our conduct, if we refuſe them the means?

censures,

cenſures, or haſty in their condemnation of fellow-creatures, miſled by a paſſion, which, however fatal and dangerous, when unmortified and unſubdued, is yet, for wiſe and good ends, interwoven in the frame of our nature; and from ſome aberrations in which, but few, it is to be feared, can plead abſolutely guiltleſs. When therefore we conſider the ſtrength of paſſion, and the imbecility of reaſon; when we conſider that the moſt generous and humane diſpoſitions have ſometimes been led captive by this deluſive paſſion; when we conſider that ſuch, many ſuch, moſt celebrated in hiſtory, have not only felt and acknowledged the ſevereſt checks of conſcience, but by God's grace, have become as eminent for their penitence as for their faults: ſuch reflections muſt ſoften the rigour of our judgments; muſt lead us not to doubt of the poſſibility of the thorough and real reformation of thoſe unhappy young creatures, who have fallen victims to a paſſion which is common to our nature; and who have much to *urge*, much to plead in their own behalf, and in requeſt of our forgiveneſs and compaſſion.

Some

Some of them will tell you, of the base and treacherous arts of merciless seducers; who, by every unlawful method, by vows, by promises, by oaths, won their unsuspecting, honest, gentle hearts; heart, yet unpracticed and estranged to guile! won and abandoned them (ah cruel and perfidious! let such boast their conquests!) won and abandoned them to sore destruction. Some of them will tell you of the afflicting and early loss of careful and affectionate parents, who left them,—left their beloved orphans, to an injurious world; left them an easy, artless prey, or ever they could distinguish evil from good, or good from evil; a prey to the inhuman barbarity of the savage ministers of lust. Others, with streaming eyes will plead, as a coercive argument for their continuance in such a state, that they could find no hand to relieve, no heart to pity; that there was no place for them to fly unto, that none cared for their souls: that their friends, nay, their dearest parents, forsook them! that they had not, they could not find where to lay, where to conceal, their wretched heads!

heads! And ſome will urge the ſtrong and irreſiſtible calls of hunger and of thirſt; appetites which muſt be ſatisfied: But,—ah truly pitiable daughters of affliction! not ſolely hunger and thirſt of their own, but of a miſerable babe perhaps, the ſad iſſue of their unfortunate guilt,—yet not on that account the leſs claiming all the tenderneſs of maternal love! And could the mother ſee the little helpleſs innocent periſh in her arms? Could ſhe behold its tongue cleaving to the roof of its mouth for hunger, and for thirſt? Oh what could not a mother rather behold! what virtue would not ſink under ſuch a trial! *Can a woman forget her ſucking child?* Pity her, oh pity her, ye happier mothers: and ſay, could ye not excuſe a crime — ſay rather, will ye not bleſs this hoſpitable charity, which relieves the inexpreſſible diſtreſs of many ſuch miſerable women?

Indeed, I cannot but obſerve here, that ſo ſcanty are the means of ſubſiſtence allowed the female ſex; ſo few the occupations which they can purſue, and thoſe ſo much engroſſed by our ſex: ſo ſmall are the

the profits arising from their labours, and so difficult often the power of obtaining employment, especially for those of doubtful character; and frequently so utter their unskilfulness in any branches of their common industry, from a mistaken neglect of their parents in their education;—several of whom, while they absurdly expend much on boarding-schools, think it beneath them to have their daughters taught a trade.—So scanty are the means of subsistence, arising from these and the like causes, that, it is but too well known, many virtuous and decent young women, left desolate with poor unfriended children, have been compelled to the horrid necessity (and we want not to be told, what numbers in this great city lie in wait to improve, and turn to their own advantage that necessity) of procuring bread by prostitution! which nothing could have induced them so to procure, but the cries and tears of hungry children, craving repeated supplies of food; which thus becomes the food of bitterness to the mother, and renders life the most oppressive burden.

But

But I dwell not now on the peculiar hardſhips, difficulties and diſtreſſes of the female ſex: I dwell not upon the temptations to which they are expoſed; in the free and unreſtrained uſe of which, cruel ſeducers even think themſelves juſtifiable: I dwell not upon the ſuperior *advantages*, (if advantages they may be called) which our ſex hath over them; whoſe reputation ſuffers no ſtain even from an avowed indulgence in this vice; while one unhappy deviation blaſts the fair beauty of female honour.—I dwell not upon theſe topics; they have been already ſufficiently handled.

Suffer me only to remark, that the ſucceſs of this undertaking ſerves above all things to recommend it, and to remove every objection which either caution or malevolence might have to urge againſt it *. Of the firſt two hundred women who voluntarily ſought this happy covert from the ſtorm, but a very inconſiderable number at this time remains in the houſe; and ſome of them ſo perfectly happy and ſatisfied with their ſituation, that they pray never to depart thence, and have intreated permiſſion from

* See the account at the end of the book.

from the benevolent governors of the charity, to paſs their lives ſecluded from temptation and danger, within thoſe walls where they have found ſafety and peace.

Of the reſt, many have been introduced into decent ſervices, where they have conducted themſelves with ſo much propriety, that ſeveral have claimed and received that bounty, which the rules of the charity aſſign as an encouragement to thoſe who continue a year in their ſervices, and meet the approbation of their ſuperiors: For, particular application is given, not only to the habituating them all to induſtry, but likewiſe to the teaching the uninſtructed ſuch branches of female employ, as may qualify them for different provinces, and enable them to get their livelihood with honeſty and credit, when they are replaced in the world.

That ſome ſhould again return to impurity, could not but have been ſuppoſed by the moſt ſanguine eſpouſers of this charity. But it ſurely deſerves attention, and is ſome proof of the right principles imbibed in the houſe, that the greater part, even of thoſe who have been diſcarded with

diſhonour

dishonour, have sought for and readily undertaken the hardest services, rather than return to their former detested way of life: nay, and some, to avoid that necessity, have even applied to magistrates to send them abroad, and thereby capacitate them to procure an honest and industrious subsistence.

While it ought to be mentioned, as a mark of the good government and regulation of the house,—and I think we may add, of the good intentions and right principles wherewith these women enter it—that since the institution of it, no acts of flagrant indecency or gross misbehaviour have ever appeared; though no punishments or corrections are ever used; for nothing but the law of reason, of religion, and of lenity, is permitted to rule in a place, designed for a comfortable and desirable retreat to the sincerely penitent.

Besides those who have been placed out in the world, several have been restored to their rejoicing parents. And could you have been spectators of the many affecting scenes, which have passed on these occasions, your sym-

ſympathetic hearts would have melted, and you would have bleſſed a charity productive of ſuch celeſtial comforts. Could *your* hearts be unmoved, if you ſaw, what the Directors of this Charity ſo frequently ſee; if you ſaw an aged parent introduce a young and hapleſs daughter; if you heard her with the voice of maternal anguiſh, thus tenderly implore your aid; "For the ſake of our "adorable and compaſſionate Redeemer, take "my wretched, ruined child, into your "kind protection; ſave her, oh ſave her "from utter deſtruction; and, in ſo doing, "ſave alſo the life of a miſerable mother! "She was once my ſole comfort, once "my moſt pleaſing hope! I truſted that ſhe "would have been the ſtaff and ſupport "of my old age, and have held me up "amidſt all the ſorrows and afflictions of "widowhood! But alas, a cruel ſpoiler "came; deceived her, artleſs as ſhe was; "deluded and withdrew her from my roof "and protection! In vain, with parental "anxiety, I ſought her: conſcious of her "crime, ſhe ſtill flew from me; and abandoned by her perfidious deceiver, whoſe

"heart

"heart was harder than the nether mill-"stone, she became a prey to the arts of "those who lye in wait to destroy the "young and the friendless! Defiled and "diseased, lost to reputation and herself, I "have at length recovered my child, ;—for "still she is *my* child, though thus unhappy! "And, on my bended knees, I implore that "you would have pity on a mother's an-"guish; that you would commiserate a wi-"dow's distress; that you would save my "dear, though polluted daughter, from that "extremity of horror and perdition, which "otherwise must unavoidably attend her! "Compassionate her youth: pardon the past: "her tears witness her contrition; let them "plead for her; let her mother's tears also "plead for her: save us, oh save us both from "the agonies of despondence! So will the "blessing of those who are ready to perish "come upon you; so will you be fathers to "the fatherless; and cause the dejected wi-"dow's heart, long unacquainted with com-"fort, to sing for joy!"

Could *your* generous hearts refuse to such a petitioner the relief she required?—I am convinced they could not. Now then, imagine,

imagine, that many fuch are pleading with you for your liberal contributions to this charity; contributions fufficient to enable its governors never to have the hard and painful tafk of rejecting petitioners of this fort; fufficient to enable them to enlarge their mercy, and to open wide their bleffed doors, like thofe of heaven, at the call of every pitiable and repenting object.

And, only think, if the benevolent heart feels fuch a guft of joy in relieving the prefent anguifh of fuch melancholy fufferers; what muft it feel, when it beholds the good effects, the full fruits of its compaffion; when it fees the top-ftone brought forth with gladnefs; fees the work perfected, in the complete felicity of thofe to whom was miniftered its firft and kindly fuccour?

Among many of this fort, let us not pafs over a ftriking inftance of the grateful parents of a young woman, who had been a confiderable time in the houfe, had behaved herfelf with all propriety, and a few weeks paft was taken home to her tranfported family. How pleafing, how tenderly pleafing was it, to fee her parents, with eyes full of tears, pouring forth, in broken accents,

accents, their thankful hearts to the governors of this charity! "Bleſſed charity, ſaid "they, which hath ſaved our child, our beloved daughter from everlaſting ruin! A "charity, for the proſperity of which we muſt "ever pray, and the benevolent ſupporters of "which we muſt ever bleſs, as (under God) "the authors of all our felicity; as the reſtorers, almoſt from death, of our loſt and "undone child! Amidſt the numberleſs obligations conferred upon us, permit us (continued they) to aſk yet one more; permit "us, with our recovered and new-born "daughter, to ſeal our vows of thankfulneſs "and devotion at the altar of your *Chapel*; "and to preſent ourſelves with our child, "at that holy table, to HIM who hath "done ſo great things for us!" Who could hear ſuch language without emotion and delight? But who, unmoved and undelighted, could behold theſe chriſtian and truly ſenſible parents, kneeling on either ſide of their daughter at the altar; preſenting their mutual thanks, and lifting up their eyes in expreſſive gratitude and gladneſs; the parents for their recovered child; the child for her reconciled parents, and with them, her God, her peace, her preſent and eternal comfort reſtored and ſecured to her!

Theſe are ſights which muſt refreſh every benevolent mind; theſe are fruits of our charity, which muſt render it amiable in all your eyes; which muſt make you anxious to communicate liberally to ſuch good; to be fellow-workers in deeds of ſuch diſtinguiſhed excellence. For, granting that many ſhould abuſe this well-intended deſign, (and what deſigns are not liable to abuſe?) granting that half, only half of thoſe who ſeek its friendly ſhelter, ſhould duly improve its proffered bleſſings; nay, granting that a tenth part only ſhould be ſaved from the moſt exquiſite diſtreſs which can affect human creatures; that only a tenth part ſhould be ſaved from an early and ſhocking death, amidſt all thoſe miſeries, which are of moſt fearful name—ſhould be ſaved from the unutterable miſeries of death eternal; ſurely it were a work well worthy all our our pains, well worthy all the approbation and aid, which the great, the virtuous, and the good can give.

But, indeed, we have all the certainty which the nature of the work will admit, that a far greater proportion properly improve the benefits of this inſtitution, and are not only made happy themſelves, but diffuſe that happineſs

happineſs through the wide circle of their loved relations: while, at the ſame time, they àre reſtored to the ſtate, and become uſeful members of it:—a circumſtance by no means inconſiderable at a period when war is ſpreading ſo widely its terrible devaſtations of the human ſpecies; nor indeed at any time inconſiderable, in a commercial nation like ours, whoſe ſtrength and proſperity depend on the number of its inhabitants.

However, reſpecting ſome of the objects, we have abſolute certainty: for it hath pleaſed God to call away ſome of them ſince their admiſſion into the houſe; who have died with ſuch marks of real Repentance, that no man could entertain a doubt of their forgiveneſs and acceptance with their Redeemer. And oh! what a tranſporting thought is that to a mind duly ſenſible of the worth of an immortal ſoul! Poſſibly, had they not been admitted within theſe charitable walls, they had periſhed, horribly periſhed, in the ſtreets, amidſt cold and nakedneſs, famine and diſeaſe, uninſtructed, unrelieved, unpitied, impenitent! periſhed miſerably in this life, only to enter on another far more miſerable!

And indeed, when this thought extends itſelf to all the women now in the houſe, bleſt with health, reſtored to happineſs, induſtriouſly employed, and chearfully ſinging praiſes to their God; many, very many of whom, moſt probably without this relief, had long ago ended their days in the extremity of ſufferings,—young and wretched victims to the deſolation of wide-waſting and unrelenting luſt,—our compaſſion muſt be moved; and the benevolent heart will want no farther recommendation of a work ſo productive of the higheſt good which mortals can aim at, or accompliſh *.

Of which, one example further before I conclude, will ſerve more fully to convince

* This ſingle circumſtance of the *preſervation of ſo many lives*, which is effected by the Magdalen Charity, ſhould alone be ſufficient to recommend it to the public attention. From the general account it appears, that but eight have died out of the number of 483, who have been received into the houſe, ſince its firſt opening. In my firſt ſermon, p. 84, I obſerved, that it is probable, *ſixty* in an *hundred* or more, of theſe objects would have been dead in two years: and upon this calculation, which I believe to be pretty juſt, what a great ſaving of lives is here to the public, and lives, in general, of ſubjects under twenty years!

you

you: one example, in which you will trace with a ſympathetic pleaſure, the tender ſtruggles of chriſtian rejoicing and parental affection.

An amiable young creature, juſt in her ſixteenth year, was admitted into the houſe: her conduct was humble and blameleſs, ſuch as became and denoted the penitent. After her admiſſion, ſhe had the happineſs to be reconciled to a mother who had felt the ſevereſt ſorrow for her miſconduct, who affectionately loved, and was beloved by her child. Not long ſince ſhe was ſeiſed with a mortal diſeaſe, which ſhe bore with chearfulneſs, fortitude, and reſignation. When ſhe perceived the hour of death approaching, ſhe earneſtly deſired to ſee her widowed parent, and to take her laſt farewell. As ſoon as it was poſſible, the afflicted mother came: the ſoul of the daughter ſeemed to revive at the voice of her parent. The interview was pathetic and affecting: none preſent could refrain from tears. But it was ſcarcely paſſed, ſcarce had the tender parent preſſed the cold and trembling lips of her child, before the fluttering ſoul quitted its earthly habitation; as if it had only ſtaid to pay this tribute, and to perform this laſt office of filial duty and love.

Parental affection then, and christian joy ſtrove with each other in the mother's breaſt. For awhile ſhe ſpoke not: ſhe could not ſpeak. Tears at length burſt forth; ſhe wept: ſhe could not but weep for her daughter once loſt, but now doubly precious to her, by having been found, and reſtored to obedience and virtue. She could not but weep for her *only* daughter, thus early cut off from her, when ſhe had formed pleaſing views of their happineſs and comfort together. "Yet "let me not weep, ſaid the parent; rather "let me rejoice, and bleſs the goodneſs of "God! Had my child periſhed in her ſtate "of ſin, had ſhe been cut off amidſt proſtitu-"tion, diſeaſe, and miſery, what could have "ſupported my ſoul? Now, by the bleſſing "of this heavenly charity, I have ſeen her die "in ſuch a manner, that I cannot doubt her "happineſs with God. I will not weep for "thee, therefore, my child, my deareſt child! "bleſſed, for ever bleſſed be God, who has "ſaved thee from deſtruction, and reached out "his merciful hand to reſcue thee from woe "everlaſting! Bleſſed, for ever bleſſed be "thoſe, into whoſe hearts he put it to open "the doors of this houſe of repentance: may "theſe our benefactors for ever be bleſſed!

"And

"And may their good hearts be refreshed "with the knowledge of many, many daugh-"ters dying true penitents like mine: may "they live to have the constant and fervent "prayers of many, many parents made happy "like me!"

As it is impossible for me to add any thing to this real and interesting relation, (more affecting far, believe me, than I can describe) I will leave it with you: nothing doubting but as parents; as christians; as lovers of your country; as full of humanity and benevolence; you will all think yourselves engaged to support and encourage an undertaking, by which the aching hearts of so many parents are comforted; by which so many souls are saved; by which so many members are restored to industry and the state; by which every office of benevolence is discharged; the hungry fed, the naked cloathed, the stranger taken in, the sick relieved; eyes given to the blind, and feet to the lame: "for the worst of blindness, that of the mind, is removed, while the wandering feet are led into the paths of peace and virtue." * Who can be indif-

* See the preface to the History of the Penitents in the Magdalen House.

ſerent to an inſtitution productive of ſuch univerſal good? an inſtitution, to which we, my *brethren*, cannot refuſe our beſt aſſiſtance! many from motives of honour; all from motives of gratitude to that ever valuable ſex, without whom life would be vapid, and every labour irkſome †. Nor can *that amiable Sex* refuſe their beſt encouragement to an inſtitution, whoſe very foundation witneſſes an high regard for the intereſt of their ſex, and a tender concern for the diſtreſſes of that part of female individuals for whom we plead. The happy virtuous will learn to pity them, from a review of the comforts which they themſelves enjoy: ſo richly fed by the bounty of providence, they will not refuſe to theſe daughters of miſery the crumbs which fall

† If the price of a *good woman* is beyond gold: if the ſincereſt joys of life flow from the conduct of *virtuous women*; and the acuteſt miſeries from the *vicious* part of the ſex: were it poſſible to drop the conſideration of a future ſtate, the converting *bad* women into *good* ones, would be a work worthy the higheſt applauſe of *men*, as the converſion of ſinners is a ſubject of joy to *angels*. Even the conſciouſneſs of ſuch a *good intention* will aſſuredly advance their happineſs who attempt it."—*Hanway*'s Reflections, vol. 2. p. 284. See alſo p. 289.

from

from their table. Nor, while they readily admit the poſſibility of reformation in our ſex, will they teach us ſo ſevere a leſſon againſt themſelves, as to deny that poſſibility to any of their own: eſpecially, when ſecluded from the world; becauſe retirement naturally leads the mind to recollection, and gives an edge to ſerious reflections.

But why ſhould I urge thus much? It is enough, that you are *great*, that you are *benevolent*, that you are *chriſtians*, to aſſure us, that this inſtitution ſhall never want your ample ſuccour: An inſtitution indeed hitherto remarkably bleſt and honoured; and at whoſe religious and affecting ſervice in the *Chapel*, we have ſeen many a *noble* eye ſhed tears of pity and generoſity! tears, which have dignified nobility, and which ſpoke the heart *good* as well as great. Won by that ſervice, and the genuine piety of the penitential votaries there, many who came thither with far other intentions, have confeſſed the humanity of the undertaking; many who ſhall hereafter come, will own, we truſt, that their objections (if yet any objections remain) are done away, and their ſcruples ſilenced: while their hearts and their eyes teſtify a perfect approbation of a charity, in every reſpect conformable to the gofpel of Chrift, and in every view honourable to the times in which we live.

I cannot in juftice conclude, without faying, " and in every refpect honourable to *you*, its benign and unwearied fupporters, directors, and managers." From the happy knowledge of many of *you*, I have been enabled to draw that picture of the BENEVOLENT MAN, which I gave you at the beginning; for you exemplify the character. Go on in that work, the eftablifhment of which abundantly teftifies the goodnefs of your hearts, and the reality of your religion: the conduct of which abundantly teftifies the delicacy of your fentiments, and the ftrength of your judgments. Go on, fecure of the eftimation and applaufe of the virtuous and the valuable: fuperior to the little taunts of meaner thinkers; fuperior to all the oppofition which *weaknefs of underftanding*, or *malevolence of heart* would throw in your way. That charity is not perfect, which is intimidated or difcouraged by difficulties in the profecution of its juft and upright purpofes. Firm in your benevolence, and extenfive in your generous profpects, go on; and you will fee the good work profper under your hands. You are engaged in an honourable, a delightful enterprize. God is

for

for you, and he will crown your endeavours. You ſhall enjoy, what is infinitely beyond every other ſatisfaction, the fervent thankſgivings of many parents made happy by your means; you ſhall enjoy the bleſſing of many, once ready to periſh, but who, thro' your charity, are now reſcued from the depth of miſery and deſpair, and reſtored to hope and comfort. Induſtry, when it hears of it, ſhall praiſe you: your country ſhall hold your names in honour and eſteem. And, what is a conſideration far ſuperior to all, the great GOD, who looks down from heaven with peculiar complacency upon acts of love and benevolence, ſhall guard you with his more eſpecial protection in this world; and reward you, thro' the merits of his Son, with diſtinguiſhed honour in the world to come.

"Yes, bleſſed Lord, may they all inherit that glory! all who contribute to this chriſtian deſign! all who contribute to the reclaiming loſt ſouls! Oh may they all enjoy thy continued protection, thy peculiar favour! ſhield them in every danger; guide them in every difficulty: bleſs them in their going out, and their coming in: bleſs them in their domeſtic, bleſs them in their public life; bleſs them with all deſirable bleſſings

 below;

below; and bleſs them moſt, when moſt they want thy benediction—in the time of diſeaſe, and at the hour of death! Do thou, O God, make their beds in their ſickneſs: do thou, graciouſly ſuſtain them in their laſt agonies! And in the tremendous day of judgment, do thou kindly remember their works of mercy, and fulfil in their behalf, thine own moſt faithful promiſe, "That they who are wiſe, and turn many to righteouſneſs, ſhall ſhine as the brightneſs of the firmament, and as the ſtars for ever and ever!" *Amen.*

A SER-

A

SERMON,

ON

JEREMIAH, Chap. XIII. ver. 23.

Preached at the

CHAPEL

OF THE

MAGDALEN-HOUSE,

By *WILLIAM DODD*, M. A.

The SECOND EDITION.

JEREMIAH XIII. 23.

CAN THE ETHIOPIAN CHANGE HIS SKIN, OR THE LEOPARD HIS SPOTS? THEN MAY YE ALSO DO GOOD, WHO ARE ACCUSTOMED TO DO EVIL.

AS unpromiſing a Text as could have been pitched upon before the preſent Audience!—But, let us not judge too haſtily: The very reaſon, why I have choſen it, is becauſe it appears ſo unpromiſing, and becauſe perhaps, it is almoſt the only Text, which with any plauſibility can be urged againſt our preſent inſtitution; or thrown out to diſtreſs the minds, and diſcourage the endeavours of the Women, who fly to this place of refuge, to reform and reconcile themſelves to God. And I imagined, that it would be an acceptable ſervice, both to them, and to the ſupporters of this humane undertaking, to ſet forth at large the genuine ſenſe and meaning of this paſſage of Scripture; and conſequently to ſhew,

ſhew, That it by no means tends to diſcourage the good endeavours of the penitent; nor of thoſe, who, with true Chriſtian benevolence, open the door of mercy to ſuch.

Low and narrow minds, when they are not inclined to contribute to the ſupport of good and laudable undertakings, in order to ſecrete the true reaſon, and to ſcreen from notice their own littleneſs,—with a malevolence as baſe as it is mean,—are uſed to throw out objections, and to ſcandalize the work, which they mean not to encourage. While others, from a weakneſs of underſtanding; an ignorance of the Chriſtian Religion; and a fond deſire perhaps to cultivate the friendſhip of particular perſons, highly extol one charity, as ſuperlatively beſt: and with a diſingenuity, and a want of judgment and piety, not leſs pitiable than deſpicable, endeavour to eſtabliſh their own favourite, upon the diſcredit and ruin of all others. In this attempt they are as abſurd as the man, who ſhould endeavour to raiſe the reputation of his friend, upon the cenſure and reproach of all mankind.

Chriſtian Benevolence is a great, a noble, a godlike principle; which leads us to rejoice in Good, of all, of whatever kind; by whom-

ſoever,

ſoever, or whereſoever it be done. And when we ſee men exerting themſelves in compaſſionate and commendable undertakings, though the greatneſs and excellence of the deſign may not ſtrike us with equal force, as it ſtrikes them; yet our hearts ſhould give their approbation; and every generous tongue will ſay, "We wiſh you good luck in the name of the Lord."

Indeed, there is not the leaſt doubt, but that whenever men undertake charitable and kind works, for the comfort and advantage of their fellow-creatures, with ſincere and upright intentions, the bleſſing of God will attend them; and every Charity, good and uſeful in itſelf, and well meant, will meet with ſufficient encouragement, in our benevolent times;—will find Men of virtue ſufficient to aſſiſt, promote, and ſupport it; nor is there any manner of need to uſe little and deſingenuous arts, or to wiſh to riſe on the ruins of a rival.

Though this might be enough, and more than enough perhaps, to anſwer to men of this ſtamp, yet I muſt be allowed to add, that when they urge againſt the poſſibility of reforming the vicious, the Text of *Jeremiah*, *Can the Ethiopian change his ſkin, or the Leopard his*

his spots *? they seem to forget entirely "the nature and end of the Christian Religion;" while they reason unfairly, and make such an use of his words, as would shock the Prophet, should he hear them.

I. For, I would ask them in the *first* place, Is not the great, the characteristic blessing of the Christian Religion, "pardon of sin;"—free and full pardon of all sin, however great or complicated, upon true Faith and sincere Repentance? Did not Christ come into the world to save sinners? Was he not named *Jesus*, of the angel, because *he should save his people from their sins?* hath he not himself over and over declared in his Gospel, that He came to call Sinners to repentance; that therefore he conversed freely with them,—as a Physician is conversant with the sick, because they want his aid and healing medicine; which they do not, who are in perfect health? and are there not instances abundant on record, in the word of truth, of Sinners, habitual, grievous Sinners, not only admitted to our Lord's presence, but pardoned by Him?—nay, and becoming in consequence the greatest

* See p. 2—9 of Mr. *Hazeland's* Sermon, preached before the governors of the Asylum, in the year 1760.

peni-

penitents, and moſt exemplary believers? And hath not this been found the caſe in every age and period of Chriſtianity?

Conſider then, that, if you underſtand this Text of *Jeremiah* in its full extent, as implying as great an impoſſibility, that they who have been accuſtomed to do evil, ſhould ever do well, as it is for the Æthiopian to change his ſkin, or the Leopard his ſpots—which is indeed an utter impoſſibility:—If, I ſay, you underſtand the words in their ſtrict, literal ſenſe; Why then, farewell the comforts of the Goſpel of Chriſt! Farewell the glad tidings of pardon and peace to the penitent! Sinners are in a deſperate caſe indeed!—Chriſt hath died in vain; and all our preaching, and all our offers of his grace and mercy, are mere babbling; are idle and inſignificant!

This, with all Chriſtians, ſhould be a very ſufficient argument, in my mind, to prove, that the paſſage is not to be underſtood in this general and unreſtrained ſenſe. But indeed, we have another argument, and that a pretty ſtrong one too, to urge againſt this interpretation; and that is "Matter of fact:" The experience, not of Chriſtians only, but of others alſo, in almoſt every age of the world, undeniably aſſuring us that many, who have been

been accuſtomed, who *have learnt*, as the original is, *to do evil*, —(underſtand the phraſe in as ſtrong a ſenſe as you pleaſe) that many ſuch, have, on the other hand, *learnt*, and *accuſtomed* themſelves to do well.—It would be endleſs to produce inſtances: *Manaſſeh* and *Mary Magdalen* may properly be mentioned, becauſe I have dwelt upon their examples in this place. We cannot look into hiſtory, ſacred or profane, without ſufficient proof: Even the divine *Socrates*, the firſt, and greateſt maſter of the heathen World, fairly confeſſed the predominance of evil paſſions and habits, and his Victory over them: And Saint *Auſtin*, whoſe name and piety are almoſt one and the ſame, lived for above the thirty-firſt years of his life not only in the darkneſs of the worſt hereſies, but *accuſtomed*, habituated to the practice of the moſt ſenſual luſts.

But, not to dwell upon individuals, I would only aſk, What can be ſo ſtrong as Saint *Paul*'s words, to ſome of his converts, whom he ſpeaks of, not only as *accuſtomed* to, but even *dead* in treſpaſſes and ſins? Nay, he ranks *himſelf* in the ſame degree; "Even when *WE* were dead in ſin, he *quickened* us, together with Chriſt." And, writing to the Corinthians, he mentions ſome of the groſſeſt

crimes,

crimes, whereof he ſays, they once were guilty, tho' now reformed—" *Be not deceived; neither fornicators, nor adulterers, nor idolaters, nor effeminate, nor abuſers of themſelves with mankind, nor thieves, nor covetous, nor drunkards, nor revilers, nor extortioners, ſhall inherit the Kingdom of God.*" Here, it muſt be allowed, is a liſt of ſome of the worſt vices to which men can accuſtom themſelves. But theſe *Corinthians*, guilty of them, were not given up, as *deſperate.*—No; the Apoſtle adds, " *And ſuch were ſome of you;—But ye are waſhed, but ye are ſanctified, but ye are juſtified, in in the name of our Lord Jeſus, and by the Spirit of our God.*"

This teſtimony, it muſt be acknowledged, is deciſive: I will only add, that, in agreement with it, the primitive apologiſts for Chriſtianity always apply to this evidence of the truth of their Religion:—They appeal to the vicious, and habituated ſinners of every degree, who, thro' the grace of God in Chriſt, had been converted to a new and holy life. And they challenge their enemies to controvert this proof, as the inſtances were numerous, and continually before them;—Inſtances, of the unclean and impure becoming chaſte and virtuous; the drunkard,

ſober:

ſober; the churl, generous; the cruel and hard hearted, tender and compaſſionate; the diſhoneſt, faithful; and the idle, diligent. This, in truth, was no more than what the Prophet, in his elegant manner, foretold ſhould be the conſequence of the coming of the Prince of Righteouſneſs; when *the wolf ſhould dwell with the lamb, and the leopard lye down with the kid; the calf, and the young lion, and the fatling together, and a little child ſhould lead them*; * that is, Savage natures ſhould be tamed, and Chriſtian virtues reign there, where the fierceſt and moſt deſtructive paſſions were before predominant.—Nay, and to theſe examples, if need were, we could add ſome from the preſent houſe of reformation; of whoſe real repentance, and thorough change of heart and life, it would be impoſſible to doubt.

II. Having then ſhewn *what is not* the true ſenſe of the Text, it may be time to enquire *what is.*

Now, in the firſt place, I would obſerve, reſpecting the eaſtern ſtyle in general, that it is high and figurative, and abounds with ſtrong metaphors and alluſions, which muſt be reduced a good deal, before we can deter-

* Iſaiah, chap. xi. ver. 6, &c.

mine

mine their precife meaning.—Again, I obferve of the prophetic ftyle, that, as it is perhaps the moft fublime of all the eaftern writings, fo are the figures, metaphors and allufions in it not lefs bold, than they are beautiful and expreffive: But they make it difficult to be underftood, and fhould render us cautious in our reafonings upon it. An example of this you have in the paffage from *Ifaiah* juft quoted, refpecting the change of difpofitions, fignified by the taming of the wildeft animals. In another place, this fame Prophet has thefe remarkable words; "*The ftars of heaven, and the conftellations thereof fhall not give their light; The fun fhall be darkened in his going forth, and the moon fhall not caufe her light to fhine:*" * Which paffage they who are unacquainted with the genius of the prophetical writings, and their frequent reference to hieroglyphical ideas, would not readily underftand in its true and undoubted meaning, of the total deftruction of the civil and ecclefiaftical polity of the Jews.

I produce thefe examples only to fhew, how figurative the prophetic ftyle is, how lofty and elevated: and confequently how much we fhall miftake, by underftanding any fuch paffages in a merely literal fenfe. Now, read the

* See Chap. xiii. 10.

paffage

paſſage in hand, from *Jeremiah*, under theſe reſtrictions, and you will perceive, That it is an high and exaggerated expreſſion of the prophet, in his great wamth for the cauſe of God; implying only, that "after all the meſſages which God had ſent by him to the Jews;—after all the mercies which their God had ſhewn to them, they were ſo hard and ungrateful, that he could ſcarcely entertain a good hope of them."—And he ſtrives to arouſe, to awaken, to ſtimulate them, by the ſtrongeſt words and arguments poſſible.—"Can the Ethiopian change his ſkin, or the Leopard his ſpots? no, they cannot; and I fear there is almoſt as little reaſon to ſuppoſe, that you, who are ſo accuſtomed to do evil, to tranſgreſs and rebel againſt God, will ever learn to do well; will ever obediently return to him, and leave your idols, and your iniquity."

This is as much as we can fairly draw from the text; for, that it includes not an abſolute denial of the poſſibility of their return, every other chapter of *Jeremiah*'s propheſy clearly proves: In which he is continually exhorting them to repent, and to return to that God, who *will abundantly pardon:* and he uſes conſequently every argument, drawn from every conſideration, and from every paſ-

ſion,

ſion, which he conceived might become effectual. Nay, and the very laſt verſe in this ſame chapter is itſelf an undeniable teſtimony, that, he meant not to ſpeak of—that he did not by any means believe, the caſe of thoſe to whom he addreſſes himſelf, to be deſperate, or all hope of their amendment vain.

Upon this verſe I could be content to reſt the whole of the argument; for, nothing can be more full and more pathetic, than the prophet's expoſtulation in it; which, ſurely, would have been ridiculous and abſurd, had it been as utterly impoſſible for them to be made clean, to repent and reform, as for the Ethiopian to change his ſkin:—*I have ſeen thine adulteries, ſaith the Lord, and thine abominations on the hills in the fields*; thy ſpiritual adultery, that is, by which is meant *idolatry* throughout the prophets.—*Wo unto thee, O Jeruſalem! wilt thou not be made clean?* wilt thou not be purified and pardoned? *when ſhall it once be?*—The original is remarkably emphatical—*When once?* as if the tender mercies of God would not allow him utterance—while he vents his paternal deſires for their return in broken wiſhes, and earneſt longings, too vehement and affectionate to be expreſſed.—*When once?* " how long wilt thou refuſe to forſake thy unrighteouſneſs? As I live, ſaith the Lord, I have no pleaſure in the death of a ſinner, but that he ſhould repent, and live: wherefore, turn ye, turn ye from your evil ways, for why will ye die, O houſe of Iſrael * ?"

After all, it ſhould be particularly obſerved, not only that this paſſage is applied to the Jews of that day, with a peculiar force and propriety,—when their idolatries and crimes had been ſo many and aggravated, that they had wearied out the patience of God, who had now determined to puniſh them with a ſeventy years captivity; and therefore, it ſhould with great caution be applied or accommodated to any other perſons:—*This* is not only to be obſerved, but we muſt remark, that it is a proverbial expreſſion, and proverbs, we all know, are never to be received or underſtood in their extenſive ſenſe. They ſerve to convey general truths, but, applied to individuals, are often found not only falſe, but prejudicial. We might eaſily produce examples enow of this, from our own language, which abounds with proverbs; many of them wiſe and excellent; but, many of them cruel

* See Ezek. xxxiii. 11.

and

and malevolent; and by which, if we were to judge or act, we should wander far from the paths which Christian truth and benevolence would approve. Indeed it is a common rule with all commentators on the scriptures, never to strain proverbial expressions, but to soften and reduce them. There is a passage very pertinent to our subject in archbishop *Tillotson*'s Sermons, where, speaking of our Text, he says, "That this expression, of *the Ethiopian*, &c., is much to be mitigated, will appear, by considering some other like passages of scripture. As, where our Saviour compares the difficulty of a rich Man's salvation, to that which is naturally impossible,—*to a camel's passing through the eye of a needle*; Nay, he pitcheth his expression higher, and doth not only make it a thing of equal, but of greater difficulty: "I say unto you, it is *easier* for a camel to go through the eye of a needle, than for a rich man to enter into the Kingdom of God." And yet, when he comes to explain this to his disciples, he tells them, that he only meant, that the thing was very difficult; "*How hard* is it for those that have riches to be saved!"—and in another place, "for those that trust in riches!" and that it was not *impossible*, but, speaking according to human probability; *with men this is impoſſible, but not with God.* And thus alſo it is reaſonable to underſtand that ſevere paſſage of the Apoſtle to the Hebrews. " It is impoſſible for them, who were once enlightened, &c. if they fall away, to renew them again to repentance :" * It is *impoſſible*, that is, it is *very difficult.*

In like manner we are to underſtand this high expreſſion, (which is very hyperbolical.) " Can the Ethiopian change his ſkin, or the Leopard his ſpots ? then may ye alſo do good, who are accuſtomed to do evil :" that is, This moral change of men ſettled and fixed in bad habits, is very difficult : though,—as the archbiſhop goes on to ſhew,—there is great ground and hope of encouragement that it *may* be done : And, when we conſider the Chriſtian Religion, and the power of divine grace, there is all the reaſon in the world to believe that it *will* be done, when we heartily ſet about it, and uſe every neceſſary and proper endeavour."

But I remark once more, that the Text itſelf may be tranſlated and underſtood differently. You will obſerve, by referring to your Bibles, that the word *then* is printed in

* Heb. vi. 4, 6.

Italic characters; which is always a certain mark, that there is nothing for the word so printed in the original Hebrew: and I conceive the passage may well be understood thus —*Can the Ethiopian? &c.* No: that is impossible:—*BUT you who have been accustomed to do evil, may learn to do well:*—and for this purpose he proceeds, *Therefore will I punish you with* temporal trials and afflictions, to bring you to this true repentance: And he adds in conclusion, *How long? when will this* true reformation and repentance take place?—Many similar methods of expression might be produced from the prophets *; But I lay no stress on this criticism, as the former arguments are quite sufficient to shew the genuine sense of the passage.

Thus then, what I have urged will, I hope, serve abundantly to remove all objections which may arise from this Text, against attempts to reform the vicious, when made either by themselves or others: And I have been led to these remarks, thro' a zeal for that first and most benign of all truths,—the

* "Can a Woman forget her sucking child, that she should not have compassion on the son of her Womb? &c. Yet will I not forget thee." Isaiah xlix. 15.

 free

free and perfect pardon of every penitent's ſins, thro' faith in Chriſt Jeſus;—that *Chriſt Jeſus, who came into the world to ſave ſinners!* Thus, pleading the cauſe of every one who acknowledges the want of this glorious ſalvation, againſt the ſelf-righteous and phariſees of our days; who would repeat the old objection againſt the Diſciples, which *they* of former times made againſt the Maſter; (and indeed it is enough for the diſciples if *they be as the maſter*)—"Why do you eat, why do you converſe with publicans and ſinners?" "They that be whole, ſaid the divine Redeemer, (and, in ſo ſaying, he hath inſtructed *us* what to reply)—need not a phyſician; but they who are ſick: But go ye, and learn what that meaneth, I will have mercy, and not ſacrifice: for, I am not come to call the righteous,—the ſelf-righteous and ſelf-juſtified—but ſinners to repentance." *

1. Theſe are declarations from the lips of infinite love, who lived and who died to ſave us. ſweeter ſurely to the penitent ſoul, ſweeter ſurely to all *YOUR* ſouls, than honey to the taſte, or the moſt raviſhing muſic to the ears!—Declarations, which muſt not only comfort you, under every gloom of doubt and uneaſineſs; but encourage you to perſevere,

* See Page 72 foregoing.

unfaint-

unfainting and unwearied, in the good way you have chosen; till your perseverance is crowned, and your happiness secured, beyond the reach of time or chance. Since nothing might be supposed so discouraging to your endeavours, and so afflicting to your souls, if really desirous to recover the lost favour of God,—as to be told, that all such endeavours were fruitless, and that it was as impossible for you to reform, as for the Ethiopian to change his skin, or the Leopard his spots; I have therefore been at the more pains to remove this discouragement; and so to assure you, that, thro' the grace and mercy of Christ, no impediments lye in your way to salvation, except such as may be laid by your own irregular passions and irresolute efforts. For, let me not by any means deceive you, nor do you on any account deceive yourselves, by imagining, that you have no difficulties to encounter, no efforts to use.—— Far, very far from this is the case.—Tho' salvation thro' Christ, is freely offered to all who will repent, believe, and amend their lives; tho' none are excluded from that general act of grace, which the Saviour procured by his own blood; tho' sins, deep in their dye as the crimson, and numerous as the ſtars in the firmament, thro' that omnipotent grace will be cancelled and done away; Yet, let us forever remember, that in conſequence of ſuch forgiveneſs of the paſt, we muſt labour for the future to ſhew forth the fruits of repentance and faith. We muſt not only ceaſe to do evil, but learn to do well; not only abandon all our former ways of iniquity, but ſerve God in righteouſneſs and holineſs all the future days of our life. And though it is undeniably certain, that God's grace, co-operating with our own beſt endeavours, is all-powerful to ſubdue and to change the worſt natures, and the worſt habits; yet it is undeniable, that great watchfulneſs and care is required on our parts, in this beſt of combats. For, bad habits and cuſtoms are ſtubborn, and not ſubdued with idle, indifferent and feeble efforts. We muſt exert all our ſtrength; we muſt apply to God for his continual aid; and while we ſtand upon our guard, in the regular uſe of all the means of grace, in the right diſcharge of our proper duties, in the performance of all things required from us, habits of virtue will then gain the aſcendency. And, ſo lovely, ſo amiable, ſo correſpondent to our nature, are goodneſs and virtue, that we need not fear,

when

when once we have tafted their delights, and made them habitual to us, that we fhall ever be induced to forfake them entirely; fhall ever be fuch enemies to ourfelves, as to quit the fountain of living waters, for the impure and unrefrefhing ftreams of poifonous vice.

2. As this houfe, MY BELOVED, was firft opened to give the objects of our prefent concern an opportunity to reform; So, their continuance here for a certain term is fixed, that they may acquire habits of virtue and induftry. And, bleffed be God, the fuccefs which has hitherto attended the inftitution, gives us no room to doubt, that the reformation of many will by this means be perfected, and fuch habits of virtue and induftry acquired, as will, thro' the divine grace, be fufficient to eftablifh them firmly in the good refolutions they have taken.—You have heard, my brethren, you yourfelves are well fatisfied, how conformable the prefent humane undertaking is, to that great and moft exalted purpofe, which caufed the Son of God "to be cloathed with human flefh and frailty; namely, that he might fave from inevitable ruin a perifhing race of creatures." And while you ferioufly reflect upon your own many imperfections and frequent deviations from the pure

law of God, you will never be defirous to with-hold that mercy from others, whereof we all ftand fo much in need: you will never be forward to clofe the door of forgivenefs and grace upon any of your fellow-creatures, knowing in how many things we offend all; and that if God fhould be extreme to mark what we have done amifs, few of us fhould be able to anfwer before him! Truth it is, and it would be well, if, according to our feveral connections, we would pay a ftrict attention to that truth,—That great is the danger of contracting, and great the difficulty of conquering, evil habits and vicious cuftoms. This fhould render us very jealous over our own fouls, and particularly anxious not to fuffer corrupt and improper paffions to grow prevalent and habitual: while, for our children, or thofe any way related to us, we fhould ufe every wife and reafonable effort, to tincture the young mind with the pureft and moft lafting tafte of religion and virtue; to inftil every lovely principle of purity and truth; that fo they may avoid the groffer offences, and pafs thro' life, with a ferene application to that law and that love, which is perfect freedom and perfect peace.

But

But, while thus careful to do all we can to guard ourſelves and others from the ſubtle ſnares of vice, to which a corrupted nature and an alluring world are continually tempting; We ſhould be as careful, on the other hand, not to cloſe the golden door of mercy, which the Son of God himſelf came down from heaven to open: We ſhould be careful not to caſt the unhappy offenders into deſpondency and deſpair; nor with a ſeverity which is as dangerous as it is unſeemly in mortals, diſcourage the convicted ſinner from attempts to reform. From ſuch attempts, we have ſeen, good may always be expected; even the reformation of the vileſt ſinners ſhould never be deſpaired of. For, it is certain, that there is left, even in the worſt of men, a natural ſenſe of the evil and unreaſonableneſs of ſin, which can hardly ever be totally extinguiſhed in human nature; and when ſuch have any thoughts of becoming better, they are apt to conceive good hopes of God's grace and mercy: and when once they reſolve, who knows not how great the power of a fixed reſolution? who knows not what man can do, when urged to it by an almoſt invincible determination *?—Well ſaid *Pythagoras*—

* See Abp. *Tillotſon.*

"that power and neceſſity are neighbours, and never dwell far from each other."

Add to this, that the grace of God is never to be deemed unattainable by us; and to that grace, which they, who ſincerely aſk it, ſhall certainly obtain, all things are poſſible.—Conſiderations theſe, which will ſerve to convince us, that the reformation of the greateſt, moſt hardened and inveterate ſinners, may well be expected: Much more, the reformation of ſuch as theſe before you, who have many circumſtances to offer, in alleviation of their guilt.—True, they have been accuſtomed to do evil; but, they have gained one ſignal victory, in that they have expreſſed their deſire to do good. This is no trifling circumſtance; they are not compelled to come in hither: it is the act of their own voluntary choice; an act which witneſſes, that they are weary of their paſt crimes, and deſirous to repent and amend; and Moraliſts have always eſteemed it the firſt ſtep to virtue, to have fled wholly from the practice of vice.

Bear with me too a few minutes longer, while I obſerve in behalf of theſe unhappy Women, and to ſhew that they deſerve not to be ranked amongſt veteran and incorrigible ſinners,

ſinners,—That many of them have never had the bleſſed and unſpeakable advantages of a ſerious and religious Education, the tender care of parents, and the wiſe directions of ſolicitous friends; but, left to be toſt on the billows of the world, they have been ſhipwrecked on vice; and no wonder, having no pilot to ſteer them aright. Others again, have been deluded into the road of ruin by the moſt flattering and deluſive promiſes, ſuch as few unſuſpecting hearts might have withſtood; and when undone, have been left by their cruel ſeducers, a miſerable prey to infamy and diſtreſs: and ſome ſo young, ſo very young, that it is impoſſible to conceive their minds hardened againſt all good impreſſions; —Nay indeed, many, I might ſay the moſt part of thoſe who have entered here, have ſhewn themſelves ſo far from being hardened, that they have expreſſed the utmoſt deteſtation of their way of life; and ſome, ſuch tender and affecting ſentiments, as would do no diſcredit to unpolluted virtue.

But alas! wretched and ruined, introduced to ſhame and ſorrow, reputation and virtue loſt, caſt off and abandoned by all—whither could they fly, or where obtain relief? They cannot, muſt not utterly periſh in want and

naked-

nakedneſs:—perhaps too, the anguiſh and misfortunes of ſome of them have been aggravated, by the neceſſity of ſupporting a little hapleſs infant, heir of its mother's infamy and ſuffering! Dreadful alternative to the mother, either to ſee her child, her much loved, though unfortunate child, periſh with hunger and with thirſt,—or to obtain its ſupport by the horror of proſtitution! yet to this dire neceſſity many broken-hearted mothers have been reduced! and thus the beſt and moſt tender parental affection has reigned in the woman's breaſt, while the poor afflicted wretch has been compelled to a way of life moſt deteſtable and ſhocking to her!

You would not doubt of the reformation of ſuch a one, if an opportunity to reform and to regain her credit in the world could be given her. But *here*, and *here only*, ſuch an opportunity is given; an opportunity, already embraced by many, and by many, we have the utmoſt reaſon to believe, truly improved.—I could eaſily mention many circumſtances more, to ſhew how great objects of compaſſion theſe women are; but I have already treſpaſſed too much on your patience: Let me only add, that one chance, at leaſt, for reformation and life, ſhould unqueſtionably be be given in a christian and humane country, like ours, to every sinner, however guilty; and no chance, no possible chance for repentance and amendment of life *is given* to these sinners, (whether more guilty than many others we enquire not now)—No other chance, but what this house of mercy affords, is given to those who once were the objects of solicitude and tender care; and who, even if betrayed by their own passions, have been betrayed by passions the most prevalent and universal—such, as we ought not to condemn too severely; and with a view to which our Saviour's words may be applied, "Let that person, who is without sin, unconscious of any irregular desire or gratification in this way, let that person cast the first stone at her *."

When we dwell upon these and the like considerations, as Christians we shall rejoice in so beneficent an undertaking; we shall pray for its success; we shall highly esteem its humane and generous Patrons and Governors, for their compassion and disinterested zeal for the salvation of their fellow-creatures: and we shall justly rank it amongst the greatest blessings of our lives, that we have an

* John viii. 7.

ability and an opportunity to concur in ſo good a deſign; nay, and to be fellow workers with our adorable Saviour, in that moſt important of all works—abundantly proved ſuch by the manner in which he condeſcended to perfect it—"The recovery and reſtoration of thoſe who were loſt to ſin, and dead to their God."—To encourage us in which, let us, in concluſion, hear what the Lord himſelf ſaith to us.—"Incline your ear, and come unto me: hear, and your ſoul ſhall live: ſeek the Lord, while he may be found; call upon him while he is near. Let the wicked forſake his way, and the unrighteous man his thoughts; and let him return unto the Lord, and *he* will have mercy upon him; and to our God, for he will abundantly pardon *."

* Iſaiah lv. 3, 6, 7.

A

SERMON,

ON

ZECHARIAH, Chap. iv. Ver. 7.

Preached in

CHARLOTTE-STREET CHAPEL,

JULY the 28th, 1769.

BEFORE THE

PRESIDENT, VICE-PRESIDENTS, TREASURER, AND GOVERNORS

OF THE

MAGDALEN-HOSPITAL,

ON LAYING

The FIRST STONE of their NEW BUILDING,
In ST. GEORGE'S-FIELDS, SOUTHWARK.

By *WILLIAM DODD*, LL. D.

The THIRD EDITION.

ZECHARIAH iv. 7.

AND HE SHALL BRING FORTH THE HEAD-STONE THEREOF WITH SHOUTINGS; CRYING, "GRACE, GRACE UNTO IT!"

IT has been a cuſtom, no leſs general than commendable, to implore, by a ſolemn Dedication, the protection of God towards thoſe works of PIETY and HUMANITY, which are erected to his Glory. Nothing can be more magnificent and awful, than the account handed down to us, of the Dedication of the *firſt* Temple at *Jeruſalem*, by *Solomon*: The *ſecond* was conſecrated with equal Piety, though with much leſs ſplendour; and it is to that event the Prophet alludes in the Text; aſſuring *Zerubbabel*, one of the leaders of the people from the *Babyloniſh* Captivity, that he ſhould accompliſh the great work which he had in commiſſion; that by the power of the Lord, he ſhould riſe ſupe-

rior

rior to every difficulty, and remove every obſtruction which might lie in the way: The *great Mountain before him ſhould become a plain*; and, triumphant over every obſtacle, he ſhould *bring forth the Head-ſtone with Shoutings:* He ſhould place the *top*, or *finiſhing-ſtone* upon the walls of the Temple; while the people with joyful acclamations ſhould cry, "*Grace, Grace unto it!*"

The prophetical aſpect of this paſſage is to the *Meſſiah*, figuratively repreſented by the *Head* or *Corner-ſtone*; whom God was hereafter to bring into the world, as the finiſhing ornament and perfection of the Church; who is ſpoken of by the writers of the New-Teſtament as the *Chief Corner-ſtone, elect, precious* *; and of whom it is ſaid, That *the Grace of God was upon him* †, and that he *was in favour with God and Man* ‡.

It is to this two-fold *favour*, of *God* and of *Man*, that the undertaking wiſhes to lay claim, which we are this day aſſembled to promote; and for the perfect eſtabliſhment of which, we are preparing to lay the foundation of that building, the *head-ſtone* where-

* 1 Pet. ii. 6. † Luke ii. 40. ‡ Ib. v. 52.

of,

of, we doubt not, will in due time be *brought forth with ſhoutings*; with the pious acclamations of all ſincere and well-diſpoſed Chriſtians, *crying*, with true and undiſſembled zeal, "*Grace, Grace unto it!*—May the favour of GOD continually protect, may the favour of man continually diſtinguiſh this Houſe of Mercy!"

For, if PIETY may demand ſuch acclamations, where can they be given more properly, than to a work, whoſe diſtinguiſhing characteriſtic is that *Piety?*—The very chief and Corner-ſtone of whoſe foundation, is laid upon that firſt and eſſential truth of *Chriſtian Religion*, "The ſalvation of Sinners, upon their true repentance?"

Other charities have, undoubtedly, their claim to the public protection, from the ſingular humanity of their deſigns, and from the ſalutary *comfort* which they adminiſter to the *diſtreſſes* of the *Body*; — But, the peculiar praiſe of the preſent inſtitution is, that while it has an equal claim with others, to regard, from its HUMANITY, (as we ſhall ſoon ſee.) It, *alone*, of all others, brings comfort to the wounded *Mind*; relieves the unutterable anguiſh

guiſh of a bleeding conſcience * ; and affords, through the pardoning Grace of Chriſt, that *peace to the Soul*, which wanting, every hope of worldly peace and ſatisfaction is vain.

So ſuperior is the *Soul*, and ſo exquiſite and important its pleaſures, and its pains, that a Charity attentive to *its* welfare only, would certainly claim the higheſt favour from rational and immortal Beings : But, while peculiarly attentive to the great concerns of the *Soul*, our Inſtitution is by no means indifferent to thoſe of the *Body* ; and I think we may fairly pronounce, that more horrible and diſtreſsful Miſery cannot fall within the reach of human mercy, than that which is the object of this admirable Inſtitution.

Called upon ſo often to plead in this cauſe, I have painted again and again, the melancholy picture of female Suffering, in a life of involuntary Proſtitution ; and I perſuade myſelf, that there is not an heart, ſoftened at all by the feelings of Humanity, which is not both ſenſible of, and deſirous to relieve, far it is able, the *complicated* ſorrows which croud around the wretched Female, unhappily ſe-

* Prov. xviii. 14.

duced

duced from virtue and from duty, and cruelly left to wander in the dark and dreadful labyrinth of ruinous Vice. " An *inextricable Labyrinth*," it might well be called, before the establishment of this Charity. And no doubt it was the general, just and humane sense of this difficulty, and these distresses, which, when the Charity was proposed, raised in the public so great an approbation of it; and procured it a supply, liberal beyond what almost any other charitable undertaking experienced, in the same compass of time.

The peculiarity of the undertaking, the delicacy necessary for the right conduct of it, the nature of the objects, and other circumstances, raised, as might well be expected, *doubts* and *fears*, *hesitations* and *objections*; and perhaps the most sanguine espousers of the good design, were not without their anxieties. *Time and experience* were what alone could answer objections, or silence scruples: *Time* and *experience* we have had; We may say, in the prophetical language, that by *God's Grace*, they have levelled the *great mountains before us into a plain*; that they have removed our *doubts* and *scruples*: For now, after above *ten Years* trial, we can with the utmost confidence declare the great utility of the undertaking,

taking, and the ſingular advantages, derived from it, to many of the moſt miſerable and forlorn of our fellow-creatures; who, in all human probability, without its aid, would long ere now have periſhed—*Soul* and *Body* have periſhed, in horrible diſtreſs, beyond the reach of deſcription.

Indeed, nothing could be wanting, to convince in the fulleſt manner every heart, of the Propriety, the Utility, the abſolute Neceſſity of this Charity, more than a ſight of thoſe pitiable Objects, who, with fervent Prayers and Tears implore at its gates for admiſſion; for refuge from thoſe ſtorms of unutterable ſorrow, which have overwhelmed them; for refuge from a life the moſt foul and deteſtable; from devouring diſeaſe; from heart-oppreſſing poverty; from infamy, cold, and nakedneſs! from the horrors of a guilty, ſelf-convicted, dark, diſconſolate mind; from the dire terrors of approaching death, and all the fearful apprehenſions of a juſtly-incenſed and omnipotent Avenger!

Of ſufferers like theſe, more or leſs calamitous, upwards of a *thouſand* have been received by the MAGDALEN CHARITY ſince its inſtitution; above half of whom have been reconciled to, and received by their friends,

or

or placed in trades, or in reputable ſervices. A gratuity is given to ſuch as continue in their firſt place a year and a day, to the ſatisfaction of thoſe they ſerve; and we have the pleaſure to find, that many have claimed and received this gratuity. Beſides thoſe ſo provided for, ſeveral poor unhappy wretches, from the fatal conſequences of a life of Proſtitution, have proved *Lunaticks*, and afflicted with incurable Fits; for whom alſo the benevolence of the Charity hath provided, in the beſt manner their melancholy circumſtances would admit. Several have finiſhed their courſe while under the care of the Charity; ſome of them departing this life in the moſt exemplary manner, with humble acknowledgements, almoſt on their dying lips, "That to this Inſtitution, under God, they owed every hope of pardon and peace eternal, through Jeſus Chriſt, the *Friend of penitent Sinners*." Sixty-five of thoſe who have left the Houſe, are ſince married, and ſeveral of them live in great decency and credit: Some of them, to the inexpreſſible ſatisfaction of thoſe intereſted in the ſucceſs of this good Work, have appeared, with their Huſbands and their Infants at the MAGDALEN HOUSE;

gratefully offering up their acknowledgements to God and their Benefactors, for every present bleſſing, and every future expectation conveyed to them by His Mercy, through the means of this Charity.

Of the reſt, ſeveral have been diſmiſſed the Houſe for faults and irregularities, as was certainly to be expected; ſome, from uneaſineſs under reſtraint, or at their own deſire; others, for ſmall offences, petulancies of temper, and diſagreements one with another, which rendered their continuance in the Houſe impracticable. Yet, even many of theſe (influenced, we hope, by the proper inſtructions they have received) rather than return to their former evil courſe of life, have gone into honeſt and induſtrious employments and ſervices, and now live with reputation.

As, after this detail, it is impoſſible to doubt of the Piety and Humanity of the undertaking; ſo is it no leſs impoſſible to doubt of YOUR good diſpoſitions towards it. For, when you conſider, that of theſe thouſand fellow creatures, in all probability the whole, or the far greater part, without the intervention of this Charity, would not only ere now have been loſt, but before they were loſt, would have lived diffuſing contagion and deſtruction:

ſtruction: When you conſider that of theſe the greater part (we perſuade ourſelves) have been ſaved by this Charity; ſaved to the Community, and made uſeful to it; ſaved to be long uſeful to it, — as the Objects admitted have, in general, been very young: When you conſider, that ſuch is the peculiar circumſtance of their Diſtreſs, that it was ſcarce poſſible to have ſaved them by any other method, —— no other mode of Relief, than an united Charity like the preſent, being able to reach their wretched Caſe; — When you conſider theſe things, You will aſſuredly ſay, That if not *Half*—if a *Quarter* only, if a *tenth Part* of theſe poor, unfortunate, deluded young Women, had been ſaved by this Inſtitution, it were well deſerving the high Encouragement it hath met with; it had amply repaid the zeal and attention of its more immediate Directors; and that it well became every humane and ſincere Chriſtian, to unite his beſt endeavours, in order to give it a firm and laſting Foundation.

It is with this hope, and with this intention, that we are *now* aſſembled, to implore the favour of the great God, the Giver of all ſucceſs, on that Work, which, we truſt, will give ſtability to the preſent Deſign.

 After

After ſo long experience of the *uſefulneſs* of our Charity, it has been reſolved to raiſe a *proper Building* for its more commodious management. *That* wherein it hath hitherto been conducted, though ſuitable enough for the firſt Eſſay of an Undertaking, in ſome degree doubtful, was yet, on many accounts, inconvenient; not only from the nature of the Building itſelf, confined, ruinous, and expenſive; but from the remoteneſs of the ſituation, * and various other circumſtances, which have been long and ſenſibly felt. A new Building, therefore, was not more neceſſary than deſirable: The intereſts of the Charity on every account called for it; and the zeal of its Friends, ever attentive to its true intereſts, has at length, not only reſolved to raiſe ſuch Building, but carried that Reſolution into act by generous Subſcriptions, and by prudent and cautious meaſures to employ thoſe Subſcriptions with the ſtricteſt œconomy. A neat, plain, and commodious Houſe, ſufficient for the Reception of more than *Two Hundred Objects*, but capable of being enlarged at pleaſure, together with a convenient Chapel for divine Service, has

* In Preſcot-Street, Goodman's-Fields.

been

been agreed for *; and, in order to carry on the Work with due ſpeed and propriety, a time is limited for the completion of it †: And *this Day* appointed for the laying the Foundation of that Houſe, the TOP-STONE whereof we hope to ſee brought forth, in due ſeaſon, with the joyful Acclamations of "*Grace, Grace unto it!*" "May the favour of God for ever protect and bleſs it. May the favour of Man for ever watch over, and pour forth the Succours of Benevolence and Charity upon it."

Yes, my Brethren, *This*, I am aſſured, will ever be *your* Prayer, who, with ſo zealous and perſevering an attention, have watched over the concerns of this truly chriſtian Charity, from the time of its Infancy, to the preſent hour! You will not remit, I am perſuaded, of that attention: for you have the good work in your Hearts; and, actuated by the beſt and nobleſt Principles—Love to God, and Love to your Fellow creatures,—will no leſs rejoice in this happy hour, which pro-

* See the Plan. The Sum ſtipulated for the Building is 5640l.

† The Building is (by Contract) to be compleated by Michaelmas, 1770.

mifes a ftability to the Object of your benevolent Care, than you will continue your generous efforts to guide, protect, improve, and perfect that Object.

Oh! could my poor Prayers or Wifhes avail, not only fhould that Object reward your folicitude with continued fuccefs; not only fhould your good hearts every day be refrefhed with the fight and knowledge of the moft abject and miferable, reftored to life, to Happinefs, and God, by your inftrumentality: but, thofe hearts fhould every Day find increafing fatisfaction by the Love of God increafing in them; and by a glorious Augmentation of Favour both with *Him*, and with *Man*, as the juft, the pleafing return of your *Piety* to the one, your *Humanity* to the other!

Nor will you, my beloved, refufe, I am fatisfied, your Atteftation to merit of this kind. For fhall they be celebrated in the annals of time, and by the flattering tongues of Orators and Poets, *they*, whofe greateft glory is the devaftation of their fpecies, and who are counted the more illuftrious, the deeper they have dyed their hands in *human Blood*: — while the milder Virtues of Humanity and Benevolence pafs unnoticed and unfung?

ſung? Or ſhall they, who, with unbounded philanthropy, continually labour to preſerve, and to bleſs their fellow-creatures lives, be counted as nothing in compariſon of thoſe who diſtreſs and deſtroy them?—It may be ſo in the ſight of falſe-judging MAN; it is not ſo in the ſight of GOD. It will not be ſo, my beloved, in *your* ſight, who, humanized by the precepts of a meek and merciful Redeemer, know well how to eſtimate, how to praiſe, and I doubt not, how to *imitate* and *aſſiſt*, the truly laudable endeavours of godlike Charity.

Nor is there a motive whereby the human heart can be influenced, which, in the preſent caſe will not operate ſtrongly upon you. The Example of ſo many of your fellow-creatures zealous and active in the good cauſe: the peculiarly pitiable and diſtreſsful circumſtances of the Objects propoſed for your Relief: the impoſſibility of their procuring relief by any other method: the propriety, the ſtrict propriety of giving every Sinner, in a land of evangelical Light and Mercy, a chance to recover themſelves from the error of their way; a ſingle chance at leaſt, which, without the interpoſition of this Charity, is utterly denied to theſe wretched Women:—the vaſt profpect of probable Good, which may be communicated; Good to the Soul, Good to the Body; Good to the Community; prefent and eternal Good: — the extenfive and affecting influence which this Charity may have on others; on the Parents, the Relations, and the whole circle in any degree connected with the Objects themfelves:—— *Thefe*, and a variety of confiderations and motives like thefe, muft have their weight with every ingenuous mind, muft awaken your liberality towards the affiftance of fo ufeful an Undertaking, muft raife at leaft a defire in your hearts to lay one Stone in a Building fo eminently confecrated to Humanity and Piety.

For generous and liberal as the affiftance of the humane and beneficent has hitherto been, there is yet wanting a further fupply to crown the Work. And let me truft, my Brethren, that you will not be backward to throw in your Aid, and to diftinguifh this day, and this *Place* *, which now, for the very firft time fince its erection, calls upon you for the difplay of your Charity, for the

* *Charlotte-Street* Chapel had not been long opened: and no Charity Sermon had ever yet been preached in it. —

tefti-

teſtimony of your Faith. And can you require a more Chriſtian, a more pious, a more humane Inſtitution, for the exerciſe of that Charity, for the teſtimony of that Faith? I attempt not to perſuade or to move your paſſions in this cauſe, which is itſelf ſo good, and carries with it, in the plain *fact*, ſuch force of reaſon and perſuaſion, That it needs only to be recommended to obtain the general Approbation.

Indeed, it would be eaſy to move your paſſions, and to affect your hearts, as well by a detail of truly pitiable and intereſting events, which the ſtory of many of theſe unfortunate wanderers affords; as by a variety of circumſtances, which have attended both their admiſſion and their future ſettlement in Life. But, not to dwell upon theſe, I would wiſh only to recommend to attention, the plain unadorned fact, the real ſtate of the caſe before us.

Luſt and Vice prevail, and will prevail: numberleſs ſacrifices to them are continually made; unrelenting paſſion, regardleſs of their woes, introduces, yearly, numbers of innocent young creatures to the moſt deplorable and diſtreſsful difficulties: they are in the utmoſt peril of utter perdition,—preſent and eternal perdition; and are without a chance of eſcaping, if tender-hearted charity hold not forth her Relief! — Would you then ſuffer ſuch miſerable young Creatures (ſeduced by all the arts of ſerpentine craft into the paths of ruin) to wander in thoſe Paths, 'till they are utterly loſt; to periſh in miſeries, which imagination itſelf can ſcarce conceive: — Or, would you reach out the helping hand of chriſtian Pity, and give theſe young, deſerted, periſhing Fellow-creatures, and Fellow-chriſtians "*one ſingle chance*," to ſave their Lives; to ſave their Souls; to recover Health, Virtue, Happineſs, Friends, Parents, Country? In ſhort to recover Life from the Dead; Hope and Salvation from Deſtruction and Deſpair!

This is the great point of view, in which our Undertaking wiſhes to be ſeen. And ſeen in this view, as it cannot fail to obtain the approbation of every Chriſtian, every humane, every thinking heart; ſo will it for ever find the protection and encouragement, which it hath hitherto ſo amply found: and which, we truſt, it will ſtill, be the charitable labour, as it is aſſuredly the trueſt Glory and Happineſs of the pious and the worthy to give it.

" Yes, GREAT GOD, whose favour alone can give stability and success to the endeavours of feeble Man ; Thou wilt continue to support with thy Blessing this Charity, which *we* have seen so happily begun, and, so fortunately prospered, to the present hour! Vouchsafe on this auspicious Day, to hear and to receive the Prayers of thy humble servants! And while we bless thee with unfeigned hearts for all the Good which thou hast hitherto enabled us to perfect, through this Work, (for which *All Glory*, *All Praise*, be to *Thee* !) Oh, crown with thy assisting Grace, and further with thy sovereign protection, our present Attempt, to give that Work stability ! Bless all those concerned in the Undertaking ; enable them to *bring forth the Top Stone with Joy* : and may we, with all the sincerity of grateful Thanksgiving, beholding its Perfection, *shout forth*, " *Grace, Grace unto it !*" Grace on the heads of all who have charitably united to erect the House of Mercy ! Grace on the Heads of all who partake the Mercies of that House ; Grace on the Heads of all, who shall ever enter within it; Grace, Grace unto it! an abundance of divine and human Favour, to give it Perpetuity and Perfection !

Frail, feeble, and ſhort-lived as *we* are, our day will ſoon be over, and our humble endeavour (O Father of Mercies) to aſſiſt our Fellow-creatures muſt reſt with Thee! But Thou, who *inhabiteſt Eternity*, art the Almighty Jehovah, for ever the ſame: Ceaſe not, therefore, thy paternal care, and love; grant to this Charity the perpetual regard of thine eſpecial Providence; and raiſe up, we beſeech Thee, through ſucceſſive generations, faithful Servants of Thine to protect and favour it; when Thoſe, who *now* watch over it, are receiving their Reward with Thee in Glory!

Thou knoweſt, Lord, *the Secrets of all Hearts!* Thou knoweſt, and wilt reward the Uprightneſs of our Intentions: To Thee, therefore, we commit ourſelves, and this good Work, in which we are engaged; intreating thee to behold it with thine Eye of Mercy; and to accept this Tribute of "our bounden Duty and Service, not weighing our Merits, but pardoning our Infirmities, through Jeſus Chriſt our Lord." *Amen.*

ADVICE

TO THE

MAGDALENS.

HEAR COUNSEL, AND RECEIVE INSTRUCTION, THAT THOU MAYEST BE WISE IN THY LATTER END.

PROV. xix. 20.

The SIXTH EDITION.

To the READER.

AS this piece was written and intended ſolely for the uſe of the MAGDALENS; the judicious Reader, it is hoped, will not only excuſe, but ſee the propriety of uſing plain language, and more repetition, than could be juſtified in a work deſigned for the Public in general.

ADVICE

TO THE

MAGDALENS.

As I live, ſaith the Lord God, I have no pleaſure in the death of the wicked; but that the wicked turn from their way and live: turn ye, turn ye, from your evil ways; for why will ye die? Ezekiel xxxiii. 11.

If ye ſo turn, *though your ſins be as ſcarlet, they ſhall be white as ſnow; though they be red like crimſon, they ſhall be as wool.* Iſaiah i. 18.

For, *God ſo loved the world, that he gave his only begotten Son, that whoſoever believeth in him ſhould not periſh, but have everlaſting life.* John iii. 16.

IT is with the greateſt ſatisfaction that we take the opportunity you give us, to lay before you theſe ſolemn and moſt comfortable declarations of the Almighty King of Heaven and Earth, the Lord of Truth, whoſe word never faileth. The happy choice you have made, and your voluntary entrance into this Houſe, fills us with good hope that you are ſenſible of your paſt miſerable ſtate, and willing to recover the loſt favour of God and your Fellow-creatures. If ſuch be your diſpoſition, you will here find every

every thing conducive to that desirable end; and we can assure you with pleasure, that no encouragement shall be wanting, to promote your present and future felicity.

But, that you may neither mistake the design of this charitable institution, nor pervert its good intention, it is necessary solemnly to inform you of that design, and of what is expected from you. And we desire that you would seriously and often reflect upon what we deliver to you; and that you would endeavour, as exactly as you may, to comply with such Rules as are laid down, if you wish to engage our esteem, and secure our protection.

TOUCHED with a tender and pitying sense of the lamentable distresses, which young women frequently suffer, unavoidably suffer in a state of prostitution; concerned, at once for the afflicting miseries that oppress their bodies, and the miseries far more afflicting, which must oppress their unrepenting Souls; Many benevolent persons have voluntarily contributed to open this hospitable House, as a place of refuge and retreat for those who are desirous to leave the pernicious paths of vice, to redeem their good name, to recover their bodies from Shame and foul Disease, to regain the fatherly protection of God, and save their immortal Souls.

And, they were the rather inclined to this humane purpose by the peculiarly-afflicting circumstances of unhappy young women, whom lost reputation deprives of every honest means to live,

live, casts out as the very refuse of the world, and gives no opportunity to retrieve and return.

Consider then, YOUNG WOMAN, of how great value to you this House of refuge is; as being the only one to which you could fly; the only place where you could have any probability of attaining present and future Bliss.

Surely then you must greatly prize it; and feel the utmost Gratitude for the worthy Governors and Supporters of it!

This Gratitude we would wish you to cherish, as it will ever be a motive to the very best conduct.

But as this House, you perceive, was designed to receive you from the storm of Distress, and to enable you to recover lost Reputation, Health, and Virtue; you must not by any means so mistake its gracious end, as to be careless in those important concerns; as to be remiss in the discharge of any duty.

It never was intended that you should pass your whole life here; much less that you should be supported in idleness and sloth. But as your continuance is temporary, so are you to esteem that continuance a singular favour: for the indulgence of which, (if you conduct yourselves properly) you may reasonably hope, till such time as you shall be enabled to return into life with a reputation recovered; no longer the scorn and contempt of your fellow-creatures; with an habit of industry, and the means to procure honestly your own bread; and with a mind, renewed in holiness, conscious of its past evils,

and

and resolved through God's grace, to forfeit no more the blessed hope of everlasting life. Agreeable to these future views must be your present conduct,

I. With regard to your *external behaviour*;

1. The most exact compliance with the rules of the House will be required: And as nothing of severity will be shewn towards you, so nothing of unseemly and refractory conduct can be allowed, or will be permitted.

2. An humble and ready obedience to the directions of your MATRON will be the method to preserve you from error, to steer you aright, and to gain the approbation of your friends and patrons. And we trust you will be very diligent and attentive in this respect.

3. As you cannot but be sensible that the expences attending such a family are great, your own reflection must shew you, that there is an absolute necessity for much *Industry* on your part; and we must inform you, that ready as we are to succour the distressed, and to contribute with all liberality to their relief, yet, it cannot be supposed that this House is designed to harbour and encourage the idle and the vicious; and therefore a want of industry will always be sufficient to lose our esteem, as it will too plainly shew your want of Principles. For if you live idly on the sole bounty of the House, you are grievously abusing the Charity of your Benefactors, and are injuring others, who would be glad to enter, and to work as well as they are capable. Besides, as idleness is the

root

root of much evil, your perſiſting in it will defeat all the good purpoſes we intend; which are to make you induſtrious upon principle, that ſo you may get your maintenance with credit. For, be aſſured, that we muſt conſider all your pretences to Reformation diſſembled, while you are deficient in that induſtry, which is the genuine fruit of true religion. And remember, that as *Idleneſs* cloaths with rags, brings to ſhame, to every Vice and every Miſery, ſo are its ſufferings never pitied; they are the juſt reward of the crime. You muſt not then expect continuance here, or comfort any where elſe, if you are not induſtrious. The Apoſtle hath declared, *If any will not work, neither ſhall they eat* *. And for your comfort, we can ſay, that the bleſſings of induſtry are always upon it: Diligence and honeſt labour carry with them their own reward. *Idleneſs ſhall clothe with rags; but the hand of the diligent maketh rich* †.

4. There is one further particular reſpecting your outward deportment, which is of great conſequence, both to your own peace, and to that of the family in general;—your Behaviour, we mean, one towards another, and particularly to your Superior ‡. Indeed, if you have any ſenſe at all of the Religion which you profeſs, and are here taught, you will ſoon know that love is its great and diſtinguiſhing command-

* 2 Theſſ. iii. 10. † See Prov. xxiii. 21. and x. 4.

‡ The *Superior* is the woman who preſides over each claſs.

ment;

ment; and that we can then only be true Disciples of Christ, when, "*we love one another, as He hath loved us* *."

We expect, therefore, that you each one endeavour to cultivate the greatest Harmony and Unity among yourselves; that you be obedient and obliging to your *Superiors*: and that you avoid all quarrelling, reproach, and upbraiding one of another; which will be most unseemly in *you*, who, alas! have so little cause to contemn and despise. Your sameness of circumstances, and sadness of distress, should awaken in each of your hearts a tender pity one for the other: with kind Love, like that of affectionate Sisters, you should endeavour to sooth each others Sorrows; and should never mention your past misfortunes, but to condole with one another, and to deplore your former miserable Estate. If you act in such an amiable and becoming manner, you will reap the fruits of it, to your present Comfort and Happiness. The situation you are in will be like a little Heaven to you: whereas disputes, discontents, and reviling, will deprive you of the best Blessings here offered. *Live in Love*, therefore, as *dear* Children of the same heavenly *Father*, who hath shewn you such mercy, who hath done so much for the *Salvation of your Souls* †.

This is the great and material point: *The Salvation of your Souls*: and which, if not attained, great part of the present good design is

* See John xv. 12, 13. † Eph. v. 1, 2.

frustrated.

fruſtrated. For we would have you reflect, that what relates to your *Soul* is of infinitely greater moment than what concerns your *Body* only: and therefore, if its welfare be overlooked, amidſt the care for things merely external, you will receive but little of the benefit intended for you, and we ſhall receive much uneaſy diſappointment. It is hoped then you will diligently attend to what follows.

II. We truſt you are not ignorant, that you have an immortal *Soul*, as well as a periſhing *Body*; a Soul, which cannot die, but which, when your mortal frame ſhall be diſſolved, and putrify in corruption, muſt appear before an Almighty Judge, and by him be conſigned to an eternal ſtate of conſummate Happineſs, or inexpreſſible Miſery!

The knowledge of this ſingle Truth is ſufficient to make us ſollicitous for our Soul's welfare.

But, alas! what ſhall they do, who have offended this Almighty Judge by repeated and aggravated Tranſgreſſions, and cannot plead innocent before his righteous Bar?

What would *you* do in that dreadful ſituation, eſpecially if you ſhould die in an unrepenting ſtate; die, utterly unprepared for ſo ſolemn a ſcene, and ſo ſad a ſentence!

All hope would be loſt. Oh then rejoice, that when all Hope *was* almoſt loſt, even here upon earth; it now again dawns upon your Soul, and you may ſecure a bliſsful Eternity!

For, gracious to his fallen Creatures, and tender

tender of their welfare, the ever bleſſed Father of Heaven has ſent his only begotten Son into the world, who ſuffered in our nature the puniſhment due to our Sins, and made expiation on the Croſs for the Iniquities of vile Tranſgreſſors: and who, having triumphed over death by his glorious Reſurrection, hath proclaimed full pardon to all Mankind, who come to him in lively faith and ſincere repentance.

Theſe bleſſed Tidings of good Things are held forth in the books of the New Teſtament, and may be there read to your exceeding Comfort.

But a *lively faith*, and a *ſincere repentance*, you muſt remember, are indiſpenſable requiſites for the obtaining this favour, for the procuring this ineſtimable bleſſing; and a future dutiful obedience muſt witneſs your real ſenſe of it.

If you do not believe * that Chriſt died for you, you can never truſt in his death, or pray to

* That Chriſt *lived* and *died*, and *roſe again*, according to the *Goſpels*, is certain beyond all diſpute; for thoſe Goſpels were written by *Men*, who were *eye* and *ear* witneſſes of the facts they deliver, and ſo could not be *deceived*: and they were men of the moſt unblemiſhed characters, who gave up their all, and even their own lives in teſtimony of what they delivered; and ſo could not be *deceivers*. They worked alſo the moſt aſtoniſhing *Miracles*, which were impoſſible to any power leſs than God's, and they communicated that power to others, who joyfully witneſſed the truth of their faith by ſuffering patiently on account of it the moſt cruel perſecutions,

to him for his mercies: and if you pretend to believe this, yet manifeſt not a ſincere *repentance*,—vain and falſe is every expectation of forgiveneſs.

Repentance,

tions, tortures, and death. Moreover, all that Chriſt was to *be* and to *do* was foretold, many years before he appeared, in the books of the Old Teſtament, and was exactly fulfilled by him: he himſelf alſo foretold many things, which were exactly fulfilled; and as none but God can foretell future events, ſo theſe *prophecies* are a full proof of the truth of the Chriſtian Religion. The *doctrine* too which Chriſt preached, is ſo excellent, and ſuperior to all other ever taught, that it could come from none but God; and the *Sacraments* which have continued in the church ever ſince Chriſt was upon earth, are clear and ſatisfactory proofs of his having been amongſt men; ſince no other perſon can be aſſigned as the ordainer of them, nor any other time of their inſtitution, than that of which the Goſpel ſpeaks. But, above all, the preſent *being* of the Chriſtian religion, and its particular *fitneſs* to the ſtate of the human race, and the wants of miſerable ſinners, prove its divine original: for we may be ſatisfied, that it could never have *exiſted* at all, much leſs have *continued* to this time, if it had not been divine; ſince it was introduced and propagated without any human aid, without *arts*, *arms*, or *eloquence*, and in oppoſition to all the opinions and religious eſtabliſhments then upon earth. Chriſt, therefore, did aſſuredly live, and die, and riſe, as we believe; and the Goſpel is the certain Revelation of God's love to mankind; of pardon and forgiveneſs to penitent, returning ſinners. And as from this pardon no ſuch ſinners are excluded; ſo they that confeſs and forſake their ſins ſhall aſſuredly find mercy.

Repentance, be informed, is not merely a word, nor doth it ſolely conſiſt in ſorrow for ſin: true and genuine repentance, ſuch as God requires, and will accept, is a ſincere and ſorrowful ſenſe of our paſt miſdoings, as diſhonourable to God, and deſtructive to our own ſouls; is a firm reſolution to leave thoſe practices, which we are ſorry for; is a putting that reſolution into act. In one word, it is leaving the *ways*, as well as being grieved for the *works* of ſin. The Prodigal Son not only was ſenſible of his own miſery, and his ill conduct to his father, not only reſolved to ariſe and go to him, but actually aroſe, went and confeſſed his unworthineſs, and declared his determination to alter his life *.

If, then, you are bleſt with this happy repentance; are ſorry for, and actually endeavour to change your life, and forſake your evil conduct; then, in true faith, then, ſincerely believing that Chriſt died for ſinners, and offers pardon to the penitent, apply to him in lowly confeſſion, and reſt ſatisfied that he *will never caſt you out.*

This is the ſtate to which we would deſire to bring you, through God's grace; and for that purpoſe, nothing is here wanting. But we muſt urge one further conſideration of vaſt moment to you; namely, that as to obtain free pardon through Chriſt, an actual forſaking of ſin is requiſite, ſo a ſtate of pardon implies and de-

* See Luke xv.

mands

mands a new life: and there is nothing which can ſatisfactorily witneſs either to yourſelves, or to others your real penitence and faith, but your future active obedience and unfeigned humility.

We muſt expect therefore to ſee,

1. In the *public worſhip* of God, the moſt ſober, ſerious, and religious deportment. The leaſt appearance of levity there will damp all our hopes. Conſider, in that holy ſervice, the eye of infinite purity is full upon you, ſeeing into the very ſecrets of your hearts; and therefore, imagine yourſelves ever in his ſight, and give place to no unhallowed and unbecoming thoughts. But, full of thankfulneſs for the rich mercies ſhewn you, join with fervent ſouls in the ſervice, and let your hearts ever keep pace with your lips.

Human nature is ſo imperfect, that, ſpite of our beſt endeavours, our wretched thoughts will but too eaſily wander, even in the holieſt duties. This ſhould not diſcourage you when it happens, but make you more humble, and more watchful: And it will be advantageous to you to be exactly careful in attending to the ſervice in your books, as well as in making the proper reſponſes, to which we muſt requeſt you to be very attentive; as alſo to read the leſſons in your Bibles. And as it is thought adviſable, that worthy people, deſirous of ſeeing this good work, ſhould be admitted to the Chapel, let that be another forcible motive to particular humility in behaviour. The humble, meek, and downcaſt look becomes thoſe who are in a ſtate of penitence, and will ever recommend; the bold and dauntleſs ſtare will give but mean ideas of reformation; though, indeed, ſuch as have any ſenſe at all of their paſt ſhame, will find little courage to animate the wandering eye.

As to the bleſſed Sacrament of the *Lord's Supper*, we ſhall ſay the leſs, as leaving it to the more particular concern of the *Chaplain*; but it would give us infinite ſatisfaction to hear, and to find, that you are all well diſpoſed, and properly prepared to be partakers of that holy feaſt, which is ſo neceſſary for every chriſtian, as well as ſo comfortable; and at which every true *penitent*, humble in ſoul, and deſirous to walk in newneſs of life, will ever be an accepted gueſt.

And with regard to the inſtructions you have from the *pulpit*, we ſhall only obſerve, that as they are calculated and delivered for your improvement, ſo we muſt require that you give good attention to them, and treaſure them up in your hearts; that you carefully apply them to yourſelves, and pray to God for a bleſſing upon them; that you always read over the text, and talk of the ſermon one with another; and, if you can write, it may be of much advantage to tranſcribe the text, the heads of the ſermon, and any ſuch remarks as may chance particularly to ſtrike you. The review of this would afterwards be of much profit to you. And if you are careful thus to regulate your behaviour, in

regard

regard to the public worſhip of God, you will not fail in the ſame conſcientious care, with reſpect

2. To your *private worſhip.*

Prayer is the moſt important duty of a Chriſtian: without a continuance in it, we can never hope to perſevere in the right path. Great are the promiſes annexed to it; and in the regular performance of it we can ſcarce fail of a bleſſing. Prayer is not mere lip-ſervice; not a labour only of the tongue, and a bare repetition of words; it is the deſire of the heart lifted up to God; it is the language of want: therefore you muſt be careful that your heart ſpeaks thro' your lips; and that your ſoul's deſire be elevated to God, when you addreſs him in the ſolemn duty of prayer. This, we hope, you will never omit to perform *morning* and *evening*, in private; for which purpoſe, two prayers are annexed, (which we could wiſh you to uſe, unleſs you have any more proper) at the ſame time not omitting to pour forth the earneſt requeſt of your hearts, in your own words, if you find particular wants not ſpecified in theſe. There is too an holy kind of prayer, which requires no particular ſeaſons, places, or forms, and which, as being the immediate language of the heart, aſcendeth moſt acceptably to God;—we mean *ejaculatory prayer:* addreſſing God in ſhort and humble petitions, wherever you are, or whatever you are doing; ſuch petitions as your own hearts may dictate, or you may learn from the word of God, or the ſervice of the church.

3. Indeed, the beſt way to improve yourſelves in this divine art, will be to read *daily* and *regularly* ſome part of God's word You ſhould determine this with yourſelves, and let no day paſs without reading ſome portion, more or leſs, of the ſacred ſcriptures, eſpecially the *New Teſtament*. This will ſtrengthen your faith, and increaſe your knowledge, and enable you to be much in the practice of that *ejaculation* which we recommend. This too will enable you to keep your minds employed upon good and heavenly ſubjects; which you ſhould endeavour to contemplate as much as you may, not only to prevent evil thoughts from moleſting you, but to convince you more and more of the excellency of the choice you have made. And for other books, if you are deſirous of reading, they will be carefully ſupplied you: We wiſh to ſee you employed, during your ſpare hours, in ſerious reading; and ſhould be glad, and much recommend it to thoſe of you who are beſt able, to read to ſuch as are leſs inſtructed; and to labour after an increaſe of knowledge, which, we doubt not, will bring an increaſe of virtue.

4. Chearfulneſs and content will always be acceptable; and how can you better expreſs it, than by ſinging thoſe excellent and inſtructive *Hymns* which are provided for you; than by endeavouring to improve in this holy employment, which gives us ſuch ſatisfaction in the houſe of God? But remember, that the heart

in

in ſinging ſhould accompany the voice; and that if you ſing thoſe ſacred compoſitions without due attention, you will receive no advantage. Endeavour to impreſs your ſouls with a due ſenſe of the ſubject: elevate your hearts to God; and then ſing with the voice of melody, and the ſoul of praiſe.

5. With reſpect to your converſation, ſomething was hinted before: of this you muſt be eſpecially careful, as well as to avoid all pertneſs to your *Superiors*: and you will be ſo, if your hearts are truly changed. *For out of the abundance of the heart the mouth ſpeaketh.* Looſe, vain, and vicious converſation, as it will be highly offenſive to your benefactors, and is immediately contrary to the rules of the Houſe; ſo will it be uneaſy and diſpleaſing to yourſelves, if you ſincerely feel and lament the ſad effects of looſe, vain, and vicious living. *Let* then *no corrupt communication proceed out of your mouths*; no profane, looſe, wicked words; no profanation of the holy name of *God*, *Jeſus*, &c. Never ſuffer yourſelves to trifle with the name of the *Almighty*, wantonly, without meaning, or on frivolous occaſions; or to uſe any thing tending to an oath, as, *Upon my ſoul,—As I hope to be ſaved*, &c. but endeavour to purify your lips from all appearance of evil. When you converſe together, let it at leaſt be innocent: if it be poſſible, we could wiſh it might be edifying; and an attention to the Rules above given, will enable you to make it ſo. But, for God's ſake, never be

ſo abandoned and deteſtable, as to glory in your ſhame; as to repeat thoſe infamous ſcenes, which ſhould cover your faces with confuſion; and which, if you glory in them, unrepenting, will be produced at the laſt day, before all the world, to your unſpeakable horror, and be the means to ſink you for ever into the bottomleſs pit of endleſs miſery.

You muſt not conceive that by entering into this Houſe your buſineſs is done, and your Salvation ſecured; this would be a fatal miſtake. The life of a Chriſtian is a continued warfare; and we have enemies, powerful enemies *within*, as well as *without*, to encounter and ſubdue. The ſad corruption of our nature is the great cauſe of our miſery; and, as long as you bear this mortal fleſh about you, you will be ſubject to temptations and infirmities. You muſt reſolve, therefore, and endeavour to vanquiſh all the evil deſires and predominant luſts of the fleſh, and muſt labour to keep under your corrupt affections: this is required of every Chriſtian, but peculiarly of you, who, in a life of penance for ſenſual enormities, ſhould be particularly careful to ſubdue the evil propenſity of the fleſh.

6. *Temperance* and *early riſing* are friends, no leſs to health and proſperity, than to virtue and piety; and we have no doubt but you will be careful to obſerve both, as well upon religious as temporal motives. Deſirous to mortify all your evil and corrupt affections, you will

will be diligent in the uſe of all proper means*, and in every reſpect will endeavour to ſubdue your worſt enemy, the enemy within; following the example of St. *Paul*, "*I keep under my body, and bring it into ſubjection; leſt that by any means, when I have preached to others, I myſelf ſhould be a caſt away:*" and if ſo great an Apoſtle, and ſo eminent a Saint, found this neceſſary for him, how much more neceſſary, think you, is it for you? for you, who, like that Apoſtle, are monuments of the mercy,—may you be eternal monuments of the long-ſuffering mercy of Chriſt Jeſus our Lord!

Such are the general heads of advice we have thought proper to give you. For immediate directions, either as to religious or temporal concerns, you will always have acceſs to our *Chaplain* and *Matron*, who will be glad and ready to ſuccour and aſſiſt you with their beſt counſel, in every particular that ſhall reſpect your welfare. We have ſaid only what we expect from you in the general; and have neither enlarged on your *Duty* as *Chriſtians*, or as *Inhabitants* of this Houſe; ſince, for the former, we have appointed regular inſtructions from the pulpit; for the latter, we have inſtituted a general plan of conduct, with which we expect you to comply; and, in ſo doing, you will ſecure to yourſelves our favourable notice:

* Amongſt which *Faſting* muſt be particularly recommended, as a Duty of indiſpenſable Obligation; and as a neceſſary branch of real Mortification. See St. *Matt.* vi. 16, 17, 18.

which, (though a bleſſing much to be prized by you) will be but ſmall, in compariſon of that loving kindneſs of God, and that protection of his providence, wherewith, for Chriſt's ſake, he will infallibly bleſs you.

Once more let us remind you, that we have no intention, either to receive into this Houſe, or to detain in it, any whoſe inclinations are averſe to its important deſign,—namely, "*their own preſent and eternal happineſs.*" We ſeek only your good; and, on your commendable behaviour ſhall be inclined to continue you, till ſuch time as you may be put into an ability to procure your livelihood properly. Yet that tender concern we have for your welfare will always incline us ſeriouſly to remonſtrate with you, and, with the gentleneſs of parental affection, to admoniſh you, if ever, through miſtaken notions, you ſhould be ſo wretchedly wayward, and ignorant of your own true intereſt, as to deſire a removal hence, with no viſible appearance of good ſucceſs, with no probability but of returning again with the ſwine to wallowing in the mire, and of plunging again deeper and deeper into wretchedneſs and miſery.

And in all ſuch caſes, nay, whenever you find a gleam of the leaſt diſcontent ariſing in your hearts,—caſt back your eyes, and reflect upon what you WERE, upon what you muſt BE, if you leave theſe friendly walls, and return to vice.

Reflect

Reflect upon the ſoul, dead in treſpaſſes and ſins, a ſtranger to its God, and loſt to happineſs: upon the body polluted with iniquity, condemned to the foul drudgery of luſt, and to its deplorable conſequences, Shame and Diſeaſe! Reflect upon yourſelf, baniſhed from all true peace, a ſtranger to ſolid comfort, abhorred by the thinking and the virtuous *, deſpiſed and hated even by the moſt abject and vicious: caſt-out, forlorn, and wretched; ſtung with the ſharp upbraidings of condemning conſcience; an alien and an out-caſt from your neareſt friends; a ſore grief to the mother that ſuckled you at her boſom; an afflicting ſhame to your father's old age; burdenſome to yourſelf, deſpicable to others, and ſpeedily about to end a miſerable exiſtence, only to enter on an exiſtence far more miſerable! wretched, unſpeakably wretched in this world; enſlaved to the abominable ſervice of the devil, whoſe only joy is the miſery of the human race; and who

* There is nothing, one would imagine, which muſt affect the mind, eſpecially a female mind, equal to that contempt and neglect, to which the loſs of reputation, and a ſtate of proſtitution ſubjects them. They can never be admitted into the company of any of their own ſex, who are worthy to be converſed with: all the virtuous *muſt* forſake and fly from them: they are neglected and deſpiſed by all; and even thoſe who *uſe* them have no true value for them, but the greateſt hatred. O miſerable ſituation! ye daughters of ſhame, reflect, and return!

for the moſt faithful ſervice, hath only flames of hell and never-ending anguiſh to beſtow!

And what if you had periſhed in this ſtate? what if you had died, and been loſt for ever? Could any thing in this life have recompenſed the loſs of your ſoul? Bleſs God, bleſs him ever more and more, that in much mercy he hath opened to you a door of grace; that he hath put it into your heart to come beneath this hoſpitable roof, which leads you as it were to the gates of paradiſe, and points out pardon, and peace, and never-failing joy! And can there be any thing tempting in the former ſtate, that ſhould move you to forfeit the bliſs of the preſent, and to plunge again into the miſeries of the paſt; plunge again, with a double weight of guilt and miſery; plunge again, *never* to emerge, *never* to be reſcued more!

For, conſider, if you return to vice, the *knowledge* you have here had of duty, will aggravate your guilt; you will be juſtly abhorred by all: nothing but the filth of vile proſtitution awaits you; diſeaſe will again come on; miſery will again overwhelm you: A wretched outcaſt, without friends, and without hope, you will ſink in infamy and diſtreſs; no eye to pity, no hand to relieve; and, worſe than the worſt of all, without excuſe, and ſelf-condemned, your loſt and ruined ſoul muſt periſh for ever in the flames of hell.

If you reflect one moment on this moſt certain conſequence of a return to an abandoned life, your ſoul will be filled with joy for your eſcape, and

and your utmoſt endeavours will be exerted in the diſcharge of every duty which your preſent *happy ſtate* requires: a ſtate, how different from that out of which Providence has ſaved you!

Heaven now lies open before you: everlaſting comforts are prepared for you: the holy Angels are glad to tune their harps on your accounts; for there is joy in Heaven, and before the Angels of God over one ſinner that repenteth: and the bleſſed Jeſus, who died to ſave you, is ready to crown your ſincere penitence, faith, and love; is ready to bleſs your happy perſeverance with immortality and glory. All the good and virtuous part of your fellow-creatures, to whom you were before an abhorrence, behold you with joy; a joy eſpecially pleaſing to all the Supporters of this Charity, whoſe wiſh and travail of heart is for your ſalvation.

And have not many of you tender parents? have not many of you affectionate friends? muſt not your hearts then feel a commendable delight in the comforts you cannot fail to give, ſome to the *father* who begat her; and to the beloved *mother* who watched her infant wants; ſome to the friends to whom you were dear, even as their own ſouls; and who, once lamenting your loſt eſtate, can now ſay with the prodigal, *She was dead, and is alive again: ſhe was loſt, and is found!*

Theſe things if you conſider, you will be filled with exceeding comfort: we recommend it to you ſeriouſly to conſider them; and deſire you to obſerve, that as, on the one hand, in the path we point out, present Peace, Heaven, and eternal Happiness, offer themselves to you: so in a deviation from it, on the other hand, are sorrow, shame, and disease; present and eternal misery.

Choose therefore; choose for yourselves: And the God of unexhausted goodness and love incline all your souls to make a happy choice! This will be an unspeakable satisfaction to Us, this will be an unspeakable comfort to Yourselves.

PRAYERS

PRAYERS

For the Uſe of the

MAGDALEN-CHARITY.

I.

The PRAYER *uſed in the* MAGDALEN-CHAPEL*.

FATHER of mercies, and God of all comfort, who has ſent thy Son Jeſus Chriſt into the world, to *ſeek and to ſave that which was loſt*; † we praiſe thy holy name for the bountiful proviſion made in this place for the ſpiritual and temporal wants of miſerable offenders: beſeeching thee ſo to diſpoſe our hearts by the powerful influence of thy bleſſed Spirit, that through ſincere repentance and a lively faith, we may obtain remiſſion of our ſins, and all the *precious promiſes* ‡ of thy Goſpel. Awaken thoſe, who

* This truly ſcriptural Prayer was received into the public ſervice of the CHAPEL, after having undergone the correction, and obtained the ſanction, of the late Archbiſhop of Canterbury, Dr. SECKER; a generous friend to the MAGDALEN CHARITY, from the beginning as well as at the end; for he left a handſome legacy to it.

† Luke xix. 10. ‡ 2 Peter i. 4.

have

have not yet a due ſenſe of their guilt; and perfect a godly ſorrow, where it is begun. "Renew in us whatſoever hath been decayed by the fraud and malice of the Devil, or by *our own carnal will and frailneſs*:" * Preſerve us, *after eſcaping the pollutions of the world, from being again intangled therein* †; and keep us in a ſtate of conſtant watchfulneſs and humility. Forgive, as we do from our hearts, thoſe who have done us wrong; and grant to all, who have ſeduced others, or been ſeduced themſelves into wickedneſs, that they may forſake the *evil of their doings*, and live. Make this Houſe a bleſſing, we pray thee, to the ſouls and bodies of all its inhabitants; and a glorious monument of thy *grace, abounding to the chief of ſinners* ‡. Strengthen the hands, direct the counſels, reward the labours and the liberality of all who are engaged in the government or ſupport of it; and increaſe the number of thoſe who have a zeal for thy glory, and *compaſſion on the ignorant, and on them that are out of the way*, § that many may be *turned from darkneſs to light, and from the power of Satan unto* thee their *God* ‖ through the merits and mediation of Jeſus Chriſt our Lord. *Amen.*

* See "the order for Viſitation of the Sick," in the Common Prayer Book.

† 2 Pet. ii. 20. ‡ Heb. v. 2. § 1 Tim. i. 14, 15. ‖ Acts xxvi. 18.

II. *Private*

II.

Private Prayer for the MORNING. *

GLORY be to thee, Lord God, moſt merciful, for all thy bleſſings vouchſafed to me, and particularly for thy preſervation of me this night paſt.

O Lord, I am not worthy to lift up mine eyes unto thee; my ſins bear witneſs againſt me: But there is mercy with thee, therefore ſhalt thou be feared: pardon and pity me for the ſake of thy bleſſed Son, my Lord and Saviour.

I acknowledge my tranſgreſſions; and truly repent before thee: Oh give me thy grace, bleſſed Lord, to perſevere in the right path, and grant that I may henceforth never depart from it.

To thee do I humbly dedicate myſelf, my ſoul and my body; earneſtly beſeeching thee, who haſt created, redeemed, and preſerved me, to fill my ſoul with gratitude and thankfulneſs for all thy mercies, and to enable me to walk worthy thy great loving kindneſs.

Let thine eſpecial bleſſing be upon all my friends, and particularly on thoſe who are engaged in the government or ſupport of this houſe: Oh make it a houſe of ſalvation, not only to my ſoul, but to the ſouls of all its inhabitants!

Aſſiſt me chearfully to perform the duties of the day following; and ſo poſſeſs me with an

* This and the following Prayer are deſigned for the private uſe of the Penitents in their cloſets.

awful

awful ſenſe of thy preſence, of thy dear Son's ſufferings, and of that future account which I muſt ſhortly give; that I may fear to offend thee, that I may continually ſtrive to pleaſe thee: and let it be thy pleaſure, Father of mercies, and God of all comfort, ſo fully to pardon all that is paſt, and ſo completely to direct me in all which is to come, that I may not fail of eternal happineſs, through the merits and mediation of Jeſus Chriſt, in whoſe holy words I further call upon thee *ſaying*,

OUR Father, who art in heaven; Hallowed be thy name. Thy kingdom come. Thy will be done on earth, as it is in heaven. Give us this day our daily bread. And forgive us our treſpaſſes, As we forgive them that treſpaſs againſt us. And lead us not into temptation; But deliver us from evil, &c. *Amen.*

III.

Private Prayer for the EVENING.

ENTER not into judgment with thy ſervant, O Lord; for in thy ſight ſhall no fleſh living be juſtified.

Bleſſed be thy name, thou everlaſting and almighty Father, for thy gracious protection and preſervation of me this day!

Lord, thy mercies are not to be numbered: under a ſenſe of them, and of my own manifold unworthineſs, I am aſhamed to lift up my face unto thee: but thou deſireſt not the death of a ſinner:

ſinner: thou didſt ſend thy dear Son into the world, that whoſoever believeth in him ſhould not periſh, but have everlaſting life. Lord, I believe, help thou mine unbelief: Lord, I repent, I grieve, I lament for my miſdoings; have mercy upon me, for thy great goodneſs; for Jeſus Chriſt's ſake, pity, pardon, and blot out all mine offences.

Graciouſly vouchſafe unto me thy fatherly aſſiſtance, and the comfort of thy bleſſed Spirit, that I may be preſerved henceforth from all the defilements of iniquity: may ſerve thee with a pure heart and quiet mind, and bring forth fruits meet for repentance.

To thee, Lord, do I humbly dedicate myſelf, my ſoul, and my body; ſtrengthen my good reſolutions, and preſerve me from all the allurements of the world, the fleſh, and the devil.

Accept my moſt unfeigned thanks, for all thy mercies vouchſafed to me, but eſpecially for the bountiful proviſion made for my ſpiritual and temporal wants, in this houſe of refuge: Oh may thy bleſſing deſcend on the heads of all its inhabitants; may we be wiſe to know our own good, and to return the kindneſs of our benefactors in unceaſing praiſe and thankſgiving. Bleſs them, O God, with thy choiceſt bleſſings: kindly remember all my friends and relations, and be merciful to all mine enemies: grant me thy full forgiveneſs, as truly, O Lord, as I forgive all thoſe who have in any reſpect injured me.

Truſting

Trusting on thy Providence, I lay me down to sleep: let my bed ever remind me of that hour, when I shall lie down in death, to awaken no more in this world. Under an awful sense of which, may I live in constant preparation for that great event; which, if it should happen this night (as every moment of our frail life is uncertain,) O Lord most holy, O God most mighty, O holy and most merciful Father, for Jesus Christ's sake, have mercy on me; pardon all that is past; deliver me not into the bitter pains of eternal death; but take me under thy divine protection, and into thy kingdom of glory. Hear me, O Lord, for thy mercy is great, and thou hast promised to receive the petitions of those who ask in thy dear Son's name: relying on whose all-sufficient merits, I conclude my imperfect prayers, in the words which he himself hath taught us.

Our Father, &c.

IV.

A Family Prayer for the EVENING.

(From Archbishop WAKE) *

REmember not, Lord, our offences, nor the offences of our forefathers; neither take thou vengeance of our sins; spare us good Lord, spare thy people, whom thou hast redeemed with

* This excellent Prayer is designed for the *public* use of the *Penitents*, and to be read by one of them in each of their *wards*.

thy

thy moſt precious blood, and be not angry with us for ever.

Anſwer. *Spare us, good Lord.*

O God, we confeſs, with ſhame and confuſion of face, that we are not worthy of the leaſt regard from thee, whom we have ſo much offended, and whoſe patience and long ſuffering we have ſo often and grievouſly abuſed.

O Lord! we have ſinned, we have done wickedly, we have broken thy holy Commandments, by thought, word, and deed, by doing thoſe things which thou haſt forbidden, and leaving undone the things which thou haſt commanded. And to make ourſelves altogether ſinful, we have gone on in a continued courſe of ſin and rebellion againſt thee; and have perſiſted in it, notwithſtanding all the motions of thy Holy Spirit, and the checks of our conſciences to the contrary. Yea, this very day, we have not ceaſed to add new ſins to all our former guilt *.—And now, O God, what ſhall we ſay, or how ſhall we open our mouths, ſeeing we have done theſe things? O LORD, to us belong ſhame and confuſion of face, becauſe we have rebelled againſt thee; but with thee there is mercy, therefore ſhalt thou be feared. Have mercy upon us, O God, after thy great goodneſs, according to the multitude of thy mercies, do away our offences; waſh us

* *Here let a ſhort ſtop be made, for every one to call to mind, wherein ſhe has offended the day before.*

thorough-

thoroughly from our wickednefs, and cleanfe us from our fins; and grant us grace fo truly to repent of, and turn from our evil doings, that our iniquities may not be our ruin. Give us a deep fenfe of our fins paft, and a hearty forrow and contrition for them And fo endue us with the grace of thy Holy Spirit, that for what remains of our lives, we may walk more circumfpectly before thee;—redeeming the time, becaufe the days are evil.

To this end, purify our fouls from all corrupt defires and affections; mortify all our carnal lufts and appetites; make us as conftant and zealous to deny, as we have been heretofore ready to gratify and indulge them. Raife up a fpirit of piety and devotion, of love and charity, of humility and felf-denial within us; and grant that thefe, and all other Chriftian graces and virtues, may increafe and abound in us. Remove from us all envy, hatred, and malice, and whatfoever elfe is contrary to our duty towards thee, or towards our neighbour; and fo eftablifh us in thy fear, that it may never depart from our minds; but be a conftant fecurity to us againft all thofe temptations which either the devil, the world, or our own flefh, fhall hereafter minifter unto us, to draw us into fin, or to hinder us in our duty.

More particularly, we pray thee to pity and pardon whatfoever we have done amifs this day: O let us not lie down to reft under thy difpleafure! But grant us that forgivenefs of our fins now,

now, which we may never have any future opportunity to aſk of thee.

[Accept our moſt ſincere thanks and praiſes for all thy mercies from time to time vouchſafed unto us, but eſpecially for thy particular providence in the ſingular bleſſings afforded us in this *Houſe*; make us duly ſenſible of them, duly thankful for them; and grant us grace ſo to improve this precious ſeaſon of mercy, that we may obtain thy favour, and recover our loſt happineſs. And be pleaſed to ſhed the riches of thy love on the heads of all thoſe, who are any ways concerned in the management, government, or ſupport of this charitable deſign; return their kindneſs fourfold into their boſoms, and bleſs their benevolent endeavours to the welfare of their own, and of every ſoul who ſhall partake of their tender and liberal bounty.]

Take us, O God, this night into thine eſpecial favour and protection: give thy holy Angels charge over us, that no evils may happen unto us, nor any dangers approach us, to diſturb our repoſe. Refreſh us with comfortable reſt; and raiſe us up in the morning with renewed ſtrength and vigour to praiſe thy name. And, now that we are about to lie down upon our bed of reſt, grant us grace ſeriouſly to conſider that time, when, in a little while, we ſhall lie down in the duſt: and ſince we know neither the day nor hour of our maſter's coming, make us ſo careful of our duty, and ſo watchful againſt ſin, that we may be always ready; that we may never live in ſuch a ſtate

ſtate as we ſhould fear to die in; but that whether we live, we may live unto the Lord; or whether we die, we may die unto the Lord: ſo that whether we live or die, we may be thine, through Jeſus Chriſt our Lord, in whoſe moſt holy name and words, we farther call upon thee, Saying,

Our Father, &c.

The Almighty GOD, who is a ſtrong tower of defence to all them that put their truſt in him; to whom all things in heaven and earth, and under the earth, do bow, and obey; be now and evermore our defender and preſerver.

Unto his gracious favour and protection, we moſt humbly commend ourſelves, and all that belong unto us; (eſpecially all of this houſe and family.) The Lord bleſs, and keep us. The Lord make his face to ſhine upon us, and be gracious unto us. The Lord lift up the light of his countenance upon us, and give us his peace this night, and for evermore. *Amen.*

V.

A Prayer to be uſed during Sickneſs. *

ALmighty, and moſt righteous Lord God, "in whoſe hands are the appointments of life and death," give me grace to conſider that this my ſickneſs is of thy ſending; and to ac-

* N. B. *If the ſick perſon is ſo very ill that ſhe cannot read this herſelf, ſhe may deſire ſome friend to repeat it to her, and then ſhe may add at the concluſion her hearty* Amen.

knowledge

knowledge as well the juſtice, as the mercifulneſs of thy viſitation, and my ſufferings. May I look up to thee for ſtrength to bear, and grace to profit by it. It comes, O my GOD, *as thy ſcourge* for my ſins, which is to make me ſee, feel, and avoid them; *as thy medicine* to cure my ſpiritual diſeaſes; and *as thy fiery trial*, which is to prove my virtues, and purge away my droſs. Let it not fail, Lord, to anſwer theſe gracious purpoſes. Bring to my mind all ſuch conſiderations, as may revive and ſuccour me, and raiſe me above all diſcouragements and fear; and let my thoughts under this viſitation, be only thoſe of love and thankfulneſs; of reſignation and obedience; of humility and hope in thy mercy. Give me patience, I beſeech thee, and a full truſt in thy moſt gracious promiſes, that I may entertain no evil ſurmiſes; nor ſhew any indecent carriage, which would add to my guilt, if I die; or to my remorſe and ſhame, if I live.

Pity thy ſick ſervant, and leſſen my ſorrows, O Father of mercies, out of compaſſion to my weakneſs. Pardon my reſtleſs complainings, and ſupport me under them by thy comforts. Direct and recompenſe the labours and kindneſs of thoſe who charitably and friendly attend me in my ſickneſs. Keep me always ſubmiſſive and devout towards thee, and no ways impatient or ungrateful towards thoſe around me. May thy bleſſing accompany all their endeavours for my good, and all the medicines I take. Put an end in due time to my diſeaſe, (*or* to my pains:) and either reſtore me to my ſtrength, health, and

and eafe, granting me the mercies of a longer life, or elfe prepare me more immediately for a bleffed and eternal life, for our Lord JESUS CHRIST's fake, who died for our fins, and rofe again for our juftification. *Amen.*

Hath God mercifully reftored you to health? Surely you cannot doubt the obligations you lie under, to be thankful for his mercies. Dreadful INDEED, THAT OUT OF TEN LEPERS WHO WERE CLEANSED, *only one fhould return to give thanks! But take fpecial care that you follow not the example of the nine, (fee* Luke xvii. 7.) *for inftances of fuch ingratitude are too common.*

VI.

A Prayer after Recovery.

MOST gracious and merciful God, the fountain of life, I return thee humble and hearty thanks for having fpared the life of thy fervant; I adore thee as the *Author* of my *Cure*, and praife thee for the fuccefs thou haft given to thofe applications which were the means of effecting it. May I remember the chaftifements, the inftructions, and the deliverance I have received; and may I be enabled to perform the good refolutions I made in my ficknefs. As thou haft condefcended to hearken to the prayer of fo finful a creature, may I "call upon thee as long as I live!" Being made whole, may I "go away and fin no more, left a worft thing come unto me!" Having known the bitternefs of affliction, may I pity, and endeavour to relieve thofe that labour under it. And may I never

never forget my obligations to thee, and the kindneſs of thoſe about me (eſpecially my Benefactors of this *Houſe*). I humbly recommend *them* and *myſelf* to thy continued mercy, and everlaſting favour, through JESUS CHRIST, my Lord and Saviour. *Amen.**

VII.

Some Inſtances of CHRIST's *Life, propoſed for Imitation,*

Extracted from *Burket*'s Expoſition of the New Teſtament.

1. HIS early piety. See *Luke* ii. 46, 47.

2. His obedience to his earthly parents. See *Luke* ii. 51.

3. His unwearied diligence in doing good. See *Acts* x. 38.

4. His humility and lowlineſs of mind. See *Matt.* xi. 29.

5. The unblameableneſs and inoffenſiveneſs of his life and actions. See *Matt.* xix. 27.

6. His eminent ſelf-denial. See *Philip.* ii. 7, 8.

7. His contentment in a low and mean condition in this world. See *Luke* ix. 58. *Phil.* iv. 11.

8. His frequent performance of the duty of private prayer. See *Luke* vi. 12. *Mark* i. 35.

* See *Stonehouſe's Advice to a Patient*, &c.

9. His affectionate performance of the duty of praiſe and thankſgiving. See *Matt.* xi. 25. *John* xi. 41.

10. His compaſſion towards thoſe who were miſerable, and in diſtreſs. See *Matt.* xx. 34.

11. His ſpiritual, entertaining, and uſeful diſcourſe. See *Luke* xiv. 7. xxiv. 13.

12. His free familiar, ſociable behaviour. See *Matt.* xi. 19. *Luke* v. 29.

13. His patience under ſufferings and reproaches. See 1 *Pet.* ii. 21, 22.

14. His readineſs to forgive injuries. See *Luke* xxiii. 34.

15. His laying to heart the ſins as well as ſufferings of others. See *Mark* iii. 5.

16. His zeal for the public worſhip of God. See *John* ii. 17.

17. His glorifying his Father in all he did. See *John* xvii. 4.

18. His impartiality in reproving ſin. See *Matt.* xxii. 23.

19. His univerſal obedience to his Father's will, and chearful ſubmiſſion to his Father's pleaſure. See *Matt.* xxvi. 29.

20. His laws, and practice of univerſal holineſs both in heart and life. See *Luke* iv. 34.

We muſt remember, "ſo to imitate *Chriſt* "for our *Pattern*, as to acknowledge him for "our *high prieſt* and *interceſſor*," as we are taught in the following excellent prayer from the Liturgy, proper to be uſed at all ſeaſons.

Almighty

ALmighty God, who haſt given thine only Son to be unto us both a *Sacrifice* for ſin, and alſo an *Example* of godly life: give us grace that we may always moſt thankfully receive that his ineſtimable benefit: may daily endeavour ourſelves to follow the ſteps of his moſt holy life; and finally be made partakers of his reſurrection, through the ſame Jeſus Chriſt, our mediator and advocate. *Amen.*

☞ See the *Advice to the Magdalens*, and the *Preface*.

PSALMS

For the Use of the

MAGDALEN CHAPEL.

PSALM V.

LORD, hear the voice of my complaint,
  Accept my secret pray'r;
To thee alone, my King, my God,
  Will I for help repair.

Thou in the morn my voice shalt hear;
  And with the dawning day,
To thee, devoutly, I'll look up,
  To thee, devoutly pray.

For thou the wrongs the just sustain,
  Can'st never, Lord, approve;
Who from thy sacred dwelling-place,
  All evil dost remove.

Then let all those who trust in thee,
  With shouts their joy proclaim:
Let them rejoyce, whom thou preserv'st,
  And all that love thy name.

To righteous men the righteous Lord
  His blessing will extend;
And with his favour all his Saints,
  As with a shield defend.

TO celebrate thy praiſe, O Lord,
We will our hearts prepare;
To all the liſt'ning world thy works,
Thy wond'rous works declare.

Thou ſhalt forever live, who haſt
A righteous throne prepar'd,
Impartial juſtice to diſpenſe,
To puniſh or reward.

Thou art a conſtant ſure defence,
Againſt oppreſſing rage:
When troubles riſe, thy needful aid
In our behalf engage.

All thoſe who have thy goodneſs prov'd,
Will in thy truth confide;
Thy mercy ne'er forſook the man
Who on thy help rely'd.

Sing praiſes therefore to the Lord,
From Sion his abode;
Proclaim his deeds, till all the world
Confeſs no other God.

PSALM XVIII.

NO change of times ſhall ever ſhock
My firm affection, Lord, to thee;
For thou haſt always been a rock,
A fortreſs, and defence to me.

Thou my deliv'rer art, my God;
My truſt is in thy mighty pow'r:
Thou art my ſhield from foes abroad,
At home my ſafeguard, and my tow'r.

Thou

Thou ſuit'ſt, O Lord, thy righteous ways
  To various paths of human kind;
Thoſe who for mercy merit praiſe,
  With thee ſhall wond'rous mercy find.

Thou to the juſt ſhalt juſtice ſhew,
  The pure thy purity ſhall ſee;
Such as perverſely chuſe to go,
  Shall meet with due returns from thee.

For God's deſigns ſhall ſtill ſucceed;
  His word ſhall bear the utmoſt teſt;
He's a ſtrong ſhield to all that need,
  And on his ſure protection reſt.

Who, then, deſerves to be ador'd,
  But God, on whom my hopes depend?
Or who, except the mighty Lord,
  Can with reſiſtleſs pow'r defend?

PSALM XIX.

THE ſpacious firmament on high,
  With all the blue etherial ſky,
And ſpangled heavens, a ſhining frame,
Their great Original proclaim.

Th' unweary'd ſun from day to day
Does his Creator's pow'r diſplay;
And publiſhes to ev'ry land
The work of an Almighty hand.

Soon as the ev'ning ſhades prevail,
The Moon takes up the wond'rous tale,
And nightly to the liſt'ning earth
Repeats the ſtory of her birth:

Whilſt all the ſtars that round her burn,
And all the planets in their turn,
Confirm the tidings as they roll,
And ſpread the truth from pole to pole.

What though in ſolemn ſilence all
Move round this dark terreſtrial ball;
What though nor real voice nor ſound
Amid their radiant orbs be found:

In reaſon's ear they all rejoice,
And utter forth a glorious voice;
For ever ſinging as they ſhine,
"The hand that made us is divine."

PSALM XXII.

YE worſhippers of Jacob's God,
  All ye of Iſr'el's line,
O praiſe the Lord, and to your praiſe
  Sincere obedience join.

He ne'er diſdain'd on low diſtreſs
  To caſt a gracious eye;
Nor turn'd from poverty his face,
  But hears its humble cry.

'Tis his ſupreme prerogative
  O'er ſubject-Kings to reign;
'Tis juſt that He ſhould rule the world,
  Who does the world ſuſtain.

The rich, who are with plenty fed,
  His bounty muſt confeſs;
The ſons of want, by him reliev'd,
  Their gen'rous patron bleſs.

With

With humble worſhip to his throne
  They all for aid reſort :
That Pow'r which firſt their beings gave,
  Can only give ſupport.

O may a choſen ſpotleſs race,
  Devoted to his name,
To their admiring heirs his truth,
  And glorious acts proclaim !

PSALM XXIII.

THE Lord my paſture ſhall prepare,
  And feed me with a ſhepherd's care;
His preſence ſhall my wants ſupply,
And guard me with a watchful eye :
My noon-day walks he ſhall attend,
And all my midnight hours defend.

When in the ſultry glebe I faint,
Or on the thirſty mountain pant;
To fertile vales and dewy meads
My weary wand'ring ſteps he leads,
Where peaceful rivers, ſoft and ſlow,
Amid the verdant landſkip flow.

Though in the paths of death I tread,
With gloomy horrors overſpread;
My ſteadfaſt heart ſhall fear no ill,
For thou, O Lord, art with me ſtill :
Thy friendly crook ſhall give me aid,
And guide me through the dreadful ſhade.

Though in a bare and rugged way,
Through devious lonely wilds I ſtray,

Thy bounty ſhall my pains beguile,
The barren wilderneſs ſhall ſmile,
With ſudden greens and herbage crown'd;
And ſtreams ſhall murmur all around.

PSALM XXV.

TO God, in whom I truſt,
I lift my heart and voice;
O let me not be put to ſhame,
Nor let my foes rejoice.

Since mercy is the grace
That moſt exalts thy fame;
Forgive my heinous ſin, O Lord,
And ſo advance thy Name.

Let all my youthful crimes
Be blotted out by thee:
And, for thy wond'rous goodneſs ſake,
In mercy think on me.

Do thou with tender eyes
My ſad affliction ſee:
Acquit me, Lord, and from my guilt
Entirely ſet me free.

Let all my righteous acts
To full perfection riſe;
Becauſe my firm and conſtant hope
On thee alone relies.

PSALM XXXIII.

LET all the juſt to God with joy
Their chearful voices raiſe;
For well the righteous it becomes,
To ſing glad ſongs of praiſe.

Moſt

Moſt faithful is the word of God,
His works with truth abound ;
He juſtice loves, and all the earth
Is with his goodneſs crown'd.

By his almighty word at firſt
The heav'nly arch was rear'd ;
And all the beauteous hoſts of light
At his command appear'd.

Whate'er the mighty Lord decrees,
Shall ſtand for ever ſure ;
The ſettled purpoſe of his heart
To ages ſhall endure.

PSALM XXXIV.

THRO' all the changing ſcenes of life,
In trouble, and in joy ;
The praiſes of my God ſhall ſtill
My heart and tongue employ.

Of his deliv'rance I will boaſt,
Till all who are diſtreſt,
From my example comfort take,
And charm their grief to reſt.

Oh make but trial of his love !
Experience will decide
How bleſt they are, and only they,
Who in his truſt confide.

Fear him, ye ſaints, and ye will then
Have nothing elſe to fear ;
Make ye his ſervice your delight,
Your wants ſhall be his care.

HAVE mercy, Lord, on me,
  As thou wert ever kind;
Let me, opprest with loads of guilt,
  Thy wonted mercy find.

Wash off my foul offence,
  And cleanse me from my sin;
For I confess my crime, and see
  How great my guilt has been.

Against thee only, Lord,
  And only in thy sight
Have I transgress'd, and tho' condemn'd,
  Must own thy judgments right.

Blot out my crying sins,
  Nor me in anger view;
Create in me a heart that's clean,
  An upright mind renew.

Withdraw not thou thy help,
  Nor cast me from thy sight;
Nor let thy Holy Spirit take
  It's everlasting flight.

The joy thy favour gives,
  Let me again obtain:
And thy free Spirit's firm support,
  My fainting soul sustain.

PSALM LVII.

O God, my heart is fix'd, is bent,
  It's thankful tribute to present;
And with my heart my voice I'll raise,
To thee, my God, in songs of praise.

Awake

Awake my glory, harp, and lute,
No longer let your ſtrings be mute;
And I, my tuneful part to take,
Will with the early dawn awake.

Thy praiſes, Lord, I will reſound
To all the liſt'ning nations round;
Thy mercy higheſt heav'n tranſcends,
Thy truth beyond the clouds extends.

Be thou, O God, exalted high;
And as thy glory fills the ſky,
So let it be on earth diſplay'd,
Till thou art here as there obey'd.

PSALM LXXXVI.

TO my complaint, O Lord my God,
Thy gracious ear incline;
Hear me, diſtreſt, and deſtitute
Of all relief but thine.

Do thou, O God, preſerve my ſoul,
That does thy name adore;
Thy ſervant keep, and him, whoſe truſt
Relies on thee, reſtore.

To me, who daily thee invoke,
Thy mercy, Lord, extend;
Refreſh thy ſervant's ſoul, whoſe hopes
On thee alone depend.

Thou, Lord, art good, not only good,
But prompt to pardon too;
Of plenteous mercy to all thoſe
Who for thy mercy ſue.

O Come, loud anthems let us ſing,
Loud thanks to our almighty king;
For we our voices high ſhould raiſe;
When our ſalvation's Rock we praiſe.

Into his preſence let us haſte,
To thank him for his favour paſt:
To him addreſs in joyful ſongs
The praiſe that to his name belongs.

For God, the Lord, enthron'd in ſtate,
Is with unrival'd glory great;
A king ſuperior far to all
Whom kings on earth we mortals call.

O let us to his courts repair,
And bow with adoration there:
Down on our knees devoutly all
Before the Lord our Maker fall.

For he's our God, our Shepherd he;
His Flock and paſture ſheep are we:
Then let us (like his flock) draw near,
His goſpel's ſacred truth to hear.

PSALM C.

WITH one conſent let all the earth
To God their chearful voices raiſe;
Glad homage pay with awful mirth,
And ſing before him ſongs of praiſe.

Convinc'd that he is God alone,
From whom both we and all proceed;
We, whom he chuſes for his own;
The flock that he vouchſafes to feed.

O enter

O enter then his temple gate,
  Thence to his courts devoutly preſs,
And ſtill your grateful hymns repeat,
  And ſtill his name with praiſes bleſs.

For he's the Lord ſupremely good;
  His mercy is for ever ſure:
His truth, which always firmly ſtood,
  To endleſs ages ſhall endure.

PSALM CVI.

O Render thanks to God above,
The fountain of eternal love:
Whoſe mercy firm thro' ages paſt
Has ſtood, and ſhall for ever laſt.

Who can his mighty deeds expreſs,
Not only vaſt, but numberleſs?
What mortal eloquence can raiſe
His tribute of immortal praiſe?

Happy are they, and only they,
Who from thy judgments never ſtray:
Who know what's right,—not only ſo,
But always practice what they know.

Extend to me that favour, Lord,
Thou to thy choſen doſt afford;
When thou return'ſt to ſet them free,
Let thy ſalvation viſit me!

O may I worthy prove to ſee
Thy ſaints in full proſperity;
That I the joyful choir may join,
And count thy people's triumph mine.

MY ſoul with grateful thoughts of love
  Entirely is poſſeſt;
Becauſe the Lord vouchſaf'd to hear
  The voice of my requeſt.
Since he has now his ear inclin'd,
  I never will deſpair;
But ſtill, in all the ſtraits of life,
  To him addreſs my pray'r.
When death alarm'd me, he remov'd
  My dangers and my fears;
My feet from falling he ſecur'd,
  And dry'd my eyes from tears.
Then, free from penſive cares, my ſoul,
  Reſume thy wonted reſt;
For God has wond'rouſly to thee
  His bounteous love expreſt.
The future years of fleeting life,
  Which God to me ſhall lend,
Will I in praiſes to his name,
  And in his ſervice ſpend.

PSALM CXIX.

TO me, O Lord, thy grace reſtore,
  That I again may live;
Whoſe ſoul can reliſh no delight,
  But what thy precepts give.
In thy bleſt ſtatutes let my heart
  Continue always ſound;
That guilt and ſhame (the ſinner's lot)
  May never me confound.
My ſoul with long expectance hopes
  To ſee thy ſaving grace;
And ſtill on thy unerring word
  My confidence I place.

Thy

Thy wonted kindneſs, Lord, reſtore,
To cheer my drooping heart;
That from thy righteous ſtatutes I
May never more depart.

PSALM CXXX.

FROM loweſt depths of woe,
To God I ſent my cry;
Lord, hear my ſupplicating voice,
And graciouſly reply.

Should'ſt thou ſeverely judge,
Who can the trial bear?—
But thou forgiv'ſt, leſt we deſpond,
And quite renounce thy fear.

My ſoul with patience waits
For thee, the living Lord;
My hopes are on thy promiſe built,
Thy never-failing word.

My longing eyes look out
For thy enliv'ning ray;
More duly than the morning watch,
To ſpy the dawning day.

Let Iſr'el truſt in God,
No bounds his mercy knows;
The plenteous ſource and ſpring from whence
Eternal ſuccour flows.

Whoſe friendly ſtreams to us
Supplies in want convey;
A healing ſpring, a ſpring to cleanſe,
And waſh our guilt away.

PSALM

TO God, the mighty Lord,
Our joyful thanks repeat;
To him the praiſe afford,
Whoſe mercies are ſo great.
For God doth prove
Our conſtant friend;
His boundleſs love
Shall never end.

To him whoſe pow'r hath made
The heav'ns with mighty hand,
And ocean wide hath ſpread
Around the ſpacious land.
For God, &c.

Thro' heav'n he did diſplay
The num'rous hoſts of light;
The ſun, to rule the day,
The moon and ſtars, the night.
For God, &c.

He doth the food ſupply
On which all creatures live:
To God who reigns on high,
Eternal praiſes give.
For God, &c.

PSALM CXXXIX.

LORD, thou my ways haſt ſearch'd, and known
My riſing up, my ſitting down;
To thee are my conceptions brought,
Ere they are form'd into a thought.

Thine eye my bed and path ſurveys,
My public haunts, and private ways;
Thou know'ſt whate'er my lips would vent,
My yet unutter'd words' intent.

Sur-

Surrounded by thy power I ſtand,
On every ſide I find thy hand;
Wiſdom for human ſearch too high!
Too dazzling bright for mortal eye!
Let me acknowledge, O my God,
That ſince the maze of life I've trod,
The bounties of thy love ſurmount
The power of numbers to recount.
Search, try, O God, my thoughts and heart,
If evil lurks in any part;
Correct me where I go aſtray,
And guide me in thy perfect way.

PSALM CXLIII.

LORD hear my pray'r, and to my cry
  Thy wonted audience bend;
In thy accuſtom'd faith and truth,
  A gracious anſwer ſend.

Nor at thy ſtrict tribunal bring
  Thy ſervant to be try'd;
For in thy ſight no living man
  Can e'er be juſtify'd.

To thee my hands in humble pray'r
  I fervently ſtretch out;
My ſoul for thy refreſhment thirſts,
  Like land oppreſs'd with drought.

Thy kindneſs early let me hear,
  Whoſe truſt on thee depends;
Teach me the way where I ſhould go;
  My ſoul to thee aſcends.

Thou art my God, thy righteous will
  Inſtruct me to obey;
Let thy good ſpirit guide and keep
  My ſoul in the right way.

THE Lord ſupports all them that fall,
And makes the proſtrate riſe;
For his kind aid all creatures call,
Who timely food ſupplies.

Whate'er their various wants require,
With open hand he gives;
And ſo fulfils the juſt deſire
Of ev'ry thing that lives.

He grants the full deſires of thoſe
Who him with fear adore;
And will their troubles ſoon compoſe,
When they his aid implore.

The Lord preſerves all thoſe with care,
Whom grateful love employs;
But ſinners, who his vengeance dare,
With furious rage deſtroys.

My time to come, in praiſes ſpent,
Shall ſtill advance his fame,
And all mankind with one conſent,
For ever bleſs his name.

PSALM CXLVI.

O Praiſe the Lord, and thou, my ſoul,
For ever bleſs his name;
His wondrous love, while life ſhall laſt,
My conſtant praiſe ſhall claim.

The Lord, who made both heav'n and earth,
And all that they contain,
Will never quit his ſtedfaſt truth,
Nor make his promiſe vain.

The poor oppreſt, from all their wants
Are eas'd by his decree;
He gives the hungry needful food,
And ſets the pris'ners free.

By

By him the blind receive their ſight,
The weak and fall'n he rears;
With kind regard and tender love,
He for the righteous cares.

The ſtranger he preſerves from harm,
The orphan kindly treats;
Defends the widow, and the wiles
Of wicked men defeats.

The God that does in Sion dwell,
Is our eternal king;
From age to age his reign endures;
Let all his praiſes ſing.

PSALM CXLIX.

O Praiſe ye the Lord,
Prepare your glad voice,
His praiſe in the joyful
Aſſembly to ſing.
In our great creator
Let Iſr'el rejoice;
And children of Sion
Be glad in their king.

Let them his great name
Extol in the dance;
With timbrel and harp
His praiſes expreſs;
Who always takes pleaſure
His ſaints to advance;
And with his ſalvation
The humble to bleſs.

With

With glory adorn'd,
His people ſhall ſing
To God, who their beds
With ſafety does ſhield;
Their mouths fill'd with praiſes
Of him, their great king,
Shall ſongs of thankſgiving
Triumphantly yield.

Thus ſhall they declare,
That ſin to deſtroy,
And men to redeem,
The Son of God came:
Such honour and triumph
His ſaints ſhall enjoy;
O therefore for ever
Exalt his great name!

PSALM CL.

LET the ſhrill trumpet's warlike Voice,
Make rocks and hills his praiſe rebound;
Praiſe him with harp's melodious noiſe,
And gentle pſalt'ry's ſilver ſound.

Let virgin-troops ſoft timbrels bring,
And ſome with graceful motion dance;
Let inſtruments of various ſtring,
With organs join'd, his praiſe advance.

Let them who joyful hymns compoſe,
To cymbals ſet their ſongs of praiſe;
Cymbals of common uſe, and thoſe
That loudly ſound on ſolemn days.

Common

Common Metre.

TO Father, Son, and Holy Ghoſt,
The God whom we adore,
Be glory, as it was, is now,
And ſhall be evermore.

To God, our benefactor, bring
The tribute of your praiſe;
Too ſmall for an almighty King,
But all that we can raiſe.

Glory to thee, bleſt Three in One,
The God whom we adore:
As was, and is, and ſhall be done,
When time ſhall be no more.

Long Metre.

To Father, Son, and Holy Ghoſt,
The God whom earth and heav'n adore,
Be glory, as it was of old,
Is now, and ſhall be evermore.

Short Metre.

To God the Father, Son,
And Spirit, glory be;
As 'twas, and is, and ſhall be ſo,
To all eternity.

As the 37th, *and ſome other Pſalms.*

To Father, Son, and Holy Ghoſt,
The God whom Heav'n's triumphant Hoſt,
And ſuffering Saints on earth adore,
Be Glory, as in ages paſt,
As now it is, and ſo ſhall laſt,
When time itſelf exiſts no more.

As

As Pſalm 100, *and many others of Eight Syllables.*

Praiſe God, from whom all bleſſings flow,
Praiſe him all creatures here below:
Praiſe him above, angelic hoſt:
Praiſe Father, Son, and Holy Ghoſt.

As Pſalm 136, 148.

To God the Father, Son,
  And Spirit ever bleſt,
Eternal Three in one,
  All worſhip be addreſt,
    As heretofore
      It was, is now
      And ſhall be ſo
    Forever more.

As Pſalm 149.

By Angels in Heav'n
  Of ev'ry degree,
And Saints upon Earth,
  All praiſe be addreſt,
To God in Three perſons,
  One God ever-bleſt;
As it has been, now is,
  And always ſhall be.

HYMNS

HYMNS

For the Use of the

MAGDALEN-CHAPEL.

HYMN I.*

For the MORNING.

By Bishop KENN.

AWAKE, my soul, and with the sun
Thy daily stage of duty run:
Shake off dull sloth, and early rise,
To pay thy morning sacrifice.

[Redeem thy mis-spent moments past,
And live this day, as if 'twere last;
Thy talents to improve take care;
For the great day thyself prepare.

Let all thy converse be sincere,
Thy conscience, as the noon-day clear;
For God's all-seeing eye surveys
Thy secret thoughts, thy works, and ways.

* This Hymn being to long to be sung at one time, all within the crotchets [ ] may be omitted.

Wake, and lift up thyſelf, my heart,
And with the angels bear thy part;
Who, all night long, unwearied ſing
High glory to th'eternal King.

I wake, I wake, ye heavenly choir,
May your devotion me inſpire:
That I, like you, my age may ſpend;
Like you, may on my God attend.

May I, like you, in God delight;
Have all day long my God in ſight;
Perform, like you, my Maker's will;
O! may I never more do ill.]

Glory to thee, who ſafe haſt kept,
And haſt refreſh'd me whilſt I ſlept;
Grant, Lord, when I from death ſhall wake,
I may of endleſs life partake!

Lord, I my vows to thee renew;
Scatter my ſins as morning dew:
Guard my firſt ſprings of thought and will,
And with thyſelf my ſpirit fill.

Direct, controul, ſuggeſt this day,
All I deſign, or do, or ſay:
That all my pow'rs, with all their might,
In thy ſole glory may unite.

Praiſe God, from whom all bleſſings flow;
Praiſe him, all creatures here below:
Praiſe him above, angelic hoſt:
Praiſe Father, Son, and Holy Ghoſt.

For the EVENING.

By the ſame.

GLORY to thee, my God, this night,
For all the bleſſings of the light:
Keep me, O keep me, King of Kings,
Under thy own almighty wings.

Forgive me, Lord, for thy dear Son,
The ills which I this day have done;
That with the world, myſelf, and thee,
I, ere I ſleep, at peace may be.

* [Teach me to live, that I may dread
The grave as little as my bed;
Teach me to die, that ſo I may
With joy behold the judgment-day.

Let my bleſt guardian, while I ſleep,
His watchful ſtation near me keep:
My heart with love celeſtial fill,
And guard from the approach of ill.

Lord, let my ſoul for ever ſhare,
The bliſs of thy paternal care;
'Tis heav'n on earth, 'tis heav'n above,
To ſee thy face, and ſing thy love.]

Shou'd Death itſelf my ſleep invade,
Why ſhou'd I be of Death afraid?
Protected by thy ſaving arm,
Tho' he may ſtrike he cannot harm.

For death is life, and labour reſt,
If with thy gracious preſence bleſt:
Then welcome ſleep, or death to me,
I'm ſtill ſecure, for ſtill with Thee!

* The three Stanzas within crotchets are commonly omitted in ſinging at the Chapel.

Praiſe God, from whom all bleſſings flow,
Praiſe him, all creatures here below:
Praiſe him above angelic hoſt:
Praiſe Father, Son, and Holy Ghoſt.

HYMN. III.

The CHRISTIAN's HOPE.

From the Spectator.

WHEN riſing from the bed of death,
O'erwhelm'd with guilt and fear,
I ſee my Maker, face to face;
O how ſhall I appear!

If yet, while pardon may be found,
And mercy may be ſought,
My heart with inward horror ſhrinks,
And trembles at the thought.

When thou, O Lord, ſhall ſtand diſclos'd
In Majeſty ſevere,
And ſit in judgment on my ſoul,
O how ſhall I appear?

But thou haſt told the troubled mind,
Who does her ſins lament,
The timely tribute of her tears
Shall endleſs woe prevent.

Then ſee the ſorrows of my heart,
Ere yet it be too late;
And hear my Saviour's dying groans,
To give thoſe ſorrows weight.

For never ſhall my ſoul deſpair,
Her pardon to procure,
Who knows thy only Son has dy'd,
To make that pardon ſure.

On GRATITUDE.

From the ſame.

WHEN all thy mercies, O my God,
My riſing ſoul ſurveys;
Tranſported with the view I'm loſt,
In wonder, love, and praiſe.

O how ſhall words with equal warmth,
The gratitude declare,
That glows within my raviſh'd heart!
But thou can'ſt read it there.

Thy providence my life ſuſtain'd,
And all my wants redreſt,
When in the ſilent womb I lay,
And hung upon the breaſt.

To all my weak complaints and cries
Thy mercy lent an ear,
Ere yet my feeble thoughts had learnt
To form themſelves in prayer.

Unnumber'd comforts on my ſoul
Thy tender care beſtow'd,
Before my infant heart conceiv'd
From whom thoſe comforts flow'd.

When worn by ſickneſs, oft haſt thou
With health renew'd my face:
And, when in ſin and ſorrow ſunk,
Reviv'd my ſoul with grace.

Ten thouſand thouſand precious gifts,
My daily thanks employ;
Nor is the leaſt a chearful heart,
That taſtes thoſe gifts with joy.

Through ev'ry period of my life
  Thy goodness I'll pursue;
And after death in distant worlds
  The glorious theme renew.

When nature fails, and day and night
  Divide thy works no more;
My ever-grateful heart, O Lord,
  Thy mercy shall adore.

HYMN V.

The Excellency of the BIBLE.

By Dr. WATTS.

GREAT God! with wonder and with praise
  On all thy works I look:
But still thy wisdom, pow'r, and grace,
  Shine brighter in thy book.

The stars that in their courses roll,
  Have much instruction given;
But thy good words inform my soul
  How I may soar to heaven.

The fields provide me food, and shew
  The goodness of the Lord;
But fruits of life and glory grow
  In thy most holy word.

Here are my choicest treasures hid,
  Here my best comfort lies;
Here my desires are satisfy'd.
  And hence my hopes arise.

Lord

Lord, make me underſtand thy law,
 Shew what my faults have been;
And from thy goſpel let me draw
 Pardon for all my ſin.
Here would I learn how Chriſt has dy'd,
 To ſave my ſoul from hell:
Not all the books on earth beſide
 Such heav'nly wonders tell.

Then let me love thy ſcriptures more,
 And, with renew'd delight,
By day read all thy wonders o'er,
 And meditate by night.

HYMN VI.

On the SABBATH.

By. Dr. DODDRIDGE.

LORD of the Sabbath, hear us pray,
In this thy houſe, on this thy day;
Accept, as grateful ſacrifice,
The ſongs which from thy ſervants riſe.

Thine earthly Sabbaths, LORD, we love;
But there's a nobler REST above:
Oh that we might that REST attain,
From ſin, from ſorrow, and from pain!

In thy bleſt kingdom we ſhall be
From every mortal trouble free:
No groans ſhall mingle with the ſongs
Reſounding from immortal tongues.

No rude alarms of raging foes;
No cares to break the long repoſe;
No midnight ſhade, no clouded ſun,
But ſacred, high, eternal noon.

O long-expected day! begin;
Dawn on these realms of woe and sin:
Fain would we leave this weary load,
To sleep in death, and rest with God.

HYMN VII.

For the SACRAMENT.

By Dr. WATTS.

HOW are thy glories here display'd,
Great God! how bright they shine,
While, at thy word, we break the bread,
And pour the flowing wine!

Here thy avenging Justice stands,
And pleads its dreadful cause;
Here saving Mercy spreads her hands,
Like *Jesus* on the cross.

Thy saints attend with ev'ry grace
On this great sacrifice;
And Love appears with chearful face,
And Faith with fixed eyes.

Zeal and Revenge perform their part,
And rising sin destroy;
Repentance comes with aching heart,
Yet not forbids the Joy.

Dear Saviour! change our Faith to Sight,
Let sin forever die;
Then shall our souls be all delight,
And ev'ry tear be dry.

HYMN

On CHRISTMAS DAY.

By Dr. DODDRIDGE.

HIGH let us ſwell our tuneful notes,
And join th' angelic throng;
For angels no ſuch love have known,
T'awake a chearful ſong.

Good-will to ſinful men is ſhewn,
And peace on earth is given;
For lo! th' incarnate Saviour comes
With meſſages from heaven.

Juſtice and grace, with ſweet accord,
His riſing beams adorn;
Let heav'n and earth in concert join?
"To us a child is born."

GLORY to GOD in higheſt ſtrains,
In higheſt worlds be paid;
His glory by our lips proclaim'd,
And by our lives diſplay'd!

When ſhall we reach thoſe bliſsful realms
Where CHRIST exalted reigns;
And learn of the celeſtial choir
Their own immortal ſtrains!

HYMN IX.

On the NEW YEAR.

By the ſame.

GOD of my life! thy conſtant care
With bleſſings crowns the op'ning year;
This guilty life thou doſt prolong,
And wake anew my annual ſong.

How many kindred souls are fled
To the vast regions of the dead,
Since from this day the changing sun
Thro' his last yearly period run?

We yet survive; but who can say,
Or thro' the year, or month, or day,
"I will retain this vital breath;
"Thus far, at least, in league with death?"

That breath is thine, eternal God;
'Tis thine to fix my soul's abode:
It holds its life from thee alone,
On earth, or in the world unknown.

To thee our spirits we resign;
Make them, and own them, still as thine;
So shall they smile secure from fear,
Tho' death should blast the rising year.

HYMN X.

On the Passion.

FROM whence these dire portends around,
  That earth and heav'n amaze?
Wherefore do earthquakes cleave the ground?
  Why hides the sun his rays?

Not thus did Sinai's trembling head
  With sacred horror nod,
Beneath the dark pavilion spread
  Of the descending God!

What tongue the tortures can declare
  Of this vindictive hour?
Wrath he alone had will to share,
  As he alone had pow'r!

See

See, ſtreaming from the fatal tree,
His all-toning blood!
Is this the Infinite?——'Tis He!
My SAVIOUR, and my GOD!

For me theſe pangs his ſoul aſſail,
For me the death is borne!
My ſin gave ſharpneſs to the nail,
And pointed ev'ry thorn.

Let ſin no more my ſoul enſlave;
Break, Lord, the tyrant's chain;
Oh ſave me, whom thou cam'ſt to ſave,
Nor bleed or die in vain!

HYMN XI.

For EASTER.

JESUS Chriſt is riſen to day,—Hallelujah!
Our triumphant holyday;
Who did once upon the croſs,
Suffer to redeem our loſs.

Hymns of praiſe then let us ſing
Unto Chriſt, our heavenly king;
Who endur'd the croſs, and grave,
Sinners to redeem and ſave.

But the pains which he endur'd,
Our ſalvation have procur'd;
Now he reigns, triumphant king,
Where the angels ever ſing,—Hallelujah!

For WHIT-SUNDAY.

By Mr. DRYDEN.

ETERNAL Spirit! by whose aid
The world's foundations first were laid:
Come, visit every pious mind,
Come, pour thy joys on human kind!

From sin and sorrow set us free,
And make thy temples worthy thee:
Illumine our dull darken'd sight,
Thou source of uncreated light.

Thrice holy font! thrice holy fire!
Our hearts with heavenly love inspire:
Come, and thy sacred unction bring,
To sanctify us while we sing.

Plenteous of Grace, descend from high,
Rich in thy seven-fold energy!
Thou strength of His almighty hand,
Whose power does heaven and earth command.

Proceeding Spirit, our defence,
Who dost the gifts of grace dispense:
Feeble alas! we are, and frail;
Let not the world or flesh prevail!

Chace from our minds th' infernal foe,
And Peace, the fruit of Love, bestow:
And, lest our feet should step astray,
Protect and guide us in the way!

Make us eternal Truths receive,
And practise all that we believe:
Give us thyself, that we may see
The Father and the Son by thee!

Im-

Immortal honours, endless fame
Attend th' Almighty Father's name;
The Saviour Son be glorified,
Who for lost man's redemption died:

And equal adoration be,
Eternal Spirit, paid to thee;
"Come, visit every pious mind;
"Come, pour thy joys on human kind!"

HYMN XIII.

On THANKSGIVING.

By Dr. DODD.

GLORY be to God our King,—*Hallelujah!*
Thine eternal love we sing:
Thou hast bar'd thine arm divine,
Wrought salvation; made us thine.
Hallelujah! &c.

Wand'ring sheep, how far from home
Sore bewilder'd did we roam;
Till the gracious shepherd came,
Sought, and sav'd: O praise his name!

Death, no more we dread thy sting;
Sin subdu'd, we joyful sing:
Grave, thy terrors we defy;
We shall live; for Christ did die.

Fir'd with gratitude, we raise
All our souls to sound thy praise;
Touch each heart, each tongue inspire,
Sing we higher still, and higher.

Down to deepeſt hell depreſt,
Jeſu reſcu'd, rais'd, and bleſt;
Open'd mercy's golden gate,
Mercy, here who holds her ſeat.

Happy manſion!—every voice,
In the bleſt retreat rejoice;
Let each voice united ſound,
"Be the walls with gladneſs crown'd!"

Elevate our ſouls to thee:
Thou our guide and guardian be;
Worthy, worthy may we prove,
Lord, of ſuch diſtinguiſh'd love!

Bleſſing, thankful all our days,
May we pray, rejoice, and praiſe;
'Till the glorious trump ſhall ſound,
And our raptur'd hearts rebound,—*Hallelujah!*

HYMN XIV.

THANKS *to* GOD.

By Dr. DODDRIDGE.

ALL glorious God! what hymns of praiſe
Shall our tranſported voices raiſe!
What flaming love and zeal is due,
While heav'n ſtands open to our view!

Once we were fall'n,—and oh how low!
Juſt on the brink of endleſs woe:
Doom'd to the heritage in hell;
Where ſinners in deep darkneſs dwell.

But

But lo, a ray of chearful light.
Scatters the horrid ſhades of night:
Lo, what triumphant grace is ſhewn,
To ſouls impoveriſh'd and undone!

Far, far beyond theſe mortal ſhores
A bright inheritance is ours;
Where ſaints in light our coming wait,
To ſhare their holy bliſsful ſtate.

HYMN XV.

A PENITENTIAL HYMN.

RISE, O my ſoul! the hours review,
When, aw'd by guilt and fear,
Thou durſt not heav'n for mercy ſue,
Nor hope for pity here.

Dry'd are thy tears, thy griefs are fled;
Diſpell'd each bitter care!
See! heav'n itſelf has lent its aid,
To raiſe thee from deſpair.

Hear then, O God! thy work fulfil!
And from thy mercy's throne
Vouchſafe me ſtrength to do thy will,
And to reſiſt my own.

So ſhall my ſoul each pow'r employ,
Thy mercies to adore;
Whilſt heav'n itſelf proclaims with joy,
One pardon'd ſinner more.

HYMN XVII.

The SINCERE PENITENT.

By Mr. LOCKMAN.

ALmighty Lord! moſt merciful,
These thanks unfeign'd, theſe vows receive;
Thou, who, when bath'd in tears I lay,
Did'ſt hear my cries, and quick relieve.

Chorus. Great God from all eternity,
O may our pray'rs aſcend to thee!

Plung'd deep in woe, of hope bereft,
Deſtruction threaten'd me around;
Remorſe was mine, and black deſpair;
And I no ray of comfort found.

Chorus. Great God, &c.

For ever, O! recorded be
The moment, when thy grace beſtow'd,
Thro' Chriſt, the ſight of pard'ning love,
And led me to this bleſt abode.

Chorus. Great God, &c.

Since

Since treading fair Virtue's ſacred paths
  Alone ſecures the mind's content,
May the remainder of my days
  In ſerving thee be always ſpent.

Chorus Great God from all eternity,
  O may our pray'rs aſcend to thee!

HYMN XVIII.

Set by Dr. HOWARD.

CHORUS.

O God of mercy! hear my pray'r,
  Thy weak, thy ſinful creature ſave;
Thy voice can raiſe me from deſpair,
  Raiſe me triumphant from the grave!

In Vanity's bewild'ring maze,
  How long my erring feet have ſtray'd!
Far from Religion's peaceful ways,
  And far from Virtue's guardian aid!

O Lord of life! O Son divine!
  Almighty Saviour! Heavenly Friend!
To me, thy pitying ear incline,
  Thy renovating grace extend!
O God of Mercy! &c.

Tho'

Tho' thus polluted and forlorn,
By thee inſpir'd, my ſoul ſhall riſe,
Fairer than fleeces newly ſhorn,
Than mountain ſnows, or vernal ſkies.

Then, let thy Spirit from above,
My Saviour, God! deſcend on me;
Correct my thoughts, my faith improve,
And make me worthy Heaven and thee!
O God of Mercy! &c.

THE

THE RULES and REGULATIONS OF THE MAGDALEN-HOSPITAL.

Incorporated by Act of Parliament, 9 Geo. III. 1769.

I. Of the GOVERNMENT;

This is composed of

The Patroness.
A President.
Six Vice Presidents.
A Treasurer.
A General Court.
A General Committee of thirty-two.

1. THE President is appointed for life, the six Vice-Presidents, the Treasurer, and Committee of thirty-two, are annually chosen, and seven of the Committee go out yearly.

2. All the Officers and Servants, are likewise chosen annually.

II. Of

II. *Of the* TREASURER.

1. He receives the benefactions; keeps an account of all receipts and payments; and accounts, at the four quarterly general courts, or oftner if required.

2. Whatever surplus money remains in his hands, at any of the said courts, more than sufficient to defray the current expences, he is to lay it out in the public funds, if the majority of the Governors then present shall think fit.

3. He pays all bills at the Hospital in the presence of the Committee.

III. *Of the* GENERAL COURTS, *and* ELECTIONS *of* OFFICERS.

1. A General Court consists of the President, or in his absence, of one of the Vice Presidents, or the Treasurer, and eight or more Governors; and in the absence of the President, all the Vice Presidents, and Treasurer, of nine Governors, who in that case chuse their Chairman. The President, Vice President, Treasurer, or Chairman presiding, is to explain the business of the assembly; to propose questions, and to put them to the vote, and, if required, by five Governors, to take the votes by ballot, such ballot to begin and be determined immediately. The Chairman may vote in common with others; and in case of an equality of votes, the Chairman is further to have a casting vote.

2. The General Courts are held quarterly, *viz.*

The last *Wednesday* in *July*.

The

The laſt *Wedneſday* in *October*.
The laſt *Wedneſday* in *January*.
The laſt *Wedneſday* in *April*.

The Anniverſary Meeting is uſually held in *May*.

3. The Secretary gives notice by letter to the Preſident, Vice-Preſidents, Treaſurer, and Governors, of the place, day, and hour of holding General Courts: and the ſame is alſo advertiſed in ſome of the public News-papers five days before ſuch Court.

4. On the annual General Court (held the laſt *Wedneſday* in *April*) the ſix Vice Preſidents, the Treaſurer, Committee, Officers and Servants, are choſen.

5. At every quarterly General Court the Treaſurer lays before the Governors the general ſtate of the houſe, reſpecting the receipts and diſburſements of the quarter; alſo the caſh which remains in hand, &c.

6. The Treaſurer alſo reports the number of women admitted into the houſe, and the number of thoſe provided for, and in what manner they have been provided for, during the quarter.

7. The general yearly account is publiſhed at the anniverſary meeting.

8. The Court orders and diſpoſes of the Common Seal, and the uſe and application thereof, and hath p wer to enter into contracts, and make ſuch rules, bye laws, conſtitutions, and ordinances, as they ſhall think neceſſary, and to revoke and alter the ſame.

9 No

9. No bye law, rule, order, or regulation, or alteration, or repeal of a bye law, &c. can have any effect, unlefs confirmed by a fucceeding General Court, either annual, quarterly, or extraordinary.

10. In cafe of death, or refignation of the Prefident, or any of the Vice-prefidents, or Treafurer, the General Court may elect another.

11. The General Court have power, from time to time to appoint fuch other Officers and Servants as they fhall think neceffary, and to fufpend or remove all fuch Officers or other perfons, or any or either of them, and appoint others in cafe of death, fufpenfion, or removal, and make fuch allowances for their fervices as they fhall think reafonable.

IV. *Of the* General Committee.

1. Of this Committee five conftitute a Quorum, and the Prefident, Vice-Prefidents, and Treafurer, are always of this General Committee, one of whom, is Chairman; but in their abfence the Committee chufe a Chairman.

2. The Meetings of the Committee are on every *Thurfday* at five o'Clock in the afternoon, from *April* to *October*, and eleven o'Clock in the Forenoon from *October* to *April*.

3. The firft *Thurfday* only in the month is for the admiffion of objects.

4. Any three of the Committee, in Committee, have power to draw on the Bankers of the Charity.

5. The Committee contract for, and infpect the

the cloathing, furniture, and provisions; and take care to prevent impositions.

6. The Committee (being summoned for that purpose,) have power to dismiss or elect all servants under the degree of Steward or Matron, and suspend or remove any such Servants, and appoint others in case of death, resignation, suspension, or removal, until a General Court shall be held.

7. When there is any particular business, the same is to be expressed in the summons, and this business is entered upon before any other.

8. The Committee admit all such Petitioners as they approve, and give orders in what manner they shall be employed, and dismiss any women from the house, as occasions may require; and in the absence of the Committee the Treasurer has the same power.

9. The rough Minutes of the Committee are read by the Secretary, and signed by the Chairman, before he leaves the Chair. These Minutes, being copied fair into a book, are also read at the next Meeting, when they are confirmed, if approved.

10. The Members of the Committee attend by turns at the Chapel every *Sunday*, and notice of their turn is regularly given. See afterwards Regulations for the Chapel.

11. The Committee have power to make such honorary Governors as they think fit.

V. *A*

V. *A* SUB-COMMITTEE.

1. This consists of any number of the General Committee appointed by them.

2. Any three of the Committee accompanied by the Matron may visit the Wards, and make their report to the next General Committee that meets.

3. They occasionally meet to examine the accounts, and to inspect into the good order and œconomy of the House.

VI. *Of* GOVERNORS in General.

1. A Subscription of *twenty* Guineas or more is a qualification of a Governor for life.

2. An annual Subscription of five Guineas is a qualification of a Governor for that year; and every person on payment of five year's successive subscription becomes a Governor for life.

3. If any annual Subscriber shall be more than two years in arrear, his power as a Governor ceases till such arrears are paid.

4. No gentlemen, except Peers, Members of Parliament, or Privy Counsellors, are admitted to vote by proxy, but every Lady subscribing as above, is intitled to vote Personally, or by Proxy, provided that Proxy be brought by a Governor; but no such Governor shall be possessed of more than *one Proxy*. Every Community giving a Sum equal to a qualification for a Governor, may vote by Proxy.

5. Any five Governors have power to require a General Court, provided they address themselves to the President, or one of the Vice Presidents, or Treasurer, by letter, signed by them, setting forth the

the bufinefs for which fuch Meeting is required, and notice of fuch Meeting is publifhed in the news papers five days at leaft before the Court.

VII. *Of the* OFFICERS in general.

1. Every perfon who is difcovered to have received any money, perquifite, fee, reward, or emolument of any kind, relating to this Charity, more than the Salary or Wages allowed by the Governors of this Charity, or their Committee, fhall be forthwith difcharged.

2. No fervant, nor any other perfon, fhall for any reafon, or on any account whatever, take any thing out of the houfe, which has been bought for the ufe thereof

3. No officer or fervant fhall lye out of the houfe, without leave of the Treafurer, or two of the Committee in writing.

VIII. *Of the* SECRETARY.

1. He prepares the accounts for the General Courts.

2. He carries on the correfpondence.

3. He is prefent at all the Meetings, and takes the Minutes.

IX. *Of the* CHAPLAIN.

1. He reads prayers, and preaches twice every *Sunday*, and alfo reads Prayers at fuch other hours in the week days as are appointed by the Committee.

2. He adminifters the Sacrament on *Chrift-*

 mas,

mas, *Eaſter* and *Whitſundays*, and on the firſt and third *Sunday* in every Month.

3. He inſtructs the women in the Principles and Duties of the Chriſtian Religion.

4. He attends alternately in the Wards every day, for ſuch time as the Committee may direct, to expound the Scriptures, and admoniſh and inſtruct each of the women in ſuch manner as may make a proper impreſſion on their minds.

5. He attends the Committee when called upon.

6. He delivers a monthly report of the behaviour of the women, and performs all other neceſſary duties of his function.

X. Regulations *for the* Chapel.

1. The Gentleman whoſe turn it is to preſide at the Chapel on a *Sunday*, hath notice in writing the *Tueſday* preceding.

2. In caſe it doth not ſuit him to attend on that *Sunday*, he is deſired to provide ſome other of the Committee to attend, and ſignify the ſame to the weekly Committee on *Thurſday*, or to the Secretary on *Friday*.

3. The Doors of the Chapel are not opened till half paſt Ten in the morning, and half paſt Five in the evening; and the gentleman preſiding is requeſted to attend before the opening the doors, and remain in the Chapel to ſuperintend the Steward and Meſſengers, and to prevent the admiſſion of improper company.

4. Such gentleman hath power to refuſe admittance to all perſons he ſhall judge improper, without

without regard to the Tickets they bring for admittance.

5. The Tickets brought by any persons so judged improper are retained by the Messenger, and laid before the next Committee.

6. The gentlemen of the Committee are requested not to deliver more than three Tickets for each *Sunday* evening.

7. The President, Vice-Presidents, Treasurer, the gentleman appointed to preside for the night (provided he attends) and Dr. *Dodd*, are at liberty to issue as many Tickets as they shall think fit.

8. No Ticket is received unless signed by a Governor, and filled up with the name of the person bringing the same.

9. No undated Tickets, or with the date altered or obliterated, are taken.

10. These regulations are printed and sent to every Governor, and hung up in the committee room, the lobby, and at the chapel doors.

11. No person is admitted after divine service is begun, except during the time of singing the first psalm.

12. Divine service begins at eleven in the morning, and six in the evening.

13. Every Governor for life, and Subscriber of five guineas per annum, during the continuance of such subscription, is at liberty to come to the chapel every *Sunday* morning and evening, and bring three persons; and every such Governor and Subscriber as aforesaid, may have a Ticket for admission of four persons, for every *Sunday*

morning and evening, by ſending to the Secretary, or to the Steward at the Hoſpital, a note in writing ſigned by ſuch Governor or Subſcriber. A collection is made at the door for the Charity.

XI. *Of the* Physician.

He attends when called upon.

XII. *Of the two* Surgeons.

1. They attend by rotation, in their own own perſons, each for a month, and do the duty of their office, *gratis*.

2. One of them is always preſent at the admiſſion of the objects, and, if neceſſary, examines into the ſtate of their health.

XIII. *Of the two* Apothecaries.

1. They attend alternately if neceſſary, under the direction of the Phyſician.

2. The medicines are contracted for at the rate of ſixty pounds *per annum*.

3. The Phyſician, Surgeons, and Apothecaries, when they viſit the wards, are attended by the Matron, or one of the Aſſiſtants to the Matron, and no pupil, ſervant, or apprentice, belonging to the ſurgeons or apothecaries, are ever admitted.

XIV. *Of the* Matron.

1. She reſides conſtantly in the houſe, and directs the œconomy thereof.

2. She

2. She is fully inſtructed in the rules, regulations, and orders of the houſe, and obſerves them ſtrictly.

3. She ſees that all the women are neat and decent in their apparel and perſons; that they are duly employed, and behave in an orderly and religious manner, and that they conſtantly attend divine ſervice.

4. She makes reports to the Committee weekly of the behaviour and conduct of the women.

5. She receives from the Steward the materials for work, and delivers to him an account of the work done by the women, that he may make a regular entry and account thereof, in proper books.

6. She takes the charge of all the houſhold linen and cloathing, of which the Steward alſo keeps an account.

7. She receives of the Steward the proviſions which are allowed for the houſe, and takes care that none be carried away, nor any waſte made.

8. She reads the inſtructions to the women, (No. 1.) the next morning after their admittance, and delivers a copy of the inſtructions to each of ſuch newly admitted women.

XV. *The two* Aſſiſtants *to the* MATRON.

1. They take charge each of their reſpective ward.

2. They inſtruct ſuch of the women as are ignorant, in reading, needle-work, and what

elſe may be neceſſary, and ſuperintend the work of all the women in their ward.

3. They are preſent with the women at their meals, and hear grace properly repeated before and after dinner.

4. They attend the women conſtantly, and obſerve their tempers and diſpoſitions; and whether they appear to be worthy objects of the charity; what offices in life they are moſt fit for; when it is proper to diſcharge them to parents or friends, or to ſervice, and what elſe occurs.

5. They are conſtantly attentive not only to prevent any improper diſcourſe, but to communicate juſt ſentiments, and encourage ſober converſation, and a regular peaceful and pious behaviour.

6. They ſee that the bed-chambers are kept compleatly clean and in good order.

7. They ſee that the beds and bedding are kept properly mended, neat and clean.

8. They ſee that the table-furniture and linen be kept clean and mended, and preſerved in good order.

9. They hear all complaints which may be made by the women in their reſpective wards, and if neceſſary lay the ſame before the Matron or Committee.

10. They duly and ſtrictly obſerve the ſeveral rules, regulations, and orders of the houſe, and the directions which may be given them from time to time by the Committee.

11. They make a report to the Committee every week, with a list of the women in their respective wards, with such remarks as they think proper.

XVI. *Of the* STEWARD.

1. He resides constantly in the house, and is not to follow any business or employment whatsoever, but such as immediately relates to his duty in this Charity.

2. He makes a weekly report to the Committee of whatever he is required to do.

3. He receives the respective provisions for the use of the house, and the materials for the employment of the women.

4. He inspects the weights, measures, and quality thereof, and makes regular entries of them, and superintends all other domestic concerns, and is diligent in observing the rules of the house, and all the orders of the committee.

5. He keeps an exact account of all the work done by the women.

6. He keeps a fair and exact inventory of the furniture as ranged in the different wards and apartments, with the cost of each article, and produces all the accounts for the quarterly payments.

7. He collects the annual benefactions, and gives security in the sum of two hundred pounds.

XVII. *Of the* Messengers.

1. They dwell in the houſe, and are employed in errands and out-door buſineſs, and give ſecurity if required.

2. They are not to bring any letter, verbal or written meſſage into the houſe, or carry out any letter, verbal or written meſſage, without the knowledge and inſpection of the Matron.

3. They attend the gate by turns, and receive meſſages and letters, and what elſe the nature of their office requires.

N. B. The Steward and Meſſengers live in apartments, which have no communication with the wards.

XVIII. *Of* Admission.

1. The Committee ſit to admit objects on the firſt *Thurſday* in every month, at five o'clock in the afternoon, during the Months of *April*, *May*, *June*, *July*, *Auguſt*, and *September*, and at eleven o'clock in the Forenoon during the months of *October*, *November*, *December*, *January*, *February*, and *March*.

2. The method of admiſſion is by petition, without any recommendation, preſented to the Committee in the form preſcribed (No II.) the blanks in which petition are filled up by the Steward from the report of the petitioner, gratis.

3. The Steward gives the petitioner the number of her petition.

4. Theſe petitions are preſented to the Committee

mittee, and the petitioners are called by them according to their number.

5. The names of the persons are not called, that if the petitioner is not admitted her name may not be known to others who attend.

6. The question being put on the admission of every object, it is decided by the votes of the majority of the Committee.

7. Every petitioner is previously examined as to the state of her health by the nurse attending for that purpose; and, if necessary, by the Surgeon also. If she is infected with the foul disease, she is not admitted; but upon her obtaining her cure, may be reconsidered by the Committee, and if then found proper is admitted.

8. If the petitioner is admitted, the Secretary gives her a note directed to the Matron, signifying her admission.

9. If more petitioners apply on any admission day than can be then received, they may apply again the next admission day.

10. Proper instructions being provided for such as are admitted, they are assembled the next morning after admission, and the *instructions* are read to them by *the Matron*, as already mentioned. And, in order to make the deeper impression, the same instructions are read, by the *Assistants to the Matron*, in their respective Wards, constantly on the first Saturday morning in the month.

11. No woman admitted is allowed to go out of the house, without special leave in writing,

 signed

ſigned by the Treaſurer or Chairman, and two of the Committee; and that for a time not exceeding the day, and this only on an urgent and extraordinary occaſion, which may relate to property: and in ſuch caſe ſhe is attended by the Matron, or one of her Aſſiſtants.

XIX. *Of the* Wards *and* Precautions.

1. The Houſe is divided into parts, in order to make a total and diſtinct diviſions of the objects.

2. The women are claſſed in each Ward, and the Aſſiſtants to the Matron appointed to preſide, are accountable for the conduct and behaviour of their reſpective Wards.

3. A proper number of the women are appointed to perform all the domeſtic buſineſs of their reſpective Wards; and the houſhold ſervice, the keeping the Chapel clean, and what elſe is neceſſary, according to the directions given by the Matron.

4. Each woman lies in a ſeparate bed, and has a box for her cloaths and linen, under a lock and key, which key is kept by herſelf.

5. Strict regard is had, by the Matron and her Aſſiſtants, that the Wards be kept completely ventilated, and the air pure; for which purpoſe they viſit the chambers and working-rooms frequently every day.

6. The relations or friends of the women (being known as ſuch) may, upon application, and by leave in writing, firſt obtained from the Treaſurer, or Chairman, and two of the Committee, be

be permitted to ſee and converſe with the reſpective women, in the preſence of the Matron, or one of her Aſſiſtants.

XX. *Of the Sick* WARD.

1. For each claſs and diviſion of the houſe, a room is ſet apart for the ſick.

2. There is a Nurſe appointed to attend the ſick, and every neceſſary for their recovery ſupplied.

XXI. *Of the* NAMES.

1. If the women are deſirous of concealing their true names, they have liberty to aſſume others.

2. Reproaches for paſt irregularities are forbidden; no enquiry into names or family is permitted; but all poſſible diſcouragement given to the making any diſcovery, which the parties themſelves do not approve.

XXII. *Of their* DRESS.

1. If, upon their admiſſion, their apparel is clean, or fit to waſh, it is ticketted, and laid by, in order to be returned to them whenever they leave the houſe.

2. They wear light grey ſhalloon gowns; and in their whole dreſs are plain and neat, and exactly alike.

XXIII. *Of their* DIET.

1. A diet for breakfaſt, dinner, and ſupper, for certain ſeaſons, is appointed at the diſcretion of the Committee; and the ſame written in a fair hand writing, and hung up in the Committee-room, and in each Ward.

2. They repeat grace by turns, each a week, in a ſolemn and ſerious manner.

XXIV. *Of their* EMPLOYMENT.

1. Each perſon is employed in ſuch needle-work or houſhold-buſineſs as is ſuitable to her abilities.

2. The chief objects in which they have hitherto been employed are, making houſhold linen of all ſorts, fine ſhirts, and alſo ſlop ſhirts and ſhifts: making all the linen for the uſe of the houſe, knitting ſtockings, making and mending all the cloaths they wear, and alſo the ſheets and table-linen, and learning to do domeſtic offices, to qualify them for ſervice.

3. In their work, as in every other circumſtance, the utmoſt propriety and humanity are obſerved; all looſe or idle diſcourſe, ſluttiſhneſs, indolence, or neglect of moral or religious duties, are cloſely attended to; and if theſe are not in the degree to occaſion a diſcharge, they are at leaſt ſeverely reprehended.

XXV. *Of Times of* REST *and* DIET.

1. From Lady-day to Michaelmas they riſe at ſix, and go to bed at ten; and from Michaelmas

elmas to Lady-day riſe at ſeven, and are in bed at nine; and after that time no fire or candle are allowed, except in the ſick ward.

2. They breakfaſt at nine o'clock, and are allowed half an hour; and dine at one o'clock, and are allowed an hour; and leave off work at ſix in the winter, and ſeven in the ſummer.

XXVI. *Of* Discharge.

1. Application being made, either by the parents or friends of the woman, if ſuch parents or friends appear worthy of being truſted, and declare they forgive paſt offences, and will take ſuch woman under their protection, the woman alſo conſenting, the Committee diſcharge her accordingly, and her cloaths are returned to her.

2. If any Houſe-keeper of ſufficient credit applies for a ſervant, the Matron recommends ſuch a woman as ſhe thinks will anſwer the purpoſe, as to abilities and good conduct; and if ſuch ſervice is approved by the Committee, the woman is diſcharged accordingly.

3. Services out of town are always preferred, as being the moſt ſafe.

4. Every woman who is placed out in a ſervice, and continues there one year to the approbation of her maſter and miſtreſs, upon its being made appear to the Committee, that ſhe hath behaved unexceptionably, they give ſuch woman a guinea, as a token of their approbation of her good behaviour.

5. The Committee, upon the good behaviour of any woman, and upon her having remained

mained a proper time in the houſe, write to her friends or relations to provide for her.

6. On the diſcharge of thoſe who behave well, whether they go out to ſervice, or to be married, if their parents or friends are not in a capacity to furniſh them with cloaths, theſe are provided for them in a proper manner.

Every means which the Committee can think of, that may conduce to the great ends of this Charity, is uſed, whether it be to ſave the ſoul, preſerve the life, or render that life uſeful and happy.

Form

FORM *of the* PETITION *for Admiſſion.*

See p. 320.

To the General Committee for Tranſacting the Buſineſs of the Magdalen Hoſpital.

THE Humble Petition of
aged years
of the pariſh of in the
County of

Sheweth,

THAT your Petitioner has been guilty of Proſtitution, and is truly ſenſible of her offence, which has plunged her into the greateſt diſtreſs, and rendered her deſtitute of every means of getting an honeſt livelihood.

YOUR Petitioner therefore humbly prays ſhe may be admitted into the ſaid Houſe, and doth ſolemnly promiſe to behave herſelf decently and orderly, and that ſhe will conform to all the Rules of the Houſe.

And as in duty bound ſhall ever pray.

N. B. *This Petition is given gratis, upon application to the Steward, at the Hoſpital in* St. George's Fields.

A LIST

A
L I S T
OF THE
GOVERNORS AND CONTRIBUTORS
OF THE
MAGDALEN CHARITY.

Governors for Life, *g*.
Governors by Annual Subſcription. *a*.
Of the Committee, *c*.
Have ſerved as Stewards, *s*.
Governors for Life who give annually. *g. a*.

PATRONESS.

g. HER MAJESTY

PRESIDENT.

g. a. c. Francis, Earl of HERTFORD, *Great Groſvenor-ſtreet*

VICE PRESIDENTS.

g. a. c. ROBERT, Lord ROMNEY, *Maidſtone, Kent*
g. a. c. HUGH, Earl PERCY, *Park Place*
g. c. ROBERT DINGLEY, Eſq; *Lamb-abbey, near Foots Cray, Kent*
g. c. RICHARD BECHER, Eſq; *Portman-ſquare*
g. a. c. s. NATH. CASTLETON, Eſq; *Cavendiſh-Square*
g. a. c. s. JOHN BARKER, Eſq; *Manſell-ſtreet, Goodman's Fields*

TREASURER.

g. c. s. MICHAEL JAMES, Eſq; *Haydon-ſquare, Minories*

The

The Annual Committee.

Hon. Henry Hobart
Sir James Cockburn, Bart.
Sir Thomas Tancred, Bart.
Sir Timothy Waldo, Knt.
Robert Allen, Efq;
Ifaac Akerman, efq;
Paul Amfinck, efq;
Samuel Athawes, efq;
James Barill, efq;
Thomas Boddam, efq;
Henry Boldero, efq;
Thomas Bond, efq;
Robert Briftow, efq;
George Briftow, efq;
Thomas Calverley, efq;
Nathaniel Cholmley, efq;
Bicknel Coney, efq;
Robert Cornthwait, efq;
John Cuthbert, efq;
John Dorrien, efq;
Henry Hoare, jun, efq.
Samuel Horne, efq;
Jonas Hanway, efq;
Thomas Hirft, efq;
William Jacomb, efq;
Thomas Jacomb, efq;
John Levy, efq;
Philip Milloway, efq;
Nath. Newnham, efq; and alderman.
John Anthony Rucker, efq;
James Vere, efq;
Jofeph Wells, efq;

Secretary, Abraham Winterbottom
Phyfician, Dr William Saunders
Surgeons, Mr. W. Blizard, Mr. J. Andree
Apothecaries, Mr. And. Johnfon, Mr. J. Harris
Chaplain, Rev. Mr. John Dobie

GOVERNORS.

A

g. JOHN Duke of Athol, *Grosvenor-place*

g. s. Willoughby, Earl of Abingdon, *Hill-st.*

g. s. Heneage, Earl of Aylesford, *Grosvenor-square*

g. s. Sir Charles Asgill, Bart. *St. James's-square.*

g. James Adair, esq. *Soho-square*

g. John Adams, esq. *Grosvenor-street*

a. Mr. John Adams, No. 12, *Chancery-lane*

g. s. George Adey, esq. *Lombard-street*

g. c. s. Isaac Akerman, esq. *Clapham*

g. James Alexander, esq. *Berners-street*

g. c. s. Robert Allen, esq. *Ironmonger-lane*

g. c. s. Paul Amsinck, esq. *Steel-yard*

g. William Archer, esq. *White-hart-court*

g. Mr. Richard Ashley, *St. Dunstan's-hill*

g. c. s. Samuel Athawes, esq. *Martin's-lane*

g. William Ayton, jun, esq; *John-street, Bedford row*

g. Abraham Atkins, esq. *Clapham*

a. Hon. Mrs. Arundel

g. Mrs. Elizabeth Ainge, *Gloucester-street, near Red-lion-square*

B.

g. Henry, Duke of Buccleugh, *Grosvenor-square*

g. John, Earl of Buckinghamshire, *Bond-street*

g. s. John, Earl Bute, *South Audley-street*

g. s. Francis

g. s. Francis, Lord Viscount Beauchamp, *Stanhope-street, May-fair*

g. s. Frederick, Lord Boston, *Grosvenor street*

g. s. Brownlow, Ld. Brownlow, *Old Bond-st.*

g. s. Thomas, Lord Viscount Boulckley, *Chesterfield-street, May-fair*

g. s. Sir Robert Burdet, Bart. *Great Mary-le bone-street*

g. s. Sir Thomas Charles Bunbury, Bart. *Privy gardens*

g. Sir Walter Blackett, Bart. *Half-Moon-street, Piccadilly*

g. Sir Patrick Blake, Bart. *Queen Anne-street, Cavendish-square*

a. Sir Roger Braidshaigh, Bart.

g. a. c. s. John Barker, esq. V. P. *Mansel-street, Goodman's-fields*

g. c. s. Richard Becher, esq. V. P. *Portman-square*

g. John Bagnall, esq. *Berks*

g. John Baggs, esq. *Shadwell-dock*

a. Richard Bagot, esq. *Lower Brook-street, Grosvenor-square*

g. Thomas Barney Branston, esq. *Norfolk*

g. c. s. James Baril, esq. *Tokenhouse-yard*

g. Jonathan Barnard, esq. *Eltham, Kent*

g. William Henry Barnard, esq. *Argyle-buildings*

g. Mr. John Barnard, *Ipswich*

a. Mr. James Barnard

g. Mr. Philip Barling, *Broad-street*

a. Hon. J. Smith Barry

g. George Baskerville, esq. *Crosby-square*

g. John Bates, esq.

a. Mr. Joseph Bayley, No. 141, *New Bond-street*

a. Mr.

a. Mr. Daniel Beele, No. 1, *Little Prescot-street*
g. John Becher, esq. *Camberwell*
a. Mr. Thomas Bell No. 262, *Borough*
g. Richard Barwell, esq.
g. William Bearsley, esq.
g. Thomas Bennet, esq. *Old Broad-street*
a. Alexander Bennet, esq. *Beaufort Buildings, Strand*
g. James Bernard, esq.
g. s. Daniel Birket, esq. *Swan-stairs, London-bridge*
g. Joseph Bird, esq. *New Lloyd's Coffee house*
g. Ebenezer Blackwell, esq. *Lombard-street*
g. William Blizard, esq. No. 12. *Mark-lane*
g. Mr. Thomas Blunt, *Cornhill*
g. Charles Boddam, esq. *East India-house*
g. c. s. Thomas Boddam, esq. *Enfield*
g. Thomas Boddington, esq. *Mark lane*
g. s. Edmund Boehm, esq. *Sise lane*
g. c. Henry Boldero, esq. *Lombard-street*
a. John Boldero, esq. *Mansion house-street*
g. c. Thomas Bond, esq. *Lambeth-marsh*
g. Charles Boone, esq. *Soho-square*
a. Richard Wilbraham Bootle, esq. *Bloomsbury-square*
g. Samuel Bosanquet, esq. No. 10. *Birchin lane*
g. William Bowden, esq. *St. Thomas's Hospital*
g. Mr. John Bowles, *Cornhill*
a. Samuel Brailsford, esq.
a. Thomas Brand, esq. *St. James's-square*

g. Gustavus

g. Gustavus Brander, esq. *Crown-court, King-street, Westminster*

g. Matthew Brickdale, esq. *Bristol*

g. c. s. Robert Bristow, esq. *Spring-gardens*

g. c. s. George Bristow, esq. *Merchant Taylors-hall*

g. Edward Brocksop, esq. *Savage-gardens*

g. William Bromfield, esq. *Conduit-street*

g. Isaac Hawkins Brown, esq. *Russel-street, Bloomsbury*

g. William Brown, esq No. 2. *Pump-court, Temple*

g. James Brown, esq. *Lombard-street*

g. s. Frederick Bull, esq. Alderman, *King's-street.*

g. James Bulcock, esq. No. 85, *Borough*

g. s. Francis Burdett, esq. *North Audley street*

g. George Burgess, esq.

a. John Burrow, esq. *New Road, Black-friars-bridge*

g. Robert Butcher, esq. *Copeland, Bedfordshire*

a. Francis Burton, esq.

a. Thomas Burton, esq.

g. Isaac Buxton, esq. No. 80, *Coleman street*

a. Countess of Bute, *North Audley-street*

a. Lady Bryan Broughton, *Cleveland-row*

g. Mrs. Barker, *Mansell-street*

g. Mrs. Diana Blake } *Queen Anne-street, Cavendish square*
g. Mrs. Jane Blake }

g. Mrs. Hawkins Brown, *Russel-street, Bloomsbury*

g. Lady

g. Lady Braidfhaigh
g. Mrs. Bull, *King's-ftreet*

C

a. Frederick, Earl of Carlifle, *St. James's Place*
g. Philip, Earl of Chefterfield, *Abroad*
a. James, Earl of Cholmondeley, *Piccadilly*
a. Marquis of Carmarthen, *Grofvenor-fquare*
g. a. s. William, Lord Vifcount Courtney, *Grofvenor-fquare*
g. a. s. William, Lord Craven, *Charles-ftreet, Berkeley-fquare*
a. Lord George Cavendifh, *Savile ftreet*
g. Lord Thomas Pelham Clinton
g. Right Rev. Bifhop of Clonfert
g. Right Rev. Bifhop of Cork
g. s. Sir Robert Clayton, Bart. *Hill-ftreet, Berkeley-fquare*
g. c. s. Sir James Cockburn, Bart. *Soho-fquare*
g. s. Sir George Colebrook, Bart. *Threadneedle-ftreet*
a. Sir John Chefter, Bart.
g. Sir Guy Charlton, K. B. *Quebec*
g. a. c. s. Nathaniel Caftleton, efq. V. P. *Cavendifh-fquare*
g. c. s. Thomas Calverley, efq. *High-ftreet, Borough*
a. Major General Carpenter, *Stable-yard*
g. John Cartier, efq. *Great Ormond-ftreet*
g. s. Robert Cary, efq. *Hampftead*
g. Charles Cartwright, efq.
a. Thomas Cave, efq. *Upper Grofvenor-ftreet*

a. Henry

a. Henry Cecil, esq. *Albemarle-street*
g. John Conyers, esq. *Copthall, Essex*
a. Henry Cavendish, esq. *Stanhope-street, May-fair*
a. William Challoner, esq.
g. s. Abraham Chambers, esq. *New Bond-street*
a. William Chaplin, esq. *Bedford coffee-house, Covent-garden*
g. Francis Charlton, esq. *Welbeck-street*
g. Charles Child, esq. *Cateaton-street*
a. Robert Child, esq. *Berkley-square*
g. c. s Nathaniel Cholmley, esq. *Portman-square*
g. Mr. William Cholmley, *Lad-lane*
g. Mr. John Barker Church
g. Mr. John Church
g. Edward Chyslin, esq. *Doctor's Commons*
a. William Cheplin, esq.
a. Jervoise Clarke, esq. *Hanover-square*
g. Mr. John Clements, *Cheapside Conduit*
a. Mr. John Close, *Tower-dock*
g. Thomas Clutterbuck, esq.
g. Mr. Henry Cook
a. Richard Coffin, esq. *North Audley-street*
g. Benjamin Cole, esq. *Copthall court*
g. Mr. Frederick Comyn, *Cornhill*
g. c. Bicknell Coney, esq. *Leadenhall-street*
g. Rev. Allen Cooper
a. Thomas Cooper, esq.
g. Thomas Cowper, esq. *Bream's-buildings, Chancery-lane*
a. Richard Combe, esq. *Harley-street*
g. c. s. Robert Cornthwait, esq. *Southampton-street, Bloomsbury*
g. s. John Cornwall, esq. *King's Arms-yard*

g. Mr.

g. Mr. Samuel Courtald, *Cornhill*
g. James Coutts, esq. *Charles-street, Berkeley-square*
a. Richard Cox, esq. *Albemarle-street*
a. Richard Hippesley Cox, esq.
g. Mr. Richard Cracraft, *Brabant-court, Philpot-lane*
a. s. Rev. John Craven, A. M. *Craven-buildings*
g. Patrick Crawford and John Dalrymple, esqrs.
a. John Crew, esq. *Grosvenor-square*
g. s. James Crockatt, esq. *Richmond*
g. Charles Crommeline, esq.
a. Mr. John Crosier, *Catherine-court, Tower street*
g. s. Asheton Curzon, esq. *David-street, Grosvenor-square*
g. s. Peregrine Cust, esq. *Great George-street*
g. c. John Cuthbert, esq. *Paper-buildings, Temple*
g. Lady Mary Coke, *Kensington*
a. Dame Mary Clayton, *Hill-street*
g. Lady Frances Coningsby, *Upper Brook-street*
a. Lady Cotton
g. Mrs. Ann Cotesworth, *Knightsbridge*
a. Mrs. Castle, *Spring-gardens*
g. Mrs. Courtald, *Cornhill*
g. Mrs. Curteis, *Wapping*

D.

g. s. William, Duke of Devonſhire, *Piccadilly*

a. John, Duke of Dorſet, *Oxford-ſtreet, near Park-lane*

g. s. William, Earl of Dartmouth, *St. James's-ſquare*

g. s. Arthur, Earl of Donegal, *ditto*

g. s. Sir Lawrence Dundaſs, Bart. *Arlington-ſtreet, Piccadilly*

g. Sir John Dick, Bart. *Leghorn*

g. c. s. Robert Dingley, eſq. V. P. *Lamb-abbey, Kent*

g. Richard Dalton, eſq. *St. James's-ſtreet*

g. John Darker, eſq. *St. Bartholomew's Hoſpital*

g. Samuel Daſhwood, eſq. *Well, Lincoln-ſhire*

a. Charles Vere Bertie Daſhwood, eſq. *John-ſtreet, Berkeley-ſquare*

g. Monkhouſe Daviſon, eſq. *Fenchurch-ſtreet*

g. William Daviſon, eſq.

a. Maximilian Daws, eſq. *Norfolk*

g. Thomas Dawſon, M. D. *Hackney*

g. Edmund Dawſon, eſq. No. 20. *Stoney-lane, Southwark*

a. Chriſtopher Dawſon, eſq.

g. John Day, eſq.

a. s. Peter Delmé, eſq. *Groſvenor-ſquare*

g. Robert Dent, eſq. *Temple-bar*

g. William Dent, eſq. *Garraway's Coffee-houſe*

g. Mr.

g. Mr. Edward De Sante, *Leadenhall-ſtreet*
a. Francis Dickens, eſq. *Mount-ſtreet*
g. Thomas Dinely, eſq. *Tower-hill*
g. Rev. Robert Henry Dingley, *Lamb-abbey, Kent*
g. James Dixon, eſq.
g. Rev. William Dodd, LL. D. *Argyle-ſtreet*
g. c. s. John Dorrien, eſq. *Billiter-ſquare*
g. Mr. Thomas Dorrien, *ditto*
a. Henry Drummond, eſq. *Pall-mall*
a. Robert Drummond, eſq. *Charing-croſs*
a s. Charles Dunbar, eſq. *Hill-ſtreet, Berkley-ſquare*
a. Thomas Dundaſs, eſq. *Arlington-ſtreet*
g. Mr. Peter Duval, *Hackney*
g. Lewis Duval, eſq. *Warnford-court, Throgmorton-ſtreet*
g. John Duval, eſq. *Throgmorton-ſtreet*
a. Ducheſs of Devonſhire, *Devonſhire-houſe*
a. Counteſs of Denbigh, *South-ſtreet*
g. Mrs. Eſther Dingley, *Lamb-abbey, Kent*

E.

a. s. Brownlow, Earl of Exeter, *Groſvenor-ſtreet*
g. George, Earl of Egremont, *Piccadilly*
g. s. Sir James Eſdaile, Knt. and Alderman, *Bunhill-row*
g. s. Peter Eſdaile, eſq. *ditto*
g. s. Mr. John Eddowes, *Cheapſide*
g. James Ellis, eſq.

g. Mr. Charles Ellis, *Almacks, Pall Mall*
g. Thomas Ellison, esq. *Westham, Kent*
a. Mr. Evans

F.

g. Hugh, Viscount Falmouth, *St. James's-square*
a. Hon. Charles Finch, *St. James's-street*
g. Sir John Fielding, Knt. *Bow-street*
g. s. Thomas Farrar, esq. *Mark-lane*
g. William Fauquire, esq. *Stretton-street,*
a. Mr. David Fenton, *Mansion-House-street*
a. Mr. Thomas Fielder, *Cross-street, St. Mary-hill*
g. Mr. William Finney, *Cheapside,*
g. Hon. Mr. Fitzmaurice, *Pall-mall*
a. John Fleming, esq. *New Bond-street*
g. Thomas Fletcher, esq. *Walthamstow*
g. Mr. William Fletcher, *Cornhill*
g. Thomas Flight, esq. *Hackney*
g. s. Freeman Flower, esq. *Clapham*
g. Charles Floyer, esq. *Bengal*
a. Edward Foley, esq. *Bentinck-street*
a. Thomas Foley, jun. esq. *Park-lane*
g. Rev. Dr. Fordyce, *Essex street, Strand*
g. Mr. Alexander Fordyce, *Harley-street, Cavendish-square*
g. Edward Forster, esq. *Broadstreet-buildings*
g. Thomas Furley Forster, esq. *ditto*
g. s. Aaron Franks, esq. *Bishopsgate-street*
g. William Franks, esq. *Percy-street*

g. John

g. John Free, esq. } *Devonshire-square*
g. Nathaniel Free, esq. }
g. Thomas Edwards Freeman, esq. *Sackville-street*
g. a. Henry Arthur Fellows, esq. *Hill-street, Berkeley-square*
g. Richard Fuller, esq. *Cornhill*
g. Countess Dowager Ferrers

G.

a. Thomas, Earl of Gainsborough, *Harley-street*
a. s. Marquis of Granby, *Piccadilly*
g. s. Sir Sampson Gideon, Bart. *St. James's-square*
g. Sir Robert Goodiere, Bart. *Sackville-street*
g. s. Mr. William James Gambier, *Aldermary Church-yard*
g. Samuel Garbert, esq. *Birmingham*
g. s. William Garrett, esq. No. 40. *Norfolk-street, Strand*
g. Peter Gaussen, esq. *St. Hellens*
g. s. William Gill, esq. No. 30. *Abchurch-lane*
g. Ambrose Lynch Gilbert, esq.
g. Ambrose Godfrey, esq. *Southampton-street, Covent-garden*
g. s. David Godfrey, esq. *Lincoln's-inn-fields*
g. s. Stephen Peter Godin, esq. *Southgate*
g. Richard Goodall, esq. *Crosby square*
g. Thomas Goodwin, esq.

g. Mr. Elijah Goff, *Old Gravel-lane, Wapping*
a. James Grant Gordon, esq.
g. Charles Gough, esq.
g. John Graham, esq.
g. John Grant, esq.
g. Thomas Gray, esq.
g. David Greame, esq.
g. Mr. Charles Green, *Limehouse*
g. Andrew Grote, esq. *Leadenhall-street*
g. Richard Grove, esq. *Paper-buildings, Temple*
g. Nicholas Gruber, esq.
g. Countess Dowager Gower, *Pall-mall*
g. Mrs. Gowland
a. Miss Hester Greville, *Bath*

H.

g. a. c. Francis Earl of Hertford, *President, Grosvernor-street*
g. Francis, Earl of Huntingdon, *Park-place*
g. a. s. Edward, Lord Hawke, *Bloomsbury-square*
g. Nathaniel, Lord Harrowby, *Park-street*
g. Honourable Thomas Hampden, *Conduit-street*
a. c. s. Honourable Henry Hobart, *Jermyn-street*
g. s. Sir Robert Hildyard, Bart. *Clifford-street*
g. a. Sir John Honeywood, Bart. *Hampstead*
a. Sir Harry Harpur, Bart. *Upper Grosvenor-street*
g. s. Sir Thomas Heathcote, Bart.
g. Sir Robert Herries, Knt. *Jeffries-square*
a. William Hale, esq. *Grosvenor-place*
g. William Hallhead, esq. *Clapham*
g. Francis Hammond, esq. *Cannon-street*

g. Mr.

g. Mr. Herb. Hancock, No. 23, *Ludgate-hill*
g. c. s. Jonas Hanway, esq. *Red-lion-square*
g. J. Harland, esq.
a. Henry Harper, esq.
g. James Harris, esq.
g. Mr. Edward Harston, *Wardour-street*
a. W. N. Hart, esq.
g. Thomas Hartley, esq. *Fish-street-Hill*
a. William Harvey, esq. *Clifford street*
g. Thomas Hervey, esq. *Bentinck-street*
g. William Hassey, esq.
a. George Hatton, esq. *Park-lane*
g. Edward Hawkins, esq. *Leman-street, Goodman's fields*
g. Samuel Hawkins, esq. *ditto*
g. a. s. William Heberden, M. D. *Pall-mall*
g. Mr. James Hedger, *Dog and Duck, St. George's fields*
g. Isaac Henkil, esq. *Fenchurch-street*
g. Thomas Heathfield, esq. *Tom's coffee-house, Cornhill*
g. John Heneker, esq. *Bank coffee-house*
g. William Hill, esq. *Borough*, No. 92.
a. Thomas Hill, esq. No. 8, *New-square, Lincoln's-inn*
g. c. Thomas Hirst, esq. *Great Russel-street*
g. Henry Hoare, esq. *Fleet-street*
g. s. c. Henry Hoare, jun. esq. *Ditto*
g. William Hoare, esq. *Bath*
g. George Hogg, esq. *Lynn, Norfolk*
g. Mr. William Holden, *Birmingham*
g. John Horne, esq. *Sise-lane*
a. Charles Orbey Hunter, *Wimpoole-street*

g. s. c. Samuel Horne, esq. *Clapham*
g. s. Charles Hornby, esq. *Coney-court, Gray's-Inn*
g. Mr. George Holland, *Strand*
g. s. James Hubbald, esq. *Suffolk-street, Cavendish-square*
g. Mr. Thomas Hudson, *Philpot-lane*
g. Mr. Thomas Hunt, *Love-lane*
a. William Hunter, M. D. *Windmill-street, Haymarket*
g. George Hurst, esq.
g. Babo. Hugercemal, *Bengal*
g. The Countess Dowager of Huntingdon, *Bath*
g. The Countess of Hertford, *Grosvenor-street*
g. Mrs. Sarah Harvey, *Golden-square*
a. Mrs. Jane Hart
a. Mrs. Elizabeth Hanmer, *Grosvenor-street*
a. Mrs. Alice Hill
g. Mrs. Grace Hill
g. Mrs. Heathcote
g. Mrs. Catharine Hyde, *Clapton*

I.

g. s. Sir Justinian Isham. Bart. *Wimpoole-street*
a. Sir William Jones, Bart. *Cavendish-square*
a. Mr. Stephen Jacob, *Cornhill*
g. a. c. s. William Jacomb, esq. *Laurence-poultney-hill*
g. c. Thomas Jacomb, esq. *King's-Bench-walk, Temple*

g. Mr.

g. Mr. Henry Jaffray, No. 65, *Strand*
g. c. s. Michael James, eſq. Treaſurer, *Heydon-ſquare*
g. Mr. John James
g. Joſeph Jekyl, eſq. *near Northampton*
g. Edmund Jennings, eſq. *Sevenoaks, Kent*
g. Loſtus Jones, eſq. *Frith-ſtreet, Soho*
a. William Jones, eſq.
g. Henry Jones, eſq.
a. Dame Iſham, *Spring-gardens*

K.

g. Edward Earl of Kingſton
g. Joſeph Kane, eſq.
g. s. Anthony J. Keck, eſq.
g. Page Keeble, eſq.
a. Dr. George Kelly
a. Thomas Kelſal, eſq.
g. s. Benjamin Kidney, eſq. *Laurence-pountney-hill*
a. Thomas Knight, eſq. *Groſvenor-ſtreet*
a. Lucy Knightley, eſq. *Groſvenor-ſquare*
a. John Knightley, eſq. *ditto*
g. John Knott, eſq.
g. s. John Koe, eſq; *Fore-ſtreet, Moorfields*
a. Mrs. King
a. Mrs. Francis Kid, *Ave Maria-lane*

L.

a. William Duke of Leinſter, *St. James's-ſtreet*
g. a. Edward, Lord Leigh
a. Earl of Lincoln, *Arlington-ſtreet*
g. James, Lord Lifford, Chancellor of Ireland

a. s. Sir James Langham, Bart. *Cavendish-square*
a. s. Timothy Lacey, esq; *Bath*
a. James Lambert, esq;
g. Mr. Timothy Lane
g. Mr. Henry Langkopf, No. 22, *College-hill*
g. s. Edmund Lardner, esq, *Borough*
g. s. Edwin Lascelles, esq; *Portman-square*
g. James Lawrell, esq.
g. s. Francis Lawson, esq;
g. Mr. John Lebreton, *Walworth*
g. George Lee, esq. *Lombard-street*
g. s. Joseph Leeds, esq; *Bridge-street, Westminster*
g. s. John Lefevre, esq. } *Stratford*
a. Leonard Lefevre, esq. } *Stratford*
g. Peter Leheup, jun. esq; *Albemarle-street*
g. c. John Levy, esq. *Borough*
g. John George Liebenrood, esq. *Reading, Berks*
a. Mr. Macey Life, *Craven-street, Strand*
g. Luke Lillingston, esq.
g. William Lock, esq;
g. Thomas Lucas, esq; *Albemarle-street*
g. William Lucas, esq. *Mark-lane*
g. John Daniel Lucadou, esq. *Old Broad-street*
g. Mrs. Ann Legrand and Mrs. Mary Legrand

M

g. s. George, Duke of Marlborough, *Pall Mall*

g. s. Anthony,

g. s. Anthony, Lord Viſcount Montague, *Queen Anne-ſtreet*

g. Charles, Lord Viſcount Maynard, *Groſvenor-ſquare*

g. Peniſton, Lord Melburne, *Piccadilly*

a. Thomas Lord Middleton, *Stanhope-ſtreet May-fair*

g. s. Sir Joſeph Mawbey, Bart. *Vauxhall*

g. Sir Horatio Man, K. B.

g. a. s. Herbert Mackworth, eſq. *Cavendiſh-ſquare*

a. Archibald M'Donald, eſq. *Lincoln's-inn*

g. Mr. Brough Maltby, No. 5, *Barge-yard*

g. Mr. Alexander Malkſtead, *Fan-court, Fenchurch-ſtreet*

g. Mr. Thomas Manby, *Low Layton*

g. s. Timothy Mangles, eſq. *Wanſtead*, or *Tom's Coffee Houſe*

g. Mr. Samuel March, *Dice Quay*

g. Rev. Dr. Robert Markham, *White Chapel church*

a. Rev. Dr. Thomas Marriott, *Beaver's-court, Baſinghall-ſtreet*

g. Samuel Marriot, eſq. *Exciſe Office*

g. Samuel Marſh, eſq. *Southampton-row, Bloomſbury*

g. Samuel Martin, eſq.

g. Colonel Flemming Martin

g. a. James Mathias, eſq. *Warnford-court, Throgmorton-ſtreet*

g. John Mawbey, eſq. *Vauxhall*

g. John May, esq.
g. George Medley, esq. *New Burlington street*
g. Mr. Herman Meyer, *St. Mary-axe*
g. Samuel Middleton, esq.
g. c. s. Philip Milloway, esq; *Abchurch-lane*
g. Mr. Charles Mills, *Tower-hill*
g. John Milner, esq.
g. Hugh Minett, esq.
g. Thomas Misenor, esq. *Lothbury*
g. ——— Mitchell, esq.
g. s. Samuel Moody, esq. No.96, *Leadenhall-street*
g. George Moore, esq. *Crutched-friars*
a. Mr. William Moore, *Bishopsgate-street*
g. Mr. Thomas Moore, *Chiswell-street*
g. s. Crisp Mollineux, esq; *Garboldisham, Norfolk*
g. Mr. James Morgan, *Broad-street-buildings*
g. William Morland, esq. *Black-heath*
g. John Mount, esq. *Tower-hill*
a. Joseph Musgrave, esq. *New Norfolk-street*
a. George Musgrave, esq. *Bond-street*
g. James Mytton, esq.
g. a. Mrs. Mauvillan, *Spring-gardens*
g. Mrs. Medley, *New Burlington-street*
a. Mrs. Letitia Munday, *Bath*

g. s. Hugh,

N.

g. s. Hugh, Duke of Northumberland, *Charing-crofs*

a. Robert, Earl of Northington, *Berkeley-fquare*

a. William Lord Newhaven, *St. James's-fquare*

g. s. Thomas Nafh efq. *Maurice-caufeway*

a. Mr. Charles Nevifon, *Duke-ftreet, St. James's*

g. c. s Nathaniel Newnham, efq. alderman, *Botolph-lane*

g. William Newnham, efq. *ditto*

g. s. John Nightingale, efq. *Lombard-ftreet*

a. Thomas Nobbes, efq. *Hampton-court*

g. James Norman, efq. *Printers-ftreet, Blackfriars*

a. John Norris, efq. *Witton, Middlefex.*

g. Duchefs of Northumberland, *Charing-crofs*

O.

g. s. Francis Lord Vifcount Orwell, *Stanhope-ftreet*

g. Robert Lord Ongley, *Great George-ftreet*

g. Mr. Jeremiah Ofborn, *Briftol*

g. Mr. Saunders Oliver, *Cannon-ftreet*

g. Mrs. Oliver } *Fenchurch ftreet*

a. Mrs. Mary Oliver, } *Fenchurch ftreet*

P.

g. a. c. Hugh, Earl Percy, V. P. *abroad*

a. Other, Earl of Plymouth, *Bruton ftreet*

a. Henry, Lord Pagett, *Savile-row*

g. s. Sir

g. s. Sir Gregory Turner Page, Bart. *Hertford-street, May-fair*
g. s. George, Lord Pigott, *abroad*
g. s. Right Hon. Sir Thomas Parker, Knt. *Bedford Row*
a. Sir John Palmer, Bart. *Mortimer-street, Cavendish-square*
a. Sir Thomas Powis, Bart.
g. s. Sir George Pococke, K.B. *Charles-street, Berkeley-square*
g. Sir Samuel Prime, Knt. *Isleworth*
g. John Page, esq. } *Tower-hill*
g. Edward Page, esq. }
g. s. Robert Palk, esq. *Burton-street*
g. a. Mr. Charles Parnell, *Somerset street, Whitechapel*
g. Mr. John Pearce, *Islington*
g. s. Jens Pederson, esq. *Wellclose-square*
g. s. Robert Pell, esq. *ditto*
g. a. Charles Pelham, esq. *Arlington-street*
g. s. George Perrot, esq. *Newington, Middlesex*
g. s. George Peters, esq. *Old Bethlem*
a. Frederick Pigou, esq. *Mark-lane*
a. Robert Pigott, esq. *Seymour-place*
g. Mr. Nicholas Peter Pillon, *Howard-street, Strand*
g. Mr. Edmund Pitts, *Swithin's-lane*
a. Mr. Peter Pope, *Fenchurch-street*
g. Thomas Plumer, esq. *John-street, Bedford-row*
g. Francis Plumer, esq. *New Exchange, Strand*

g. Mr.

g. Mr. William Pocock, *Devonshire-street, Queen's-square*
a. Sacheverel Poole, esq. *near Derby*
a. John Porter, esq.
g. Mr. James Portis, *Nicholas-lane*
g. Rev. Littleton Powes, *Letford, Northamptonshire*
a. Thomas Powys, esq. *Albemarle-street*
a. Rev. Newdigate Poyntz, *Bucklebery, Berks*
g. George Prescott, esq. *Threadneedle-street*
g. The Countess of Pomfret
a. Lady Powys
g. Mrs. Poyntz
a. Mrs. John Pitt, *Arlington-street*

Q.

a John Quick, esq. *Cornwall*

R.

g. a. c. Robert, Lord Romney, V. P. *Arlington-street*
a. George, Lord Rivers, *Hertford-street, May-fair*
g. Sir Thomas Robinson, Knt. and Bart. *Chelsea*
a. Sir John Rouse, Bart. *Wigmore-street*
g. John Randall, esq. *Rotherhithe*
g. Charles Rebotier, esq. No. 11, *Exchange-alley*
g. John Reed, esq.
g. s. John Regnier, esq. *Richmond, Surrey*
g. Charles Reinholt, esq.
a. Thomas Reynolds, esq.

g. William Reynolds, esq. *Church-court, Fenchurch-street*

g. Bateman Robson, esq. *Lincoln's-inn New-buildings*

a. William Rose, esq.

g. James Rowles, esq. *Adelphi*

g. c. s. John Anthony Rucker, esq. *Suffolk-lane*

g. Thomas Rumbold, esq. *Queen Anne-street*

g. Edward Russel, esq. *Borough*

g. The Marchioness of Rockingham, *Grosvenor-square*

S.

g. s. Richard, Earl of Scarborough, *South Audley-street*

g. John, Earl of Sandwich, *Admiralty*

g. s. John, Earl Spencer, *St. James's-place*

g. William, Earl of Shelburne, *Berkley-square*

g. George Earl of Stamford, *Sackville-street*

g. Philip, Earl Stanhope, *Queen Anne-street*

g. William, Earl of Strafford, *St. James's-Square*

a. Charles, Earl of Sefton, *Mansfield-street*

g. s. Nathaniel, Lord Scarsdale, *Cavendish-square*

g. Lord Robert Spencer, *Berkeley-square*

g. Sir George Savile, Bart. *Leicester-fields*

g. Sir

g. Sir Frank Standish, Bart. *Lancashire*
g. Mr. William Sainsbury, *Bread-street*
g. s. Robert Salmon, esq. *Limehouse*
g. s. Joseph Salvador, esq.
g. Mr. Herman Samler, *St. Andrew's hill*
g. s. Richard Sampson, esq. *Mansion house*
g. s. James Scawen, esq. *Dean street, South Audley-street*
g. Mr. Claud Scott, *Prescot-street, Goodman's-fields*
g. John Seare, esq. *Berkhamstead*
g. Hugh Seton, esq. *Leicester-square*
g. Mr. Samuel Sharpe, *Bishopsgate-street*
g. Henry Shiffner, esq.
g. s. John Shiffner, esq.
g. Thomas Skipwith, esq *Upper Brook-street*
g. Joseph Shrimpton, esq *Mark lane*
a. s. Robert Shuttleworth, esq. *New Burlington-street*
g. s. John Rogers Siebel, esq. *Abroad*
g. Mr. Joseph Simms, *Blackman-street*
g. Joseph Skinner, esq. *Whitechapel*
g. Russel Skinner, esq.
a. Colonel Skinner
g. Alexander Small, esq. *Clifton, Bucks*
a. Richard Smallbrook, LL.D.
g. John Small, esq.
g. a. s. John Smith, esq. *Little St. Helens*
g. E. Smith, esq.
g. Brigadier General Richard Smith, *Harley-street*
g. Mr. Samuel Smith, *Cannon-street*
g. Mr. Benjamin Smith, *ditto*

a. Mr.

a. Mr. Thomas Sparſhot, *Ivy-lane*
g. Richard Spencer, eſq. *Parliament-ſtreet*
g. Samuel Spencer, eſq. *Lewiſham*
g. Captain John Stables, *at Mr. Child's, Soho-ſquare*
g. Joſeph Stackpoole, eſq. *Soho-ſquare*
g. Richard Stannier, eſq. No. 54, *Cannon-ſtreet*
g. John Staples, eſq. *Stepney-green*
g. Roger Staples, eſq. *Cornhill*
g. Henry Steers, eſq; } *Figtree-court, Temple*
g. John Steers eſq; }
g. s. William Stead, eſq.
g. Mr. Robert Stewart, *Fenchurch-ſtreet*
g. s. William Stow, eſq. *St. Mary-hill*
a. Hon. Stephen Digby Strangeways, *Burlington-ſtreet*
g. s. Lawrence Sulivan, eſq. *Quene-ſquare*
a. Mr. —— Summers, *Ironmongers-hall*
g. Francis Sykes, eſq. *Brook-ſtreet*
g. Manoel Francis Sylva, eſq. *St. Mary Axe*
g.Ounteſs Spencer, *St. James's-place*
g. Hon. Mrs. Ann Shirley
g. Miſs Stannier
a. Hon. Mrs. Steuart
a. Mrs. Hannah Stone, *Privy-gardens*
g. Mrs. Sulivan, *Queen ſquare*

T.

a. George, Earl of Tyrconnell, *Hanover-ſquare*
a. The Rt. Rev. Biſhop of Down and Conner

a. c. Sir

a. c. Sir Thomas Tancred, Bart. *Lincoln's-inn New Buildings*
g. Sir Charles Kemys Tynte, Bart. *Hill-ftr.*
a. Sir John Trevilian, Bart. *Nettlecomb, Somerfetfhire*
g. Sir John Thorold, Bart.
a. Mr. John Tarris, *St. James's*
g. a. John Tafker, efq.
g. John Taylor, efq.
g. James Taylor, efq. *St. Peter's, Ifle of Thanet*
g. John Taylor, efq. *Queen Ann-ftreet*
a. s. John Tempeft, efq. *Wimpoole-ftreet*
g. Mr. John Terry, *Crediton, Devonfhire*
g. s. Andrew Thompfon, efq. *Auftin-friars*
g. Richard Thompfon, efq.
g. George Thompfon, efq. *Duke-ftr. Weftm.*
g. Harry Thompfon, efq.
g. s. John Thornton, efq. *Clapham*
g. Samuel Thornton, efq. *ditto*
a. s. Oliver Toulmin, efq. *Crutched-friars*
g. s. Kirkes Townley, efq. *Suffolk-lane*
g. s. John Townfon, efq. *Grays-inn*
g. Rev. John Tozor, *Gravefend*
g. Rob. Cotton Trefufis, efq. *Little Cannons*
a. Hon. John Trevor, *Argyle-buildings*
g. George Fofter Tuffnell, efq. *Dover-ftreet*
g. a. William Turner, efq.
a. Robert Turner, efq. *Friday-ftreet*
g. Mrs. Jemima Turnpenny, *Black-heath*
a. Mrs. Anna Maria Tracey
a. Mrs Turner
g. Mrs. Thornton } *Clapham*
g. Mifs Thornton }

a. Mr.

V.

g. Benjamin Vaughan, esq. *Lawrence Pountney-hill*
g. c. s. James Vere, esq. } *Bishopsgate-street*
g. John Vere, esq. } *Bishopsgate-street*
g. James Vere, jun. esq. } *Bishopsgate-street*
g. Harry Verelst, esq. *St. James's-square*

W.

a. s. George, Earl of Winchelsea, *Grafton-street*
a. George, Earl of Warwick, *St. James's-square*
a. Lord Viscount Wentworth, *Savile-row*
g. a. Sir Watkin Williams Wynne, Bart. *St. James's square*
a. Sir Richard Worsley, Bart. *Berner's street*
a. Sir George Warren, K. B. *Grafton-street*
g c s. Sir Timothy Waldo, Knt. *Clapham*
g. Hon. William Ward, *Grosvenor-gate*
g. s. Samuel Wathen, M. D. *Great Cumberland-street*
g. Mr. Jonathan Wathen, *Bond-court, Wallbrook*
g. Thomas Wake, esq.
g. Thomas Wale, esq.
g. Joseph Walls, esq. *Lincolnshire*.
g. Mr. John Ward, No. 21. *Borough*
g. Colonel George Ward, *Ireland*
g. Henry Wass, esq. *Lad-lane*

g. Tho-

g. Thomas Watts, eſq. *Sun-fire-office, Threadneedle-ſtreet*

g. Mr. Edward Watſon, No. 31, *Cannon-ſtreet*

g. s. Benjamin Webb, eſq. *Martin's-lane*

g. c. s. Joſeph Wells, eſq. *Ludgate-ſtreet*

g. Thomas Wentworth, eſq.

g. s. Mark Weyland, eſq. *George-lane, Eaſt-cheap*

g. s. John Weyland, eſq. *Hill-ſtreet, Berkeley-ſquare*

g. s. James Whitchurch, eſq. *Twickenham*

g. Mr. John Whiſton

g. John Wickenden, eſq. *Abchurch-lane*

g. Walter Wilkins, eſq. *Maiſlow, Radnorſhire*

g. s. Jacob Wilkinſon, eſq. *Abchurch-lane*

g. George Williamſon, eſq. *Eaſt Indies*

a. ——— Willis, eſq. *Kenſington*

g. William Willis, eſq. *Lombard-ſtreet*

g. Henry Wilmott, eſq. *Bloomſbury-ſquare*

g. Robert Wilſon, eſq. *Lombard-ſtreet*

g. Mr. Charles Wilſon, *Ditto*

g. Mr. Titus Wilſon, *Bridge-ſtreet, Weſtminſter*

g. Mr. Francis Wilſon

g. Mr. George Wilſon, *Cannon-ſtreet*

a. Mr. John Winter

g. Abraham Winterbottom, No. 32, *Threadneedle-ſtreet*

a. Dr. Samuel Withers, *Sun Tavern-fields, Shadwell*

g. Francis Wood, eſq.

g. s. Michael

g. s. Michael Wodhul, esq. *Berkeley-square*

a. John Wodehouse, esq. *East Lexham, Norfolk*

g. s. George Wombwell, esq. *Crutched-friars*

g. s. John Wowen, esq. *Hertford-street*

g. Mr. Charles Wray, *Fleet-street*

g. s. Thomas Wright, esq. No. 30, *Abchurch-lane*

g. Paulet Wrighte, esq. *Greek street, Soho*

a. George Wrighte, esq. *Grayhurst, Bucks*

g. Thomas Wroughton, esq. *Warsaw*

a. J. William Wynne, esq.

a. Lady Wentworth

a. Mrs. Wentworth, *Clerges-street*

g. Mrs. Anne Wheeler, *Park-street, Grosvenor-square*

a. Miss Wynne, *Grosvenor-street*

g. Mrs. Webb

Y.

g. Honourable John York, *Berkeley-square*

g. Edward Roe Yoe, esq. *Normington, near Leicester*

LEGACIES

LEGACIES *Received.*

1759	The Executors of Mr. Hill,	10	10	0
1761	Mrs. Martha Prynne,	30	0	0
	Peter Lewis Levius, of *Liſbon*,	44	15	0
	Joſhua Warde, Eſq;	21	0	0
1762	Richard Spooner, Eſq;	100	0	0
	Mrs. Mary Beriman, in *Eaſt-India* Annuities,	100	0	0
	Mr. Thomas Warde,	20	0	0
	Mrs. Elizabeth Beal,	4	4	0
1763	Mr. John New,	100	0	0
	Mr. John Redman,	5	5	0
1764	Mr. John Stow,	50	0	0
1765	Mrs. Henrietta Wolfe, of *Greenwich*,	100	0	0
	John Parminter, Eſq;	100	0	0
	Mrs. Elizabeth Erwin,	10	0	0
1766	Mrs. Mary Middleton,	200	0	0
	Mr. Timothy Helmſley, a Legacy and two Mercers Bonds,	115	8	2
1797	Dr. Bowles,	100	0	0
	Counteſs of Montraith,	500	0	0
	Hele Dyer, Eſq;	313	10	0
1768	Miſs Mary Weſt,	1000	0	0
	Henry Allen Eſq;	400	0	0
	George Newland, Eſq;	30	0	0
	Thomas Meadows, Eſq;	200	0	0

1769 James

Year	Name	£	s.	d.
1769	James Farquerharſon,	500	0	0
	Mrs. Mary Parkhurſt,	100	0	0
	Charles Rabotier, Eſq;	25	0	0
	Mr. Henry Thompſon,	50	0	0
1770	Rev. Richard Somaſter,	100	0	0
	Thomas Hanſon, Eſq;	500	0	0
	Andrew Regnier, Eſq;	50	0	0
	The Rev. Mr. Beriman,	50	0	0
	Mrs. Rebecca Vick,	200	0	0
	Philip Delahaize, Eſq;	100	0	0
	Albert Michelſon, Eſq;	100	0	0
	Hon. Mr. Hume Campbell,	300	0	0
	Richard Briſtow, Eſq;	100	0	0
1772	Part of a Legacy by the Hand of the Counteſs Dowager Gower,	500	0	0
	John Brown, Eſq;	100	0	0
	Mrs. Ann Hunt,	500	0	0
	Mrs. Catherine Dowdall,	50	0	0
1773	Peter Burton, Eſq;	200	0	0
	Earl of Cheſterfield,	200	0	0
	Richard Dalton, Eſq;	50	0	0
	Ferdinand Nerton, Eſq;	300	0	0
	Mrs. Frances Thornhill,	200	0	0
	Richard Chyſlin, Eſq;	600	0	0
1774	Robert Baldy, Eſq;	100	0	0
	Charles Jennings, Eſq;	200	0	0
	Thomas Pike, Eſq;	1000	0	0
1775	Paul Blagrave, Eſq; 3 per Cent.	500	0	0
1776	Eliſha Biſcoe, Eſq;	10	10	0
	John Delmé, Eſq;	50	0	0
	Peter Bataille, Eſq; 3 per Cent.	100	0	0

General

Disbursements as aforesaid, from Ditto to Ditto.

	£.	s.	d.	£.	s.	d.
Additions to the new Hofpital fince the building —	327	10	4			
Cloathing for the Women in the Houfe, and others admitted	491	1	2			
Ditto for 77 Women difcharged to Service or Friends —	186	16	6			
Paid 12 Women who had remained in their Places one Year —	12	12	0			
Furniture — — —	158	14	10			
Apothecary Bills for Medicines by Agreement —	60	0	0			
Stationary, Printing, and Advertifing — —	63	15	0			
Rent of the Old Houfe and Salaries — —	626	9	1			
Houfekeeping and other Houfe Expences —	1660	0	3			
Loft by bad Silver collected at Chapel — —	7	15	9			
Infurance on 150*l.* the Value of 1500 Rupees, on board the *Anfon*, fince arrived, — —	1	1	3			
				3595	16	2
Balance				3160	6	1
Paid the Surveyor of the new Hofpital out of the General Fund, the Building Fund being infufficient, — — —				162	8	0
Reduced Balance				2997	18	1

MAGDALEN-HOSPITAL, April 24, 1776.

General Account of the *Receipts* and *Disbursements*.

	£.	s.	d.	£.	s.	d.
Total Receipts from the Commencement of the Charity, to *December* 31, 1775,	70314	16	11			
Disbursements from Ditto to Ditto,	67154	10	10			
Balance				3160	6	1
Advanced out of the General Fund to pay the Surveyor of the new Building in full, the Building Subscription having proved insufficient,				162	8	0
Reduced Balance				2997	18	1

Receipts, from the 31*st* Dec. 1774, *to the* 31*st* Dec. 1775.

	£.	s.	d.	£.	s.	d.
Balance of last Year,	3925	10	9			
Collected at the Chapel at the Anniversary	84	1	6			
Ditto at Dinner	157	1	6			
General Benefactions,	299	13	2			
Legacy, being the Produce of 500*l.* 3 *per Cents.* reduced Bank Annuities,	436	17	6			
Annual Benefactions	860	10	0			
Profits on Mr *Ward's* Medicines	20	3	0			
Collection at the Chapel	730	1	4			
Dividends on Stock and Mercers Bonds	138	6	0			
Work done by the Women	103	17	6			
				6756	2	3

Titles in This Series

MARRIAGE

The General Nature of Marriage

1. Thomas Salmon. A Critical Essay Concerning Marriage. London, 1724.
2. Letters on Love, Marriage, and Adultery; Addressed to the Right Honorable the Earl of Exeter. London, 1789.

The Forms of Marriage, Legal and Illegal

3. Henry Swinburne. A Treatise of Spousals, or Matrimonial Contracts. London, 1686.
4. Simon Dugard. The Marriages of Cousin Germans, Vindicated from the Censures of Unlawfullnesse, and Inexpediency. Oxford, 1673.
   with
   John Quick. A Serious Inquiry into that Weighty Case of Conscience, Whether a Man may Lawfully Marry his Deceased Wife's Sister. London, 1703.
   with
   James Johnstoun. A Juridical Dissertation Concerning the Scripture Doctrine of Marriage Contracts, and the Marriages of Cousin-Germans. London, 1734.
   with
   John Fry. The Case of Marriages between Near Kindred. London, 1756.
   with
   John Alleyne. The Legal Degrees of Marriage Stated and Considered, in a Series of Letters to a Friend. London, 1775.
5. Henry Gally. Some Considerations upon Clandestine Marriages. London, 1750.

with

A Letter to the Public: Containing the Substance of What hath been Offered in the Late Debates upon the Subject of the Act of Parliament, for the better Preventing of Clandestine Marriages. London, 1753.

with

Henry Stebbing. An Enquiry into the Force and Operation of the Annulling Clauses in a Late Act for the better Preventing of Clandestine Marriages, with Respect to Conscience. London, 1754.

with

Henry Stebbing. A Dissertation on the Power of the States to Deny Civil Protection to the Marriages of Minors Made without the Consent of their Parents or Guardians. London, 1755.

Divorce and Adultery

6. Marriage Promoted. In a Discourse of its Ancient and Modern Practice, Both under Heathen and Christian Common-Wealths. London, 1690.

   with

   A Treatise Concerning Adultery and Divorce. London, 1700.

   with

   Conjugium Languens: or, The Natural, Civil, and Religious Mischiefs Arising from Conjugal Infidelity and Impunity. London, 1700.
7. George Booth, Earl of Warrington. Considerations Upon the Institution of Marriage. London, 1737.

   with

   The Present State of Matrimony: or, the Real Causes of Conjugal Infidelity and Unhappy Marriages. London, 1739.
8. F. Douglas. Reflections on Celibacy and Marriage; in Four Letters to a Friend. London, 1771.

   with

   Considerations on the Causes of the Present Stagnation of Matrimony. London, 1772.
9. Trials for Adultery: or, the History of Divorces. (In seven volumes). London, 1779.

SEX

General Sexual Knowledge

10. Nicholas Venette. Conjugal Love; or, the Pleasures of the Marriage Bed. London, 1750.

11. Aristotle's Masterpiece or the Secrets of Generation. London, 1700.
with
Aristotle's Masterpiece in Three Parts. London, 1725.
with
Aristotle's Problems. London, 1710.
with
Aristotle's Last Legacy or His Golden Cabinet of Secrets Opened for Youth's Delightful Pastime. London, 1720.

The Dangers of Masturbation

12. Onania, or the Heinous Sin of Self-Pollution and All Its Frightful Consequences in Both Sexes Considered. London, 1710.
with
Onania . . . London, 1723.
with
A Supplement to the Onania. London, n. d.

13. S. A. Tissot. Onanism. London, 1766.
with
M.D.T. Bienville. Nymphomania, or, a Dissertation Concerning the Furor Uterinus. London, 1775.

Venereal Disease: Causes and Treatment

14. A Treatise of All the Degrees and Symptoms of the Venereal Disease in Both Sexes. London, 1708–09.

15. Jean Astruc. A Treatise of the Venereal Disease. London, 1737.

16. William Buchan. Observations Concerning the Prevention and Cure of the Venereal Disease. London, 1796.

Prostitution and the Sexual Life of the Town

17. The Wandring whore. Parts I–VI. London, 1660–61.
18. The London-Bawd, with her Character and Life. London, 1711.
19. John Dunton. The Night-Walker: or, Evening Rambles in Search of Lewd Women. London, 1696.
    with
    Edward Ward. The London Spy. London, 1709.
    with
    Edward Ward. The Amorous Bugbears: Or, The Humours of a Masquerade. London, 1725.
20. Hell upon Earth: or the Town in an Uproar. London, 1729.
    with
    Satan's Harvest Home, or the Present State of Whorecraft. London, 1749.
21. Select Trials at the Session House in the Old Bailey. London, 1742.
22. Robert Dingley. Proposals for Establishing a Public Place of Reception for Penitent Prostitutes. London, 1758.
    with
    Saunders Welch. A Proposal to Render Effectual a Plan to Remove the Nuisance of Common Prostitutes from the Streets of the Metropolis. London, 1758.
    with
    John Fielding. An Account of the Origin and Effects of a Police Set on Foot by His Grace the Duke of Newcastle in the Year 1753. London, 1758.
    with
    An Account of the Rise, Progress, and Present State of the Magdalen Hospital. London, 1776.
23. The Covent Garden Jester, or the Rambler's Companion. London, 1775.
    with
    Harris's List of Covent-Garden Ladies: or, Man of Pleasure's Kalender, For the Year, 1788. London, 1788.

Sodomy (Homosexual Behavior)

24. The Tryal and Condemnation of Mervin, Lord Audley Earl of Castle-Haven. At Westminster, April the 5th 1631. For Abetting a Rape upon his Countess, Committing Sodomy with his Servants, and Commanding and Countenancing the Debauching his Daughter. London, 1699.
with
The Women-Haters' Lamentation. London, 1739.
with
A Faithful Narrative of the Proceedings in a Late Affair between the Rev. Mr. John Swinton and George Baker. London, 1739.
with
John Kather. Genuine Narrative of the Conspiracy, Kather, Kane, Alexander, Nickson, etc. Against the Hon. Edward Walpole, Esq. London, 1751.
with
The Trial of Samuel Scrimshaw and John Ross, for a Conspiracy in Sending Threatning Letters to Humphry Morice, Esq; of Dover-Street: With an Intent to extort Money from him. London, 1759.
with
The Trial of Richard Branson, for an Attempt to commit Sodomy, On the Body of James Fassett. London, 1760.
with
Robert Holloway. The Phoenix of Sodom. London, 1813.

THE FAMILY, CHILDREN, AND SERVANTS

Childbearing and Childrearing: The Role of the Physician

25. Jane Sharp. The Midwives Book. London, 1671.
26. Francis Mauriceau. The Diseases of Women with Child and

in Childbed. London, 1710.

27. Guillaume de la Motte. A General Treatise of Midwifery. London, 1746.

28. Jean Astruc. A Treatise on All the Diseases Incident to Women. London, 1743.

29. Walter Harris. A Treatise on the Acute Diseases of Infants. London, 1742.

with

The Nurse's Guide: Or, the Right Method of bringing up Young Children. London, 1729.

with

William Cadogan. An Essay upon Nursing, and the Management of Children, From their Birth to Three Years of Age. London, 1750.

30. James Nelson. An Essay on the Government of Children. London, 1756.

31. John Hill. On the Management and Education of Children. London, 1754.

32. William Buchan. Domestic Medicine. London, 1772.

33. Lady Sarah Pennington. An Unfortunate Mother's Advice. London, 1817.

Children and Servants: The Advice of the Clergyman

34. William Fleetwood. The Relative Duties of Parents and Children, Husbands and Wives, Masters and Servants. London, 1705.

35. A Present for Servants from their Ministers, Masters, and Other Friends. London, 1787.

with

Eliza Haywood. A Present for a Servant Maid. London, 1743.

36. Thomas Seaton. The Conduct of Servants in Great Families. London, 1720.

DATE DUE

MAR 4 1986			
FEB 1 2 1986			
MAY 3 1 1991			
Interlibrary Loan			
3 WEEKS USE			
OR			
IL 3709266			
10-21-90			
NOV 1 0 2003			